MW00911576

Christian Counseling:
Healing the Tribes of Man

By

Joseph B. Lumpkin

Christian Counseling:

Healing the Tribes of Man

Copyright © 2005 by Joseph B. Lumpkin

For information regarding first time authors, address Fifth Estate, Post Office Box 116, Blountsville, AL 35031.

Second Edition

Printed on acid-free paper

Library of Congress Control No:
2005910502

ISBN: 1-933580-07-0
ISNB13: 978-1-933580-07-04

Fifth Estate 11/05

TABLE OF CONTENTS

PREFACE

"Cure" comes from the Latin word "cura," which means care. There can be no cure in this discipline without first caring for the lost or troubled soul sitting before you. If there is no compassion on the part of the counselor, there will be damage to those under his care as the fragile, wounded soul is treated roughly. Care – even if you are unsure of what to do next – simply care and you will be amazed at the power of compassion. Listen intently, for the telling of the story begins the healing.

We are about to take a journey into the rewarding and challenging world of ministerial counseling. This work is presented as a reference and guide for the Christian-based counselor. We will examine basic concepts of psychology and guidelines of counseling. We will delve into personality typing in order to quickly identify and classify basic personality traits, strengths, and weaknesses. We will look at the hopes, fears, and motives of the 12 personality types as revealed in the sons of Jacob and tribes of Israel. We will understand how the personality operates and malfunctions. We will find we have one basic motive driving us. It is our reason and our call. It will be our major strength, and, if not balanced and controlled, it will cause our downfall. We will discover how to understand, help, and heal.

INTRODUCTION

As we begin to penetrate the minds and personalities of the twelve tribes, we will see ourselves in them. There will be insights, pain, realization, and sorrow. However, it would be irresponsible to reveal the potentials and deficits of a personality without equipping the person with the tools to forge a path from the dysfunction to the place of true potential. For this reason, part of this work is devoted to the understanding and resolution of problems that may be encountered during the study and subsequent revealing of one's true nature. Please read, study, and ponder the psychological rules and guidelines before subjecting yourself or others to the sometimes-harsh reality of the personality profiles and revelations found in this manual.

I encourage you to completely digest this entire book before beginning the task of counseling or self-examination. Confronting a problem without the knowledge of how to handle the issue can exacerbate the situation.

Remember, understanding may come in the instant knowledge is revealed, but application and change come only from the repetition of self-discipline. Be prepared with the proper tools when you come across something in need of change. Do not go into the forest without your breadcrumbs.

To successfully help those under our care, we must address the complete person. The person must be balanced in the areas of his or her spiritual, personal, family, and community views. An incorrect view of God can lead to spiritual weakness. This condition can be as damaging as an imbalance of family life or the lack of morality and commitment needed to sustain a marriage. As counselors we must attend to all of these areas.

It is no mistake that the New Testament word "save" means to heal. Salvation means to make a person whole, complete, and healthy. Mental health is the absence of all that warps or blights the human personality and prevents full fellowship with God.

To restore the soul to health and fellowship with the Lord we must first stop the immediate crisis. This is not the same as stopping the pain or healing the injury. Those they must do on their own in time. It is up to us to provide food, shelter, safety, and hope. Only then do we guide and counsel.

JAM 2:15-17 If a brother or sister be naked, and destitute of daily food, and one of you say unto them, Depart in peace, be ye warmed and filled; notwithstanding ye give them not those things which are needful to the body; what doth it profit? Even so faith, if it hath not works, is dead, being alone.

"Pray about it" and "Read this verse" are not answers. They show no sign of caring or compassion. Listening, understanding, and wise counsel are food and shelter to the destitute soul. A person in pain or panic cannot settle spirit or mind enough to utter anything more than a cry to God. Until they can pray, it is the counselor who should be praying for them. We should pray for their healing and God's guidance as we minister. Prayer should be used to seek and accept the will of God, not to change the mind of Him who is all knowing. We can bring our needs and desires to the Lord in prayer but we should be very cautious about asking God to change His perfect will, as if we know better. The main purpose of prayer is to mold the heart of man to the heart and will of God. In this light, some internal unrest is a good teacher. It shows God is instructing us. Wait, watch, minister, and encourage. God is doing His work as He molds our hearts to His.

THEOLOGY AND PRACTICAL APPLICATION

MAT 5:44-45 But I say unto you, Love your enemies, bless them that curse you, do good to them that hate you, and pray for them which despitefully use you, and persecute you; That ye may be the children of your Father which is in heaven: <u>for he maketh his sun to rise on the evil and on the good, and sendeth rain on the just and on the unjust.</u>

To become a healthy person there are three areas that must be healthy and balanced. We must have a healthy relationship with God, we must have healthy relationships within our family, and we must have healthy relationships within our community. To have any and all of these, we must first be a mentally and emotionally healthy person. Another definition of mental health is "integration". When all of our psychological parts are fully integrated we are healthy.

As we examine the relationship between God and ourselves or our patient, we may find that in the religious community we are often told, "God is in control." With this philosophy and the knowledge that God rewards the good and punishes the evil (or the doubters), we bravely go out to conquer the world. At the first onslaught of fate, many fold up their tents of faith and go home. With the help of counseling and a slight correction in personal philosophy, life may become a little more tolerable. For those who have lost the faith, and for those who stand with questions in hand, I offer the answer to Job in one hundred words or less.

Our purpose here, as described in most holy books, can be broken down to just two statements: We are here to love. We are here to serve. To do these things in the truest sense, we must have free will. Love is not love if it is not offered of its own accord, and service is slavery if forced. To have free will, we must be exposed to all of the consequences of all our actions. To be sheltered from some is still to be controlled, even if benevolently. Assuming the acts are the same, an evil act of a good man will have the same effect as the evil act of an evil man. Likewise, a good act of an evil man will have the same result as the good act of a good man. I am not suggesting God is not all-powerful; I am saying with His power He has endowed us with free will. The confusion enters when we neglect to take into account that all wills interact. We are all tied together in the actions and reactions of our decisions and how they affect each other. This dance of timing and types is "the only dance there is."

It is the "dance" of personal interaction that makes many theologies taught today so toxic and in error thereby making the common man lost to God completely. Many theologians teach that with enough faith we can protect ourselves and our families from the onslaught of the world. There is a Chinese proverb that states, "The traveler prays for fair skies while the farmer prays for rain." The view of man controlling the actions of others has too many errors to address here, but we will take two points as examples.

Let us use a scenario of a man bent on rape or murder. If your faith were to affect his action either directly or through God, it would mean a violation of the man's free will. For love and salvation to work in most theologies, there is a direct need for free will. Even if a man's will is evil it must continue to be free so if he were to repent and turn to God, his decision would also be free and he would be saved.

In a second scenario, if your faith and prayers were to simply turn the murderer's hand to someone else, it would mean you had chosen to have someone else hurt or killed instead of you or your family. This is not consistent with the Christian principle of sacrifice for others.

What this theology does is give a sense of control. To those who feel out of control, this doctrine and way of thinking may be a salve in the short term, but when something bad or unforeseen happens, the person must blame himself for not having enough faith to prevent the event. The result is failure and blame added to the trauma of the event. That kind of faith is toxic.

There are types (personality categories) of people drawn to this theology. Each personality type will have a certain area of theological error the person will have to be careful to avoid. It is important to have a balanced and workable belief system. God IS in control. God IS omnipotent, omnipresent, and He is our savior. He has a plan for our lives. It is up to God to communicate His plan to us. It is up to us to live it in a healthy, loving way. He will reveal it to us in time. First, we must make sure our relationship with God is healthy, and then we must work on being healthy people. Only after that can we hope to and have healthy relationships with others.

In this book we will discuss beliefs, personalities, and personal pitfalls. As Christian counselors, we must take into account the individual's personality, environment of family and society, and relationship to God. All of these must be healthy and in balance to produce a healthy person. As we begin to study the personality, we must begin with our society and its effects on the person.

ROM 12:4-5 For as we have many members in one body, and all members have not the same office: So we, being many, are one body in Christ, and every one members one of another.

Paul likened the church to a body. This simile applies equally well to a society. A society could be defined as a group of people living under common laws or sharing a common culture. A society functions as a body working to feed, clothe, educate, and propagate itself. If the body or the society is balanced and healthy, it will grow and flourish. If it is not healthy, it will show signs and symptoms of its imbalance, but once symptoms are observed it is too late to prevent the disease. The faster we recognize an event as a symptom, the more likely the disease can be controlled. This is true with diseases of the body as well as social maladies. With a disease in our own bodies, we are likely to feel or observe a symptom.

Sicknesses in our society are likely to be ignored until it is too late, unless they affect us directly. So it begins that our society is infected, becomes sick, and worsens to a point we are personally affected before we rise to the challenge of doing something about it. If there is no personal pain, there is usually no impetus to act.

The gospel of Jesus Christ is a preventative of social disease. Salvation is the only cure. Once the knowledge of Christ and communion with God through Him is impaired, the social equivalent of the immune system is compromised and the society is open to malaise. As we have been forced to distance ourselves from God in our daily lives, we have been forced further and further from our source of strength and health. We, as a society, become weak and sick. It is very important we recognize how we are being forced further from God, how it opens us up to social and personal disease of sin, what the symptoms are, and what to do to restore wholeness.

In a free society it is important to protect personal freedom, yet there are passive and active ways to do so. In the past we sought to protect personal freedom by using a more passive approach which allowed an individual to avoid those things he found to be undesirable. If a person did not want to pray at the beginning of school or at a ball game, it was up to him to endure the time as hundreds or thousands of others did as they wished. In the twentieth century, there was a dramatic shift in the way personal freedom was viewed and a more aggressive approach toward protection was leveled against society. In this school of thought, it was necessary to protect the individual freedom at the expense of the masses.

The logical and reasonable approach to protecting the wishes of the many is being outweighed by our courts as they bow to the eccentric wishes of the few, or even the one. Our legal system began to insist on the wishes of the one being upheld at the expense of the wishes of the many. It was at this point that we lost moral balance and began to allow our society to be affected by the whims of the few.

Previously, our society had been based on a belief system that was almost entirely Christian and Bible-based, but we began to experience impediments or, at times, a cessation of our ability to express this belief system; thus followed a lack of proper reinforcement and propagation of the Christian way of life by our society. Without self-enforcing practice and transmission of these beliefs in our daily life, the way of life and application of the tenets began to die.

We now stand at this crossroad: to do as our legal system seeks to force us to do, or to practice and propagate the Christian beliefs and way of life against the will of recent legal interpretation. This is the age in which we now live, facing either the death or the resurrection of Christianity. To use the prior analogy, we lost the ability to protect the social body from moral disease and began to evolve into a sick society.

It is the difference between what we consider a personal space and what we view as society, which allows the sickness time to grow. If we were personally attacked by the implosion of personal freedom, we would begin to fight against the intrusion much sooner. Instead, we allow the desires of the few to take over the direction of the many because it seems removed from us. The laws are like a python slowly crushing our personal freedoms. We should not wait until we are personally restricted before we act. Any law restricting the society restricts the individual.

There are two primary views on the subject of how to improve society. One view offers the solution that each man must raise society to his level; thus the level of each one in society averages out to be at the level of society. In this view it is up to the individual to control the growth of society by growing individually. This point of view needs to allow individual freedom in order to encourage personal growth and thereby raise the "level" of the society.

In the other view, it becomes society's responsibility to raise each individual to a higher level and thus raise itself. This is a more socialistic concept and can be related in some ways to the teachings of Confucius. In this society there is a duty to society as a whole. One does what is best for society and conforms to a predetermined social structure. The individual is groomed and formed into what society esteems as a good citizen.

To my Western mind, it is difficult to see how any single person could easily challenge established ways that may need improving or abolishing if the society is his only standard and if individualism is forbidden. This society tends to be stagnant and slow to change except through "coup d'etat" or painful rebirth. Look to China and the old empire of the USSR for the examples. How individuals can be raised to a point beyond what society has to offer is a difficult point to comprehend.

Let us consider the first argument since it is a Western/democratic model and seems to apply most to the United States. Within the Western society, there are two ways of personally benefiting society. These two views can be termed "the generalist and the specialist." In a society of generalists, each man has a body of knowledge broad enough to perform functions numerous enough to fill, create, or sustain many places in society. Through carpentry, soap-making, farming, hunting, leather tanning, or weaving, each man could personally create a level of society. Even though each man may have a special area of expertise, he is multi-faceted.

In the paradigm of the specialist, on the other hand, each man has a certain place in society that has been determined and focused on to the exclusion of most other courses of study. In this type of society each man has a narrow but deep area of knowledge. This has become the template of our society. We have doctors, lawyers, and other specialists, many of who cannot build, farm, hunt, weave, or even prepare meals. In this society there is great depth but interdependence. Due to this interdependence, we are held together more tightly and are more affected by any shift in culture or society. Thus, specialists form dependent links in the chain of society, each trying to achieve higher levels and greater depths of knowledge as they attempt to better themselves and become more marketable. In doing this, we raise society to higher levels as we grow.

This system works well, but the self-interest driving each man to find a way to better himself, make more money, acquire more possessions, and gain prestige is the same thing making us blind to the sickness of our society. Our society promotes a self-concerned attitude of greed so, unless our money, jobs, or personal pursuits are affected, we turn a blind eye. In this society, symptoms become severe before most notice.

A firmer connection between self and society can be established by understanding the way in which we relate to one another. As Christians we must learn to relate to others as Christ relates to us; one on one, on an individual basis, looking into the hearts of others.

JOH 13:34-35 A new commandment I give unto you, That ye love one another; as I have loved you, that ye also love one another. By this shall all men know that ye are my disciples, if ye have love one to another.

MAT 22:36-40 Master, which is the great commandment in the law? Jesus said unto him, Thou shalt love the Lord thy God with all thy heart, and with all thy soul, and with all thy mind. This is the first and great commandment. And the second is like unto it, Thou shalt love thy neighbor as thyself. On these two commandments hang all the law and the prophets.

In Martin Bubers's work, *I and Thou*, we have a description of various approaches to personal relationships. On the first and most shallow level, we function as if the other person is a "unit" for the input and output of information to make appointments, schedule events, and act as an extension of our will. This stage we will call "Me and the Other." The "Me" does not view the "Other" as an equal. Whether we admit it or not, the "Other" is beneath or separate from us. Sadly, this is the way we conduct our businesses and even our marriages. We communicate needs, schedules, and timelines in order pick up the kids, take them to ball practice, make it to the doctors' appointments, and shop for things we need to run the household. It is the language by which we run our lives. It is a heartless or superior attitude which communicates no feelings. The only feelings functioning here are ancient callings from the body that disturb our flow of work on the same level as eating and sleeping. This is the level of eros.

The second stage we will call "You and Me." In this stage of relations, we view others as persons but still not equals. We acknowledge them as other beings with "similar" rights, but still they do not carry the same spiritual weight as we do. When it comes to discussion or argument, we do not see the equality of the others or their opinions. This is a state of philo, a friendship that may make the heart feel something, but it does not change the heart. It is from this state we conduct most close friendships and decent marriages. It feels adequate but falls far short.

The third and deepest stage of communication is called "I and Thou." In this stage we transcend ourselves and become keenly aware others are no more or less than we are, and we are a reflection of God and His Grace. We speak heart to heart as if we are communing with ourselves and with God. We deeply care about feelings and opinions. This is a state of agape' that reaches into the heart and alters it to the point where we no longer have two hearts but we are one. The heart of the other person matters as much as our own. This state is a state of Grace, imparted by Grace, sustained by Grace, in which we act, move, and feel toward another as Christ feels toward us. To sacrifice for them is to sacrifice for us. To love them is to love ourselves. This is the highest state. If we were to conduct our marriages and our personal relationships from this level, we could not easily hurt or betray our family, friends, or society.

In a society that promotes titles, position, and acquisition, it becomes very difficult to function more deeply than at the most shallow level. Our fast-paced way of life pushes us to exchange "just the facts" and move on quickly to the next issue. Our deepest beliefs and our lack of ability to have deep or meaningful relationships affect the structure of our society. The society affects our way of life. Our way of life affects our interpersonal relationships, and our interpersonal relationships affect the structure of society. Thus the circle of the life of a society goes. It is up to us to minister within this paradigm, so we had better know its structure well.

In the never-ending cycle of entropy regarding human relationships, sits the minister trying to hold the hearts of the people together while many try to self-destruct. We and those we are trying to help work too hard, drive ourselves too far, and lose sight of the true goal of what we are trying to do. We get into the mode of damage control and fire fighting, all the while overlooking the solution to the problem. We are called at all hours into the midst of grief, suffering, and human tragedy. We spend time trying to comfort and negotiate when many of the situations in which people hurt other people would not happen if Jesus were in their hearts and the best interest of others were kept in mind.

An open and compassionate heart stops many tragedies. A heart remade in the image of Christ would save us from ourselves and many of our worst mistakes. If we cared for our children as we care for ourselves, there would be far fewer divorces, affairs, and domestic violence. Mind you, I am not saying, "Get saved and all of your problems are over." Indeed, I believe much the opposite. I believe we take on many different problems when saved. Some are old problems we wish would disappear but will not. The spirit of God may change us immediately but more often than not, we will be remade in the image of Christ day by day, little by little. The good news is the spirit and power that is forming us, is in us to guide us and comfort us.

A friend approached me very distressed. Her husband had asked Jesus to be Lord of his life and had been saved. He was going to church right along, but during the week he was still drinking and at times was drunk. Congratulations, I said. You have yourself a saved drunk. Now, I know many of my more fundamentalist brothers and sisters are gathering stones and looking for my address, so before they arrive I will try to explain my stance. Jesus died for our sins because we are not perfect. We still sin and sinners are forgiven. That is not to say we shouldn't avoid sinning. We should. We should attempt to conform ourselves into the likeness of Christ. But we cannot. If we could, He would not have had to die for us. The Holy Spirit must do that for us. The timing and progress is up to him. If we know a person who still gossips a little, stretches the truth to make himself look better, or still hasn't quite laid down a vice, like smoking, even though he knows God wants him to, then we know a person as bad or good as we are. There are no degrees or magic numbers of sins. All sins are forgiven if we have faith in Him. If this is not the case, none of us will be in Heaven.

There are those who believe once a man is saved he does not sin. They are the most dangerous of all since they have somehow lost the ability to see deeply enough inside themselves. Conviction is God revealing our sins and sinful nature to us. Salvation is His forgiveness of those sins. It is not the removal of the sin nature. Yet, as God transforms us little by little, we revisit our sins less and less often over longer and longer intervals. By this we know He is working in our hearts to make us conformed to His image.

Let us be honest for a moment and speak the unspeakable. The Christianity of today does not work. The church is hurting its own people because it is lying to them. Some churches are experiencing a great falling away. The church has told us to come and all will be made right. We will be changed. It has not and we have not. Some are changed instantly into new creatures. That is a miracle. Most are not. They continue to struggle day by day as the Spirit works its slow and patient process, which will not end until "we are made perfect over there."

Christianity is not a fix, it is a path. Jesus is not a panacea. Jesus is our savior. Faith is not a magic wand. It is the key to the door of salvation. Mental and emotional injuries are inflicted when the espoused theology does not match reality. Even though it is said we walk by faith and not by sight, if our faith does not do what it is supposed to do then we do not understand the nature of faith or we have faith in the wrong thing. In short, we are saved from our sins and set free from the (spiritual) laws of sin and death, but we are not free of sin or its natural consequences.

ROM 7:14-25 For we know that the law is spiritual: but I am carnal, sold under sin. For that which I do I allow not: for what I would, that do I not; but what I hate, that do I. If then I do that which I would not, I consent unto the law that it is good. Now then it is no more I that do it, but sin that dwelleth in me. For I know that in me (that is, in my flesh) dwelleth no good thing: for to will is present with me; but how to perform that which is good I find not. For the good that I would I do not: but the evil which I would not, that I do. Now if I do that I would not, it is no more I that do it, but sin that dwelleth in me. I find then a law, that, when I would do good, evil is present with me. For I delight in the law of God after the inward man: But I see another law in my members, warring against the law of my mind, and bringing me into captivity to the law of sin which is in my members. O wretched man that I am! who shall deliver me from the body of this death? I thank God through Jesus Christ our Lord. So then with the mind I myself serve the law of God; but with the flesh the law of sin.

8:1-2 There is therefore now no condemnation to them which are in Christ Jesus, who walk not after the flesh, but after the Spirit. For the law of the

Spirit of life in Christ Jesus hath made me free from the law of sin and death.

Those who minister to others are strung up between heaven and earth, trying to ease pain and stop the cycle of hurt. To reach people the counselor must understand and be compassionate. He must see things from angles previously unknown to him. He must look at our hurting brothers and sisters and be able to understand why they may have made their decisions. This does not mean he would agree with them, only that he is familiar with their "type" of person and how they "tick." This knowledge will allow us to know how to minister to their needs and how to best approach them with the salvation of Jesus that will help them overcome their issues, as the Spirit heals them in His own time.

We must also be brutally honest and admit that telling the lost soul to pray and read scripture will not heal the hurting heart or stop the suicidal thirst to end one's own life. Bible thumping and quoting verses will only make things worse. When a person comes for help they rarely need to be convinced that they did something wrong. They are there because they know it. Although people usually will not change unless pressure is brought to bear on the personality, the pain must be bearable before the hurting heart can listen and accept God. Extreme pain can cause immobility. First assure the patient they are not alone, but let God do His work. Let it boil. Even Christians can get hurled off course and lose their way. Sin is temporary insanity. It brings all of the pain of insanity with it.

Insanity takes a toll. Please have exact change.

Sanity is seeing and accepting patterns in reality. Intelligence is adapting to those patterns. Insanity results from imposing false patterns on reality. The type of insanity is based on the imposed patterns and the reactions to them.

This needs to be repeated:

JAM 2:15-17 If a brother or sister be naked, and destitute of daily food, And one of you say unto them, Depart in peace, be ye warmed and filled; notwithstanding ye give them not those things which are needful to the body; what doth it profit? Even so faith, if it hath not works, is dead, being alone.

THEOLOGY AND THE INDIVIDUAL

Individuals are affected by their theology. Our perspective of God is often influenced by our view of the parent image. In some ways our theology perpetuates itself as a "parental voice" within the adult. Whether a person's beliefs are passed down from his parents, impressed upon him as he is raised in a certain church, or whether it is a result of where and when the spirit of God touched his heart, the personality is drawn toward certain expressions of faith as we subconsciously relate God to our relationship to authority figures in our life. The individual and his beliefs are intertwined. An extreme theology can be an indicator of an unhealthy psyche. An extreme theology can exacerbate and feed an unbalanced personality.

Generally speaking, most people have not done any deep study in theology to arrive at a point of faith or belief system. Their faith is more affected by experience and influences within their family and church. However, the expression of faith is partially a learned experience and partially a function of personality. Because of these issues, it is important for us as counselors to examine the theology of those seeking our help. Core beliefs drive our attitudes and decisions. Certain beliefs, if taken to extremes, cause extremes in action and attitude. For example, hyper-fundamentalism in any faith always leads to intolerance of others because it is the nature to believe the fundamentalist is following the letter of the law closer than anyone else and is therefore closer to God.

There are other common theologies that can lead to error if taken too far. The belief that the church or denomination to which the person belongs is the only true or real way to salvation leads to an elitist, condescending outlook and overlooks the narrow and finite understanding of man. The belief that any sin will revoke your salvation leads to insecurity in life and oneself, which could become obsessive/compulsive in nature. If one believes what is done in the body does not affect the spirit, it can lead to dealing selfishly and sinfully with others. The belief that God is a punitive god without mercy may lead to a feeling should anything go wrong in life, it is the person's fault for not living well enough. Likewise, this gives way to a strange and backwards feeling of being in control because if one could just be good enough, life would work out as it should. As mentioned earlier, this is very close to the effect the hyper-faith movement has on certain personalities.

The belief that the strength of our faith can control what happens to us leads to the illusion of control. This may be reassuring to some, until such time as tragedy strikes and one must take responsibility for what fate dealt, since their faith was not strong enough to stop it. If taken to the fullest degree, this theology would have us believe the person with the strongest faith would never be sick, never die, become wealthy, and be a god. Those that preach this doctrine would also have us take the burdens of guilt, blame, and despair for all of those things we let happen to ourselves and our families, due to our human limitations.

The belief that the amount of a person's tithe or offering is somehow tied to the depth of that person's faith leads to destitute members and rich preachers (we should ask those preaching this doctrine to give all they have to the poor in accordance to their own teachings).

Denominational doctrines must be respected. At the same time we must be keenly aware of the effect beliefs can have on certain personality types, especially if the belief or the personality is not reasonable or balanced.

There are times the counselor must focus the person's faith away from doctrine and back to God. Sometimes theology and doctrine must be tossed aside and stripped away until all that remains is Christ, His crucifixion, His resurrection, and His salvation of us. To restore God to His proper place in a person's life may be the first step in healing the person if they are addicted to a toxic doctrine. Doctrine is like glass. You can see the truth through it, but it keeps you from touching the truth. Christianity results from a "heart condition." It only functions properly when there is a communion between our heart and the heart of God. Like any relationship, it is a living, spontaneous, and ongoing communication. No doctrine can describe or contain it. After all, He is our parent.

Doctrine can serve to restrict and stifle our interactions with God by limiting what we accept as His will or actions. Toxic doctrine imposes rules and patterns on our worship or belief that are harmful to us because it distorts our relationship to God. We should strive toward a mystical relationship with God which is not very different to a healthy relationship with a parent. The relationship should be trusting, open, loving, and it should sustain an ongoing dialog. A loving, trusting relationship with a parent has no rules or doctrine. There is no need for a rule book in a relationship of this type. God will do what He wants to do. He is, after all, God.

We trust His decision will be for our best interest. After all, He is our "Parent."

THE QUEST

Any journey in life must have at least a general direction and path. If one does not have these things, he is simply wandering. The problem is how to chart and travel the course.

Keeping in mind the journey, or rite of passage in life, is that of the soul from its pristine, unaware state to the full, healthy self-aware expression. It is easy to see anything that would force the soul to deny this would stop the journey short of its completion and is a type of defeat.

The journey itself is one of overcoming the obstacles standing in the way of reaching the precious goal. Anything preventing union or restoration must be dealt with.

Healing comes in the telling of our story. Each time we tell it we leave a crumb of the pain behind. Each time we tell our story we tell the world we have overcome and made it through.

The last step in this odyssey is to reunite with that thing which is so cherished or to obtain the goal and win the battle. This is the stage needed to reach a healthy, whole, and integrated being. At this stage we know our own souls, understand what place self control holds, and have an intact psyche capable of self-expression.

We are the heroes, and ours are the quests. At the time of the dispute and trauma in our childhood, a splintering or separation occurred which stifled and stole a piece of our soul from the integrated being we were before the blow was delivered. Much like a shard falls from a crystal when it is traumatized; a shard of the psyche is taken from us. We are then no longer whole. We feel this amputation and manifest the feeling through pain, emptiness, anger, sorrow, or distrust. We wander around aimlessly trying to feel better until one day the fact of our separation dawns on us. At that time, another different, yet incredible, journey begins. We, the heroes, start on a sojourn of restoration. Having survived the disruption, separation, and recognition, we must overcome the monsters of hurt, anger, and fear in order to reach the place of forgiveness and win back the prize of wholeness and integration lost so long ago.

In the dark, half-hidden times of childhood, the deed was done, and in this postdiluvian age we must return to find the clues showing what went wrong and who did it. We must walk the obscure paths of memory, feeling our way into its wilderness further and further until the footprint is found. Then, with the skills of the bravest brave, we must trail the beast to its den. Armed with the sword of understanding and the arrows of forgiveness, we must kill the beast and take back what is rightfully ours – ourselves. From age to age and from hero to hero, from disruption through separation, recognition, journey, and victory, with all of the battles along the way, we are the heroes, and ours can be the victory.

Who we are, in the complete sense of the word, can only be understood when we examine ourselves separated from the influence of outside forces. This is because any disturbance causes a reaction. That reaction is based primarily on what part of us might be affected. This part of us is thus exaggerated, and the remaining part is eclipsed.

We may think we can fight off the world, but the fight itself causes a great distortion. We may think we have free will, and some of us, through our arrogance, suppose the life of the individual is fully controlled by the individual. But this is only a half-truth, and thus only as effective as half a boat. We will never be completely detached from the world until death, but there are ways to understand and sort out the distortions caused within us.

Consider a pond during a soft southern shower; each raindrop has its own path. Whether the individual or God chooses the path is left for the theologians to debate. Every drop enters its watery world and begins to integrate smoothly with perfect circles; that is until the area surrounding it receives another raindrop. At this point the integration and symmetrical effects of the first are interfered with by the free will of the second. The integration and symmetry of both are changed against their wills and a reaction begins. The reaction is strongest in the area where the two interact, causing distortion. This distortion is the first thing that must stop before our true face can be revealed.

Let us use the analogy of peeling an onion to symbolize the stripping away of our false faces. These faces are reactions learned by us in order to cope with the various effects and distortions brought to bear on us. To strip away these distortions is to see and know our very soul. Before the onion can be peeled it must be removed from the dirt, that place where the rocks, insects and other onions affected its growth and symmetry. Who we are can only be discerned when we are still and calm inside. We must first find the place on the inside and on the outside where we may learn to be still and thus, in a fashion, remove ourselves from the effects of the world for a time. When the dirt falls away and we recognize what is dirt and what is real, we can begin peeling the onion.

Like an onion with its dry, shining face, we present a general persona to the world. False, protective, and brittle, it hides our true nature. This extra skin was developed to allow us to better cope, not with the outside world, but with ourselves. Although it shields part of us from the environment of interaction, its purpose is to separate and shield us from the stimuli which cause the reaction of negative feelings in us. When the skin has become sufficiently thick, we feel as if we have succeeded in coping with the environment, but we have artificially stopped our own growth: no stimuli, no reaction – no reaction, no feeling – no feeling, no idea there is a problem, and no growth, no maturing. The skin we wear gives an indication of what it is we are trying to protect, what our motives are, and where the area of maturing needs to be concentrated.

The first layers are quickly identified and may seem to slough off easily, but what is revealed underneath, like the onion, is an infinite number of more and more defiant and cloying layers, substructures to which the same patient observation, identification, and dismantling must apply. For every repeated exposure to an environment there is formed a habitual reaction; another layer, another persona. A face for every situation, another little "ego." These faces serve only two purposes: to protect us and to enable us to get what we want. These faces hide our true motives from others. They are the methods used to obtain the thing we are ultimately in search of. This search is called the motive.

Like someone threatened, who winces and flails in self-protection, our persona is turned and contorted in a thousand postures forming different personas. As one protective habit is set and another situation is encountered, layer upon layer of these sub-persons are built. This is how the protective faces are formed. These layers are made up of fear of rejection, abandonment, or abuse. They normally make up a small number of the outer layers, but they are the more difficult to see through.

Far more numerous are the faces built to obtain our selfish ends. As the child grows, he learns what postures to take to get what he desires. This positive reinforcement quickly builds into a habit, a mask, a method. This means the methods we use depend partly on our own personalities and partly on our parent image and what best worked to manipulate them. Between the protective methods and the manipulative methods, before long the central or seed persona is obscured completely and all we see are the layers which are false faces or masks. We identify ourselves as the layers or masks but we are not. We are that core. Who are we? What is our true face? Let's peel the onion and find out.

One of the saints once said as he followed his thoughts back to the beginning, the path turned to a trail and the trail disappeared, leaving nothing but dragons beneath his feet. What he was referring to was his own motivation. He came to the realization: every thought he had and every action he took could always be traced back to a selfish motive. Even if the actions were benevolent, the motives could always be traced to what he thought would make him feel better, or what would look better in the eyes of his God or his peers. It wasn't the deeds which were any less "good," only that the motives were based in some part on selfishness. He discovered for himself, very few thoughts or actions sprang from a pure, selfless, spontaneous desire for good, and I suspect the same can be said for you and me. We all have motives, and the measurement of our emotional maturity may be how in touch we are with these motives. To accomplish our goals, we change our faces, adapt our methods, and become less ourselves because to get what we want is more important to us than to be faithful to what we are.

There is an old song that speaks of a woman who keeps her face in a jar by the door. I would hear that song and think, "How sad." Now I think, "How lucky." She only has one face, and she can keep up with it. I realized I had a hundred faces and they hung on every situation. I changed faces with each circumstance. All of this was cloaked under the guise of "me." It was a different face in this situation or that situation, but I still called it "me." The thing that made no sense was the lack of consistency. There is impulsive gentleness in one circumstance, anger in another, internal postures that turned and contorted like a flag in the wind. I am not suggesting we not feel, but what I am suggesting is we acknowledge that we are responsible for the reactions to our feelings. We can allow ourselves to feel more if we are in control. We must be authentic and understand our faces may be a mask worn by the same person, but it is not the same persona underneath.

A person can be cloaked in a plethora of personas. All personas he refers to as "I" or "me." The change of faces is driven by a knee-jerk reaction in response to the situation. From the time we are born we encounter similar situations or parts of similar situations. We recognize the situation or part thereof and respond to it. At first the response is spontaneous, but according to the outcome and emotional triggers, we modify our response. After encountering similar situations enough times, our response becomes habitual. With the habit of response comes the assumption of outcome. Even if the outcome is not the same and the emotional triggers of the past are missing, the habitual response continues.

This is now a face, a persona, another "I." To halt or change the reaction and eliminate the "I," we must realize, even though our reactions are habitual, we can bring them under our control again. As we encounter a situation, there is a moment in time we change faces and choose to react in a certain way. At first these reactions were conscious, then subconscious and habitual, but the reactions must be made conscious once again. That which is conscious can be controlled.

To bring the change of persona to a conscious level, the sequence of internal events must be traced back to their roots. Before reaction there is decision. Before decision there is feeling. Before feeling there is input. During all of this, part of us is watching, objectively watching, and continuing step by step from situation to reaction. The moment this sequence is fully and continually identified, the struggle to regain control begins.

On some level, we all realize this "choosing of the face." In moments of objective clarity, we have seen the sequence with perfect insight. In a blink of an eye, we know our true face and the freedom of making our own choices. We have chosen to ignore these insights because we don't want to consider ourselves to be manipulative or false. We are.

IGNORANCE IS NO EXCUSE, BUT IT IS A GOOD EXPLANATION

Like an arrow released from the archer's bow, our emotions follow the path on which they are released. And like the shooting of an arrow, there is always a span of time between the release and the flight. A brief moment passes between the archer's giving the arrow permission to fly and the damage that follows the decision. In that moment of perfect mental balance, we see everything: the draw, the tension holding the draw…holding it, holding it… the release, and the kill. If we would look objectively within, we would see the same occurrences in our emotional world. If we would, we could see we give ourselves permission to fire.

Want proof? Proof is all around. Each time we deal differently with a child than we would deal with an adult, we display the paradox. If a one-year-old child were to accidentally break your favorite vase how would you react? If a teenager or adult were to break the same vase, would you react differently? If a child of three years says something to hurt your feelings, wouldn't you tend to deal with it differently than if an adult were to do the same? If the same person draws a different response from the same event, the response must be a choice.

Insight upon insight, glimpse upon glimpse, we will start to recognize a pattern. Within the pattern are two crucial details – motive and method. Method is how you react. Motive is why you react.

Motive is always more important than method. The same method may be used for a number of motives. To understand the motive is to understand and control the action. If you are confused about right and wrong, examine the motives.

Whether the motive is anger, love, fear, or any of the other basic emotions, the rules are the same, and so is the question. What are you really after? What are your deepest motives? *Method and motive make us who and what we are.*

On the surface it may appear the motive changes from situation to situation; on the surface it does, but not at the "soul" level. To get to this level you must be totally honest with yourself and ask, "What was I trying to accomplish when this happened?" You must continue to ask "why" until there are no more answers. The end answer will reside in a well-veiled selfishness, and the motive. This is called *"peeling the onion."* Each person has one basic motive, although there can be a number of methods. *To identify the motive is to understand your own actions.*

Because we all have a primary motive throughout life, we develop tunnel vision. Due to this tunnel vision there are feelings and modes of operation with which we are out of touch. We don't understand them, and they can blind-side us. These are called *Inferior functions. Superior functions* work on an integrated and conscious level. We are in control of them. The inferior functions tend to control us. Until we understand this, our condition as humans will yield twelve diseases, many symptoms, and no cure.

STILL WATER REFLECTS TRULY

Finding the truth in any situation is based on objectivity. There must be a detachment, not a dullness, nor a repression of feelings, but a spontaneous loss of ego which produces an equality in points of view. The point of view loses the normally self-centered origin and is then balanced in an objectivity which allows a person to see things from the vantage point of a journalist's unbiased reporting of the events. That unbiased objectivity is the key to revealing the true face.

Consider the pond and the raindrops described earlier. If a single raindrop were to fall into the pond, the ripples would go out from the center, undistorted and undisturbed, until they faded away. After being absorbed and fully integrated into the pond, the raindrop would become a part of the pond. There would be no difference between the drop and the pond. The raindrop would have become the pond. If the pond then remained undisturbed, all events around the pond would be reflected with perfect clarity as the smooth surface of the pond became like a mirror. *There are only three basic steps toward wholeness: interrogation, understanding, and integration.*

From an objective, truthful, and detached point of view, you watch yourself interact with others. You watch with the perspective of a spy. You watch for your false faces and unreal responses. Interrogate yourself. Ask why you lied to yourself and others in a situation. Ask yourself what you were really after or what you were really afraid of. Keep asking why until there are no more answers. There are no more answers only when you have arrived at your own basic motive. This is the motive driving you constantly throughout your life.

Understand the true and basic set of motives driving us subconsciously from event to event. To help with this, look for patterns and repetitions in life. The type of partners chosen or repeated occurrences may give clues to hidden motives and drives. Be cruelly honest when searching for the "whys" behind the choices. Soon the unconscious motives and drives will be brought to light. Integrate those unconscious motives and drives into the conscious awareness. Make them conscious and keep vigil over them so they will never be allowed to control from an unconscious level again.

HOW TO BE STILL AND WATCH

Stalking the Wild Dragon: Motives, Masks, and Mayhem

It's just another day in paradise as you stumble to your bed. You'd give anything to silence those voices ringing in your head....You thought you'd find happiness just over that green hill. You thought you'd be satisfied, but you never will. Learn to be still. We are like sheep without a shepherd. We don't know how to be alone, so we wander 'round this desert, and wind up following the wrong gods home. But the flock cries out for another, and they keep answering that bell. One more starry eyed messiah meets a violent farewell. Learn to be still.

Taken from the album, "Hell Freezes Over" by the Eagles. Written by Don Henley

PSA 46:9-11 He maketh wars to cease unto the end of the earth; he breaketh the bow, and cutteth the spear in sunder; he burneth the chariot in the fire. Be still, and know that I am God: I will be exalted among the heathen, I will be exalted in the earth. The LORD of hosts is with us; the God of Jacob is our refuge. Selah. O clap your hands, all ye people; shout unto God with the voice of triumph.

On the path to self-discovery, many times the first step is the most difficult. It could be because it takes the most motivation, or maybe it is because before one starts down a path, the full directions are not understood. In our hassled, pretentious world, masks and motives are easy to come by, and truth about oneself is a rare commodity. Watching yourself with patience and objectivity is the first and most important step in our process of growth. We must struggle to keep the revelations gained from these objective glimpses of ourselves fresh in your minds from the inception of the journey until the very last moment of life. Between one moment and another, through what at first will seem to be an act of grace, the door to objectivity will inch open. If it is watched with an unwavering gaze, the cracked door can be pried open a bit further.

DESERT MYSTICS

In the early Christian church, we find a group of brave souls referred to as the desert mystics or desert fathers. They followed an inner calling but acted it out in such a way to make it external. They journeyed into the desert for their soul's sake, seeking desolation, a place to be alone with one's self and God to such a degree that each one was forced to become familiar with each thought and pattern of mind and heart. It was a place of revelation for the heart-wrenching present condition of the very soul. This self-imposed hero's journey was taken on by the grace of a higher calling which refused to be silenced, the need of a spirit-to-spirit communion with God, a need to know the love and sustaining hand of their source.

They knew the first step was to diminish themselves in order to make room for God. Thus, the search into the uncharted corridors of the heart was acted out through the physical hermitage in the desert. The desert became a place where many stayed for years, a place where some died, and a place where some went insane. Many surrendered to the enemy of loneliness never to complete the journey and win the prize of freedom from self. Those who returned from the desert, returned having faced fear, pain, and loneliness; supplanting the self and its ego with the agape', unconditional love of God. They are the heroes of the early church.

On the surface it may be said their journey was more esoteric, but whether internal or external, the hero's journey is the same, following the same steps and milestones as any hero's journey: realization of a missing piece, making the decision to find that which is desired, the journey and trials, the learning and wisdom it brings, the attainment of wholeness which is the victory. All heroes, real or not, religious or mundane, esoteric or physical, are linked together on a common sojourn, and so are we. In this example we have crossed from the common idea of the second journey, which many dismiss with a wave of the hand saying it is a mid-life crisis, into that which is spiritual by nature. Actually, all second journeys are spiritual in nature; some just go further or deeper than others. We are unique and have unique journeys.

The three journeys of life are with us always. We see them acted out in our families and ourselves. First we go forth to conquer the world. We subdue our environment. We build and acquire. We work.

In the second journey we understand the first journey has left us empty and lacking. We turn within to conquer ourselves. It is a time of truth, inner questioning, and self-discovery.

In the last journey, we turn from the world and ourselves and face our own mortality and death. We make peace with God once and for all.

Although these journeys may overlap in time, each is distinct and separate in nature. If we are to mature as people and as Christians we will complete these journeys. We will face our world, our selves, and our God. We will overcome through Christ and through Him we will become the heroes and saints we were made to be.

Our Father, our God, our Savior, please show us your heart. Let us go beyond beliefs and doctrines. Lift us up higher than our limited faith can reach and let us go straight into your arms. Allow us to know you and your grace, mercy, healing, and love.

A MATTER OF FAMILY

The sins of the parents are visited upon the children...(and their children, and their children, and their children...)

Having the opportunity to meet and counsel with hundreds of people throughout the years will open one's eyes to patterns. I saw some of these patterns firsthand when I was recently confronted with a group of five young ladies. Each was finding it impossible to maintain a meaningful personal relationship. Each was working in the adult entertainment industry, and each had been neglected or abused by their fathers.

I understand my view may be dismissed by various parts of our society. The view is not in vogue, however studies show the hypothesis to be true and observation back up the information. In recent years I have seen an accelerated decline in acceptable societal behavior that followed an equally precipitous decline in the soundness of the traditional family unit. I think there is an unmistakable connection here. I believe each parent represents an area of learning for his or her children. A child instinctively looks to the mother for lessons in nurturing, care, compassion, balancing self with others in relationships, and diplomatic interaction. A child looks to the father for lessons in justice, discipline, the placement and use of sex in a relationship, the self-image that comes from his approval, and certain applications of conscience.

It is not that single parents cannot raise healthy children. They can, but it is a difficult thing to do well. A single, primary parent must try very hard to instill the lessons of the other parent into the child while keeping balance in the lessons they would normally teach. This is a fight against

35

nature, as a single individual can only offer what he or she knows, not the lessons another's experience teaches.

The young girls with whom I met were between the ages of nineteen and twenty-five. Each had a story to tell of how her father had abused her, neglected her, or was perpetually unkind and distant. Each could find no way inside of herself to open up to anyone else. Each was emotionally closed, but all used the adult entertainment industry to provide a type of false closeness and openness. They performed, exposed themselves, and got physically very close to their patrons, but were unable to share anything of emotional depth with anyone in their personal lives. Attempting to find closeness without being close, trying to have intimacy without trust, substituting attention for love, none could find fulfillment.

I contend the lack of bonding with their fathers caused this inability. Even though each had a mother there who seemed to provide a loving influence, the lack of a balanced father image during the formative years caused a void in them. They struggle to fill the void.

Girls, whose father was critical, hostile, overly strict (having many rules), rejecting or neglectful, or who withholds love or approval if dissatisfied, tend to raise daughters who are overly anxious or obsessive in their relationships. Oddly enough, mothers who are overly lax and permissive in their discipline and mothers who were thought of as lacking warmth raised daughters equally as anxious or obsessive. If father and mother fight often the same anxiousness may result. The more hostile and rejecting the father was the more depressed the daughter is likely to be after a romance ends. The more unreliable or unpredictable the mother is perceived the more insecure the daughter will be.

Sons are affected just as easily. Achievement driven, controlling, dominant fathers produce romantically insecure sons. Rejecting, aloof, critical mother affect their sons in the same way. If both father and mother are too permissive, the son will grow to be romantically obsessive.

Fathers and mothers, we fill a place and we teach lessons in the lives of our children which no other person on earth can teach. It is difficult enough to raise healthy, balanced children within a traditional family. Putting them through the absence of such makes them suffer in numerous ways throughout their lives. We all need family and will build a type of family unit when and where possible. It is sad and should not be, but sometimes our family is not kind or compatible. In today's society, seldom are members of a family born under the same roof. In those times when families are splintered and at odds, we find our real family not in our homes but along the way. Parents, if we do not want our children building their families around others we must nurture them, encourage them, celebrate them as unique individuals, and keep them close to our hearts.

The Bible tells us that the man who does not discipline his son hates his son. Likewise, it says that children are our treasure, like arrows in our quiver. The balance between these two positions is the secret to raising a healthy child. Equal amounts of love and guidance will produce a loving, secure child, who will in turn grow into a loving, balanced, secure adult.

HOMOSEXUALITY,
THERE IS NOTHING GAY ABOUT IT

A person's lifestyle defines what is known about them. To the outside world, we are known by what we do. A man or woman is defined by his or her actions. He is a good person, she is a good mother, he is gay, she is a thief, he is a liar, you can't trust them, you can count on their word…these are the things people say about one another based on the person's actions. The word "gay" is one, which for most homosexuals, is a misnomer. There is nothing happy or gay about the lifestyle. It is usually cloaked in secrecy and shame. So, why would a person choose this lifestyle? Or, is it a choice?

There is much anecdotal evidence that indicates there may be more than one reason that a person is gay. Some, although it is a very small percent, are born with incorrect chromosome configurations. Some have an abnormal hormone balance. However, it stands to reason that if there were clear genetic markers they would now be easy to identify. Furthermore, within certain boundaries, nature itself would eliminate genetic traits from the human gene pool since the very basis of homosexuality is NOT to reproduce. This would mean if the gene had isolated itself, (not passed itself on), it would have disappeared within a very short time. Most people are gay because of trauma early in childhood. Great confusion caused an identity crisis.

The relationship between mother and father and the relationship between parent and child come together to form a template for how the child will interact with others. The father figure, in the form of father images such as father, stepfather, uncle, and priest or pastor seems to influence the sexual pattern more than the mother images. I do not know why. When the relationship between father images and the child go wrong – terribly wrong – the sexual patterning of the child is corrupted. It makes some sense that when a daughter is hurt and molested by a man, she may reject the male image and cling to a more comforting female pattern, becoming a lesbian. Often a male child is abused by a father, uncle, stepfather, or priest and patterns the same trait, becoming gay. Many become abusers of children, just like those that abused them. The abused male child grows to become an angry, enraged, abuser. Many times he grows into a gay man.

Why both girls and boys may become gay after abuse by a father image is not clear. It may be due to the differences in what boys and girls acquire from the father – child interaction. Boys tend to mimic the actions of the father. They learn their position in life and love from the father's actions. Girls tend to draw self-worth from the relationship they have with their fathers. They do not tend to mimic the father but to associate love, respect, and worth with how they were treated by the father. This may be why girls who were abused as children grow up to choose abusive mates, or to reject men all together and become lesbians.

The question is, "After the abuse distorts the personality and sexuality of the child, can he or she have a healthy, heterosexual relationship?"

Psychologist George Rekers writes of considerable evidence that change of sexual orientation is possible. In a number of papers citing a sizable number of cases, he writes, "the gender-identity disorder resolves fully."

Dr. Robert L. Spitzer, a psychiatric professor at Columbia University, created a firestorm in the gay community. In May 2001, he released the results of his research at a meeting of the American Psychiatric

Association. Spitzer spearheaded the APA's decision in 1973 to declassify homosexuality as a mental-health disorder. The APA came under a tremendous amount of pressure from the gay community and buckled under. The convergence of science and politics makes for very poor results. Now out from under direct pressure, Spitzer says his findings "show some people can change from gay to straight, and we ought to acknowledge that."

One should not wonder about the flack created from the gay community. The only way to sustain the lifestyle is to form an acceptable image. That image is made more respectable if one were to embrace the fact that children are born gay. This does not seem to be true in most cases. Sexual and emotional trauma during childhood is the biggest factor in the development of homosexual behavior.

But, how does one help a person "go straight?" The easiest way is to see the signs in childhood and help the child properly define his or her sexual identity.
According to Dr. James Dobson, there are signs that a child is having issues. They are:

- Repeatedly stated desire to be, or insistence that he or she is, the other sex.
- In boys, preference for cross-dressing, or simulating female attire. In girls, insistence on wearing only stereotypical masculine clothing.
- Strong and persistent preference for cross-sexual roles in make-believe play, or persistent fantasies of being the other sex.
- Intense desire to participate in stereotypical games and pastimes of the other sex.
- Strong preference for playmates of the other sex.

If the signs are not heeded, the children may continue to stray. In one study of sixty effeminate boys aged four to eleven, 98 percent of them engaged in cross-dressing, and 83 percent said they wished they had been born a girl. The most important thing to remember is that there is no such thing as a "gay child" or a "gay teen." But of the children showing signs and left untreated, these boys have a 75 percent chance of becoming homosexual or bisexual.

Simply put, look for traits that set them apart from their male peers and contributed to a distortion in the development of their normal gender identity. But make no mistake. Boys can be sensitive, kind, social, artistic, gentle – and be heterosexual. God created a vast sea of individuality.

The father plays an essential role in a boy's normal development as a man. From birth to about age 5, both boys and girls are emotionally attached to the mother. She meets all her child's needs.

Girls can continue to grow in their identification with their mothers. Boys must switch from identifying with their mothers to identifying and bonding with their fathers. The stage starts at about a year and a half and continues until the boy is about five years old. A little boy will not only begin to observe the difference, he must now decide who he will become. He looks to his father image to guide his next step. According to Robert Stoller, "The first order of business in being a man is, 'don't be a woman."

To quote Dr. James Dobson, "In 15 years, I have spoken with hundreds of homosexual men. I have never met one who said he had a loving, respectful relationship with his father." However, I must add that I have seen fathers who loved their children but who were by their nature, reserved, removed, distant, worked to the exclusion of the family, or could not make an emotional connection whose sons became gay. Sometimes these disconnects are made due to family or marital strife. If the parents focus on their own problems they are abandoning the child.

The fathers place is to form an attachment with his son to guide him away from his attachment with his mother. Male identity starts there. According to psychologist Robert Stoller, masculinity is an achievement. Thus Dr. James Dobson is quoted as having said, "Growing up straight isn't something that happens. It requires good parenting. It requires societal support. And it takes time."

So, now we can break homosexuality down into three separate causes.

1. Abuse, emotional or sexual trauma during early childhood.

2. A father who was not emotionally connected in a positive way to the child.

3. Genetic or hormonal anomalies. (Although these represent a very small percentage of patients.)

In seeking a cure for the condition, we should decide which of these has caused the child to become homosexual. We can see that children do not tend to be born gay. Neither do they consciously choose to be gay. Rather, it is a twisted road they are usually pushed down by abuse, dysfunctional families, lack of connection or direction of a father at a sensitive time, or some kind of deep-seated confusion coming from the environment. It is in the treating of the cause that we find a cure. The older a patient is, the more difficult it will be to break old habits and establish new emotional traits. In younger patients, we can help them along the path to recovery by addressing the underlying issues.

The reaction of society poses a resistance to healing the very lifestyle it opposes. By isolating the homosexual person, society guarantees they will be driven back into the gay community where the lifestyle will be reinforced. Often Christians quote the Bible to prove homosexuality is wrong.

- Leviticus 18:22-23 You shall not lie with a male as one lies with a female; it is an abomination. Also you shall not have intercourse with any animal to be defiled with it, nor shall any woman stand before an animal to mate with it; it is a perversion.

- Leviticus 20:13 If there is a man who lies with a male as those who lie with a woman, both of them have committed a detestable act; they shall surely be put to death. Their blood guiltiness is upon them.

Notice that these are Old Testament verses. In the Old Testament there were distinctions in degree of sin. Some sins were punishable by death, while others took the sacrifice of a dove as payment. We are now under the grace of the New Testament covenant where we are told, "ALL have sinned."

"All have sinned and fall short of the glory of God."   Romans 3:23

If this is true and all sin is the same since it all separates us from God, and Jesus died for all so all who will could be reconciled to the Father, then we who gossip, judge, lie, cheat, or commit adultery are as far from God as any homosexual. Yet, we must also apply caution and reason, being wise as serpents and innocent as doves.

Let us look at pedophilia for example. Not all gay men sexually abuse children. However, 100% of men who sexually abuse boys are gay by the very nature of the act. God can and will forgive. We should not sacrifice our children to test the resolve of a pedophile. This is one of the only conditions that have such a low "cure rate" as to be considered incurable. Thus, in the worse possible scenarios, we find ourselves wedged between the hope of restoration for pedophiles and the necessity to protect others from them.

In most cases we are dealing with a gay lifestyle that may bring judgment and condemnation from a society that does not know how to reconcile the balance of the twin truths "all sin is the same" and "it is an abomination." The balance and truth is simply this: We have all sinned. We all need Jesus. He can forgive all sin. All we have to do is stop believing what we are doing is right, ask for forgiveness, and cease the sin. Whether homosexuality is considered a choice or not, anything that goes against the will of God is a sin.

Three things are needed before a new life can be lived. The person must want to change from the deepest level. The true sexuality of the person must be confirmed and encouraged…in other words, breaking away from the gay community completely. The underlying issues and causes must be addressed. This may mean the establishment of positive male role models. Above and beyond all of these things, I am firmly convinced that our relationship and position with our heavenly Father, when truly understood, can lead the way to complete healing.

DRAGONS AND DRAGON ... DUNG

Deu. 24:13-14 Thou shalt have a paddle upon thy weapon; and it shall be, when thou wilt ease thyself abroad, thou shalt dig therewith and shalt turn back and cover that which cometh forth from thee. For God walketh in the midst of thy camp to deliver thee.

(Modern translation: If you have to poop, cover it up. God doesn't want to deal with your poop... and neither does anyone else.)

One of the more difficult calls to make is figuring out whether our distorted reactions are from our own dragon or from the attempt to avoid stepping in the dung left by the dragons of those around us. This is seen primarily within the family structure where the members dance around each other so as not to force any member to face his own dragons or sins. It seems easier that way since the dragons are usually related; therefore, if one member were to face his true motives, fears, or abuses, all members would be affected and would have to deal with their own motives on some level. God is not in the midst of some families because of "dung in the camp." Family secrets are kept in the family, taught or passed down from parent to child, hidden from others but known to the family. The secrets are unspoken truths lying there, stinking. To avoid the dung we walk in a false manner tiptoeing around some issues and avoiding others all together.

Since everyone has hidden agendas, motives, fears, or dragons, untrue and distorted signals are sent to those around us. When we get drawn into this lie, we begin reacting to the falseness in a correspondingly false way. We become "not real." We live a lie and we suffer from the stress of it all. This "unrealness" is a present left by the dragon of someone else. It is dragon dung. Dragon dung is very slippery and can cause one to fall. After a while it hardens into a false face. Many families live to sustain a false face, so everyone is always wearing a face full of dragon dung. Simply put, families have secrets and abuses which keep out mental health and God's blessings. The "dung" keeps God, and the health, peace, and love He brings, out of the family.

To recall the metaphor of the onion, this dung is dirt on the onion. It must be washed off. It is another mask to wear, albeit a rather smelly one, and it must be removed first before the onion can be peeled and any other personal masks can be dealt with. *If you accept another person's insanity as reality, you will become insane.*

LANDMARKS AND SHORTCUTS

Instead of setting out on a journey that will take years to complete, we can use a road map to speed up our progress. Instead of spending years waiting for enough objective glimpses of our motives to identify what they are, we can be painfully honest one time and with that information use the system in this book to lead us to a deeper understanding of our motives. We can obtain freedom from self-delusion, lies, and falseness. There is a process to be followed:

- Realize that you choose your reactions.
- Take responsibility for them.
- Watch yourself from a detached perspective.
- Trace the thoughts and reactions to a central, consistent motive.
- Use this book to understand the motive and cause of the action or feeling.

Once the subconscious motives are brought to a conscious understanding, actions will be better understood and controlled. Motives are based in fear, anger, trauma, or loss. Motives deal with how to survive or overcome in life. Motives are basic and primal. They always deal with the fear, anger, need, or greed of the child inside of us.

PSYCHOLOGY AND COUNSELING

Out of the hundreds of books written on the subject of personality, there is much overlap and much confusion. It is not my aim to add another whit to the confusion and differences in this field, but instead to attempt to unify the voices using new terminology which, when explained, will set a common, or at least familiar, ground to the many theories and ideas herein. Let us consider the most common points of view we have in the abundance of books out there. In the Freudian arena we have the id, the ego, and the superego. In the more modern view we have the child, the adult, and the parent.

Although I do not agree with many of Freud's theories, (I am "Jungian" at heart), I believe we can see a correlation between Freud's theory of the interplay of id, ego, and superego with the comparable concept of the child, parent, and adult as purported by Whitfield (author of The Inner Child) and others. As with any recurring theme that appears to work, we must assume there is a truth within, and this truth is described differently according to the way the author sees it. Truth, then, is like a jewel which offers many facets to be viewed according to the observers' perspectives. The observers then describe what they see, and we call them enlightened.

Some definitions should be established so we will all be speaking the same language. These terms recur throughout this work and will be used to define a common ground for many theories today. The theories brought together here have commonality and validity thus can be grouped and named. This is done to keep the work under a thousand pages, and to not put the reader to sleep.

1. There is a beginning state of the psyche. It is "hard-wired" by nature in the form of the heredity of personality and brain structure. It is the primal, selfish side of us that Freud labeled the id. This uninfluenced child state is called *the soul*.

2. The rite of passage for all people is that voyage between the child state which is called the soul, and the adult state. It is during this time that outside forces affect one's inside evolution and growth. This influence determines the self-expectations and self-image which act to change the natural way the soul would express itself. It is the referee that keeps the childish impulses within social norms. The combined influences appear as a single composite voice to the child. It is comprised of all the authority and parental images in the child's life. To Freud this was the super-ego. This internalized parental influence is called *the quiescent self*.

3. Becoming an adult is an ongoing process. The quiescent self influences the soul. The constant interplay between the soul, (what we are), and the quiescent self, (what we think we should be), becomes how we conduct ourselves. It is the adult image we present to the world. Freud called it the Ego. We will call it *the expression*.

As with most things, whether within or without, there are only three basic postures taken regarding any influence. In external situations you may accept, reject, or compromise. Since we are speaking of the way the soul will react to the influences called the quiescent self, we must view the reaction to see what posture is taken. These internal postures are to mimic, oppose, or compensate for the effects of others upon us. As the soul will have insufficient data to use in comparison when it is young, it will always accept the parental influences and thus attempts to mimic the ideals expressed by those we watch.

Parents can do much damage here even though they may possess no malicious intent. The reason is so simple it is usually overlooked. The parents are of a certain personality type or types which may not be compatible with the child's type. If parents insist a child who is not like them be like them, there will be a loss of the child's full expression as the soul seeks a way to obey the quiescent self. As parents we must nurture and discipline the child within the context of his own personality.

If the soul struggles to identify and express its true nature, having seen itself as a separate entity, it will compensate instead of mimic. This is an attempt to keep its identity and still satisfy the quiescent self. When no common ground can be reached, or when the expression of the soul becomes stifled to the degree that identity is lost, we can expect opposition. If the parent is too strong-willed and insists the child comply, or if the child is exposed to something in the environment that is overwhelming, there may be damage and splintering as the child is forced into a mold not made for him.

Once the soul loses its ability to express itself, it has no way of dealing in a healthy manner with the world around it. This is emotional conflict. It is because of this structure that, in childhood, we expect mimicry. In adolescence there is the push to establish selfhood and, therefore, more opposition. Once selfhood has been established, in the phase society refers to as adulthood, we find more compensation as we walk the balance beam between what we are and what we think we should be.

> Accept, agree, mimic.
> Compromise, negotiate, compensate.
> Disagree, reject, oppose.

These are the only postures or reactions in the world, whether political or psychological.

THE RULES

IF THEY HAVEN'T ASKED THE QUESTION, THEY AREN'T READY FOR THE ANSWER

Because we are human, we want to think of ourselves as individuals, but it is not so. Although it is true no two people are the same, it is also true a homogeneous basis of objective and subjective reality keeps us, as a species, capable of social intercourse. If a person is within a socially accepted boundary of behavior, he is considered sane; if not, he is considered insane. The problem of deciding if a person is normal, eccentric, or insane occurs in the numerous directions and degrees of imbalance within the accepted norm. One reason for the rising number of people needing counseling and mental health treatment is the removal of basic Christian guiding principles in their lives. With a common set of rules and boundaries it was easy to know when we were getting too far away from accepted conduct. The person or society could correct their course with accuracy. Now, with no principles to live by, our society has no lighthouse. It risks shipwreck.

Let us identify and explain certain common imbalances, the "games" used to express them, and ways to work out their effects and lessen their existence in our lives. Let us begin by establishing a few ground rules. First, there are no perfect people, so there are no perfect parents, so there are no perfect children, so there are no perfect people who grow up to be perfect parents. If you don't think your parents affected you, or your deficits will affect your children, let me remind you of the fact that a large percentage of people with drinking, abuse, or marital problems raise children who continue the trend. These are easily identified phenomena, but there are other patterns transmitted from parent to child which are not as easy to recognize. When we know where to look and what to look for, we can pinpoint, understand, and correct these problems in ourselves.

Let me stress that it is necessary for us to endeavor to change only ourselves. It is not for us to change others. The surgery must be done from the inside out. Do you want a healthy relationship? Then be a healthy person. If two healthy people love each other in a healthy way, then they can have a healthy relationship. Thus, rule number one is – Change happens from the inside out. Worry about yourself.

We have all heard it said it takes two to make a relationship, and it takes two to break it. That is one of the most ridiculous statements ever uttered. If we overlook the fact unhealthy people tend to choose unhealthy people for mates, as like seems to attract like; then without a doubt many marriages are ruined by one, as the other fights to understand and battles to keep it alive. I have seen unbalanced mates tear down as the healthy mate tries to repair. It takes both to make it, but it only takes one to ruin it.

That leads us to rule number two: Don't get into other people's affairs. Before you start your work, you must realize it is easier to identify the problems of others than those of yourself, but you cannot change the problems of others. You can only change yourself, and it will take all of your energy to identify and control your own "speck in the eye."

There are three divisions of emotional and physical property in the world: "my stuff," "your stuff," and "our stuff." Generally, if the emotion or situation is "my stuff" it is controlled only by my choice. This does not mean it would not affect others, but it does mean I am directly involved and responsible. If some thing, action, or feeling is mine, I must take responsibility for it. It should not be changed, altered, or squelched without my full consent. If some thing, action, or feeling is yours, I should keep my hands and words off it. It is not my place to change your mind if it doesn't involve me. The tricky part is where it is "ours". This occurs when mutual action, or consent is needed, or when the action or decision of both people are involved.

Since we are individuals, we will see things differently, especially given our varied backgrounds and postures from which to relate. It is necessary to understand the true intentions of each person regarding disagreements. Most people do not understand the posture through which they view the world, so they are unclear as to what is their true intent. Much like two people who view the same things, one lying down and the other standing on his head, posture can make all of the difference in how things are seen.

Try to understand both sides of a situation, but remember, it is only you who can be changed by you, so concentrate your efforts in trying to see yourself more clearly. If you can understand your own vantage point, you will be able to compensate and gain more balance. It may seem uncomfortable at first, but the benefits will outweigh the stress, and as you maintain the proper attitude it will become natural. The important thing is to fully understand what happened to help mold you into the person of today, and to rid yourself of the poor internal posture it has caused. If an impasse is reached in the discussion of "our stuff" it is good to unravel it into "yours" and "mine."

At this point the next rule comes into play. There are only three things that you can do in any given relationship:

1. Accept the situation. This is not to say you will have no problem living with the actions or the results.

2. Change your thinking about the situation. This means reaching a frame of reference resulting in the first point being achieved.

3. Change your relationship to the situation. This is achieved by a physical or emotional positioning that allows you a comfort

zone, and an easing of stress. It may result in becoming less involved with the situation. It may involve giving a project or situation completely over to the other person. It may require getting out. Whatever you do, make sure it is not done out of frustration, anger, or revenge. Otherwise, it will come back to haunt you. Any problem not dealt with to the point of resolution will require dealing with it again. It is at this point most problems get stuck.

To illustrate, if you are involved with a drug addict, the act of taking drugs is their "stuff"; however, it affects you. If you have gone to the addict and explained that his actions are causing you harm, yet he has not chosen to change his ways, you have two choices. You may decide the situation is one with which you can live. If this is truly your choice, then you should abide in peace. If not, then you will end up nagging and being unhappy. You will be covertly trying to change the person, or punishing him by your words, tone, or attitude, and that's against the rules. Your other choice is to leave. If this is your choice, make sure it is not done to intimidate or coerce. It is your right to make the decision to leave, but not to blackmail, punish, or pressure.

You have the right to cease all contact with another, but make sure it is a clean break. All will be done properly if you can say you have chosen this path based on another's actions. It should be done not to change them but to protect yourself, with no expectations of them. If you have chosen to stay in a situation yet there are bursts of anger or resentment, it is likely you still have certain expectations the other person isn't living up to. It is a fairly steadfast rule that unmet expectations will lead to anger, frustration, or resentment. If this is a problem, ask yourself what you really want from the situation, then ask what the other person is doing or not doing that goes against your expectations.

You may then take a second look at your choices of dropping your expectations and living with the situation, or getting out of the situation, assuming a compromise cannot be reached.

This is painful at times. You have to realize just because a person is dysfunctional doesn't mean you don't love them. As a matter of fact, it could be precisely because of their anomalies that you are attracted to them. What they represent is another chance to fix a problem we encountered in our past, and make it right. If they represent the parent that was emotionally distant, or the alcoholic parent or abusive parent we tried to get to love us we are drawn to attempting the struggle again, through this person. Possibly the dysfunctional person represents us in our time of greatest need and we are fulfilling in them what we wished could have been done for us. However, people cannot be helped until they are ready and very willing to receive help. Whatever the reason we are attracted to the dysfunctional person, we can rest assured the answer comes from one of our three internal voices.

There are three voices driving our decisions: the child/soul, the parent/quiescent self, and the adult/expression. The child is the part of us that never grew up. It got stunted by some trauma or abuse that stopped part of the child's growth at that point.

The parent is the part of us which internalized the perceived values and expectations of the parental image toward the child. The adult is the logical, reasonable part of us. It is the part which is capable of putting aside feelings and using facts to make choices. It is this voice upon which we must learn to rely. To do this we must understand and make plans to squelch the other voices within us.

When it comes to decisions and attractions, these three voices compete. For example, we seem to be split as to why we are attracted to certain people. It may be because these attractions can be initiated by our child within, or our adult. If the adult is attracted to a person, it is usually due to a part of the person's personality we desire to integrate into our own in order to make ourselves more complete or better people. This is why so often we marry types which are opposites.

Since the quiescent self, (the parent image inside of us by which we gage our actions), is what we are striving for in ourselves, it only follows it is also what we admire in others. We are drawn out of a need or a desire to be more like that person and to learn from him in some way. The quiescent self is also associated with the parental part of us, since it is what we value. Part of the process of becoming healthy is to be sure what we value and expect from others and ourselves is realistic.

As a relationship progresses, we can grow less and less tolerant of differences, and trouble can erupt when we lose sight of the reasons we married our mates. We need to remind ourselves why we chose our mates, and from time to time concentrate on and appreciate the differences and variety they bring. If the "child" in us is attracted to a person, more often than not, it is in order to resolve a problem the child has been working on since his exposure to emotional injury.

The "child" usually has a number of these it has gained throughout life. At each point in time when a trauma occurred, we leave part of ourselves there to worry, wonder, and try to understand how to make it go away.

This is not easy to explain to the adult, but there is no time except the "now" for the child. It is a subconscious entity to whom all things, past and present, are all still happening now. If we understand this, we then can understand why the child is so driven to solve the problems of its dysfunctional family. To him, Daddy and Mommy are still doing what they were doing so long ago, and it still hurts, it is still inflicting pain, it still must stop, and it still must be fixed. To correct the problems of the past in the present, there must exist a child and the parent who harmed it. If we choose a mate who makes us feel in some way like we felt during the time of pain in our childhood, we have set a stage that will allow the replay of some tragic times. Sadly, the replay of tragic times is often at least as tragic as the original scene.

Children are emotional creatures, even subconsciously. They don't solve life's problems very well, so this scenario can be played out over and over. Each time the odds are better for lightning to strike than of getting released from this cycle.

There can be another twist to this scenario. We have all heard of transference, and this is the classic form of it. The identification with a person in trouble brings about a sympathetic response within us, as we remember feeling similarly. Our child identifies with the other person so strongly he feels if he could help the other person it would be helping himself. All of the need to be loved, helped, or accepted the child once had that was unrequited is now heaped upon the other person, who by definition is also not whole. We would now do anything to help him.

Our time, money, love, and all our resources are at the disposal of the issue. Furthermore, since we have transferred part of us to the other, we begin to lose the line of delineation between our needs and his needs. We become less distinguished as an individual.

Loving the other person is tantamount to loving ourselves, as the hurting child we were. Many people with this urge to rescue, which is called the "white knight syndrome," experience this peculiar twist. They are often accused of collecting any stray that comes their way. The less diplomatic critic may use the term, "scum magnet." If you have been involved in a series of dysfunctional relationships, or relationships with partners who were abusive, alcoholic, or addicted, emotionally cold, liars, or those who were unfaithful, you should examine the possibility this might be a feeling of low self-esteem, abuse, or neglect engendered in your childhood affecting you today. After all, to the hurting little boy or girl, the injustice is still in the present.

Another voice inside us is the "parent," the internalized, perceived attitudes of our guardian and parental/authority images. The voice is generally strict and demanding. It is by measuring ourselves against the parents' expectations that we judge ourselves against what we perceived to be the proper state or condition. The problem is not a real voice or person. It is a perception of an imperfect person, or the opinion of an imperfect parental image. It cannot possibly be a perfect part of our psyche. Since no parent is perfect, we have no choice but to concede we are hearing a voice that is not balanced, and our image is even further thwarted because our perception is colored by our own near or far-sightedness as imperfect watchers.

The only question becomes which direction the imbalance will lean. Was our perception of the parental image that he was abusive, intolerant, critical, or impossible to please? Were there messages that may have caused obsessive or compulsive behavior? It could be something as simple as, "Can't you do anything right?" or something as complicated as the act of a parent withholding love when not pleased. Whatever the pattern, it is internalized in childhood as what is normal and expected from the parent within. To a child the parents are never wrong, and their judgments and expectations are beyond question, so if the expectations are unrealistic, the stage is set in our adult lives for frustration, low self-esteem, and even anger.

The internalized voice of our parent can make us hear criticism when none is intended, make us defensive when not attacked, make us feel everything is our fault when it is not, make us feel unloved, or that there is a price to be paid for favors and affection. These are easy parallels to see in a parent who told the child, "You were an accident. We didn't want you. You can't do anything right. I had a life of my own before I had you kids. You are stupid and lazy. You have no talent..."

A thousand others could be listed. Attitudes speak volumes. They can be seen in common exchanges such as a parent doing a favor for a child, or a parent giving a gift to a child. If the favor or gift comes with a statement of complaint about cost, time, or energy, then the child within will interpret this as meaning he is not worth the time, energy, or money that was spent. This is very obvious when we look at a typical scenario.

The child's birthday has arrived and presents are given. The parent hands a present to the child and says, "Don't expect any more of this stuff. It was just too expensive and hard to find." The simple rule for anyone is a rule of common courtesy. If you don't want to do it, then don't do it. If you have decided to do it, then do it graciously. That means don't do it and then extract an emotional payment for it. Chances are it will be appreciated a thousand times more if you don't try to demand appreciation.

Then there are actions, which always speak louder than words, actions such as beating, neglect, abuse, yelling, confining, restricting… all done with a hair trigger temper. The child who was hurt by them internalizes each of these, and they become the voice of the parent. There is the voice of the hurting child alongside the voice of a hurtful parent with only the voice of the adult, which we have grown to be, to keep them in place.

PSYCHOLOGICAL PRINCIPLES

There are certain psychological principles to observe during counseling. One is no matter what the personality type, it will have a feminine and masculine influence in part according to the sex of the person.

There is more eros/feminine/"relater" in the female matrix, and more logos/thinker/provider in the male matrix. Remember, the superior function is the area in which the person naturally functions, and the inferior function is that area in which the person must put forth effort to function. In our culture today, there may be stress for one to abandon part of his nature in order to build the inferior part. This can happen to an emotional person who gives up feeling in order to just think. This will produce an unhappy and stressed persona. The more the superior function is suppressed, the more stress is produced. This stress will come out in the weakest point of the personality.

The id is made of basic urges and instincts. It is driven by the pleasure principle, eros, and survival instincts. Most of its energy is directed toward the discharge of tensions associated with sex and aggression. This energy is called libido. Although there is not an exact match in meaning, the id is very similar to the influence of the child or the soul.

The ego is the executive, taking the primary mental images from the id and balancing them with external reality. It is the thinking, planning, and deciding part of us. It is the consciousness that puts things off until they are appropriate, or squelches unwise actions. This part of the psyche is the adult. Since the adult is the only logical, reasonable part of our inner voices, it is the only one which should make our decisions for us. It roughly equates to the adult in our makeup or the expression.

The superego is the judge, the referee, or censor of the ego's thoughts and actions. It is the conscience, that part which draws conclusions as to what is right or wrong based on past punishments and reactions. The superego contains the ego ideal, which is all of the things we perceived our parents or authority image approving. It is referred to as the parent voice, the quiescent-self, or the internalized parent. Since children view parents as the ultimate authority, this part of our psyche is directly related to how we view God. A distorted parent image can lead to a distorted view of God and religion in general. The superego matches the ego's ideal of action, accomplishment, and success.

When it is underdeveloped, the superego allows for criminal, delinquent, or sociopathic behavior. If overly strict, the superego yields rigidity, inhibitions, and guilt. The superego and the id are unconscious, while the ego is partly conscious and partly not. It is, however, the personality we see. It seems sociopaths are people with weak links between ego and superego. It could be the ego is not functioning as a referee, or the proper parental image is not being supplied by the superego. In other words, the connection between conscience and action is not there. They have no moral compass to tell them what they intend to do is wrong. The Bible speaks of those whose conscience has been burned as with a hot iron. These people are those generally regarded as evil.

Sadly, we seldom recognize the more intelligent sociopaths until the damage is done. They are usually personable, pleasant, and articulate. They are masters of manipulation without the brake or wheel of conscience to limit their actions or correct their course. These men and women ascend to greatness on the backs of others. They sometimes become the politicians, power brokers, and televangelists of our society. Thus, we may think we know the extent of brutality of the sociopath, but we may find ourselves dealing with only the common variety of manipulator and user. The violent, the robber, the liar, the thief, the thug...none can compare to the amount of misery and loss a master sociopath can inflict. Without a conscience the liar can believe his own lies and be as convincing as the most truthful man. All the time, the only guide is their own best interest. To quote Don Henley, "A man with a briefcase can steal more money than any man with a gun."

The id is the child, the superego is the parent, and the ego is the adult. The ego, however, is divided into three parts. First is that which is seen; this is our persona. Second is the subconscious; we need it to deal with our feelings. The third is the interface between the id and the superego; this interface is called the planes of expression. It is the arbitrator between the parent and child, and it is responsible for finding a way to please both child and parent.

The ego decides if the time, place, and request are possible under parental restraints. It then uses this information to subdue the id (child). When the interface is weak, then the child seems to run wild, not hearing the parent as it should. For those of us who think in terms of charts and pictures, this description of the layout and workings of the psyche may make things easier to envision and understand.

EMOTIONAL BOOKKEEPING

THE GOLDEN RULE AS SEEN IN MONETARY TERMS

In our emotional lives, between family and friends, there is a scorecard filled with plusses and minuses. It works like an emotional bank account. Each essential item has a subjective worth and acts as currency. Each of these emotional items given to another person acts like a deposit. Each item missing from the list of essential needs is like a withdrawal from our emotional bank account. The rules of finance are the same inside and out. You can't have more going out than coming in without overdrawing. You cannot stay overdrawn for long without getting into trouble. If you overdraw, the penalties will really hurt.

Usually, if we are deprived of more than two items of our essential needs, we get into serious emotional trouble. This must be stated loudly and clearly; it does not matter how religious you think you are or how controlled you perceive yourself to be, if you do not have the majority of your emotional needs met, you are in danger of having an affair. The affair, although obviously meeting a physical need, is more importantly an attempt to meet the person's perceived emotional deficit. It is stressful to live without love and these emotional items are the currency of love. Listed below are the items needed for a happy relationship:

Affection. To men this usually means sex and closeness. To women it is personal time, wooing, dating, and romance.

Companionship. To women this means talking and snuggling. A mate that is attractive and responsive is more important for men since they are more visually stimulated.

Openness. Men take this to mean spontaneous, fun, and sexually open. Women take it to mean emotionally open and honest.

Respect. Men need respect in the form of admiration. Women need to be treated chivalrously and with caring and equality.

Security. This includes trust and reliability, especially within the relationship. It is important for all of us to feel secure in our relationships if love is to deepen.

Support. To men this is important in all legitimate pursuits in their lives, be it hobby or vocation. Women especially need stability and emotional support. The need of monetary and financial stability tends to be higher on the woman's list than the man's.

Judging from this list, it seems obvious some of us are overdrawn from the beginning. We need more emotional input, but we are trapped inside our own habits and expectations – those of serving and not being served. It is important for each party to maintain a balance in the emotional bank account. When all areas are summed up, the results should always be somewhat even between the people in the relationship. So much hurt can accumulate over time as one partner stops listening or caring about the needs of their partner. In time, out of anger or frustration or pain the partner in need will begin to close their emotional doors. They will become remote or emotionally aloof. They will build up resentment and in turn stop fulfilling the emotional or physical needs of their mate. Now, the circle is set to perpetuate itself as both partners are in emotional bankruptcy.

It will take pure determination and will power to break the cycle. There will be no guarantee that opening ones heart will yield anything but more rejection, but the open heart is the prize for the effort. The reaction of the partner is a secondary result. We open our hearts because that is what

God wants from us. He works in a humble and contrite heart. If the partner does not respond that is their issue. They must work on themselves. We must work on the simple act of loving without expectation.

Most counselors have not fully applied the list of emotional needs to children, but the needs are the same. Children are an investment. We are putting currency into the accounts of our children so later they can have a full emotional account when they enter adult life. We are investing in society. If a child has *Affection, Companionship, Openness, Respect, Security, and Support* they will likely treat others that way. They will have it in their account to give.

ADULTERY:
IT'S NOT JUST FOR MEN ANYMORE

Of all the sins and injuries given and taken within the church and among Christians, adultery ranks as number one. Adultery is the most common problem a minister or counselor will encounter. It may appear as a simple visit by a couple in which one partner is complaining about the other partner being cold, aloof, distant, unpleasant, critical, or emotionally abusive; but underneath many of these cases lurks adultery. The counselor may suspect the sin but the sin may be denied…until the full truth is discovered. Be prepared for the truth. The damage to the relationship will be massive.

People seem to look at sex and adultery in different ways. It may mean very little to them, almost a recreation. They may claim there is no emotional connection to the person they were having sex with. They may wish to dismiss the entire event, until their partner cheats on them, then the playing field is evened. Some have the ability to partition or segment their minds and feelings. Like rooms in a house, what goes on in one room does not directly affect what happens in another room. An affair will not directly affect feelings about the partner…or so they believe. But the heart is divided, and so are resources of time, action, and thought. The idea comes home when the person is confronted by the partner's indiscretions. Then the betrayal, pain, and anger make perfect sense.

The counselor is likely to hear, "It was just a little fling. It didn't mean anything. I don't love her, I love you…" To the mind of the person saying these things it is true. But, it is all founded in selfishness or a feeling of emptiness, or both. Now, you may be thinking, "this sounds just like a man," and it is likely you would be correct, but things are changing. As more and more women have entered the work place and taken their positions outside the home, the number of women who seek out and begin extra-martial relationships has come close to equaling those of men. After all, it makes sense there would be some type of balance since it takes two to have a relationship.

Adultery destroys the fabric of trust in a relationship. This is the primary damage done. The person caught in the act of adultery will try to diminish the sin and its effects but there is no sweeping this under the rug. It is a blow to the partner on several levels. The act speaks in a voice loud and clear. It says:

I didn't care enough to think of your feelings before I acted.
You were not woman/man enough to fill my needs.
You trusted me and I betrayed you.
I do not love you anymore.

These words, if spoken aloud would crush the heart of the partner. Adultery shouts these lines over and over through the actions of the sin.

Yet, there are two victims here, and we cannot lose track of that. The marriage may have been in trouble for a long time. One partner may not have been supplying the emotional needs of the other. Sex could have been used as a bargaining chip to punish the partner if the other did not get his or her way.

More than likely there is one partner who chooses passive/aggressive tactics to inflict damage while avoiding repercussions. The signs are obvious. The partner will say something insulting, hurtful, or demeaning. If there is a negative reaction to the comment the person defending against the barb will be reprimanded for their defense by such lines as, "I was just kidding. Can't you take a joke?" Such exchanges must be stopped. There should be no "joking, kidding, or quipping" that makes another person feel ill at ease.

After a period of time living with these barbs, anger and resentment builds up to a point where the relationship is damaged. Coldness and lack of sex within a marriage also damages the relationship. Men view sex as a statement of love and desire as admiration, the absence of these in a marriage tells the man he is not wanted or loved. Women view conversation and togetherness in much the same way. If warmth and closeness are missing from the relationship, women may seek it some place else.

Of course, the counselor might want to inquire as to why the person throwing the barbs or withholding love feels the need to hurt the other partner. There could be unresolved issues in which the person is hurt or angry and has no way of "safely venting" the hurt except in this kind of retaliation. These endless cycle of hurt, anger, pain, and emotional distancing are very common. The cycle must be stopped so healing can begin.

The hard work undertaken to repair the marriage will not be worth your time and trouble if the underlying issues are not addressed. To talk the couple into reconciliation may be committing the adulterer to a life of constant ridicule and browbeating. This is especially true if essential needs were withheld as a punishment to begin with and that is what opened the door to adultery.

Think, counselors and ministers….think. Do not look at the sin. Look at the sinner, and ask yourself, "What was missing? Why did this happen?"

Some people are naturally promiscuous. Most of us are, but most of us are able to control our urges. Those raised in the free love days of the 60's and 70's were taught a relaxed standard by society. This conditioning competes with God's word on the subject of marriage. If the partner is not from the same mindset, the damage caused by the action will shock, stun, and surprise the adulterer. Look for the instant of realization and work from it. The moment of the utterance of: "Oh God, what have I done?" is the beginning of understanding and healing.

One of the only ways to save a marriage after adultery is to set up a safe and verifiable environment for the hurting partner. The person who has committed adultery should always be where they say they are, do what they say they will do, and call when they say they will call. All of these things should be done and verified within the bounds of common sense and not to the damage of employment or reasonable daily freedoms. After a while, trust can be re-established.

Even after proving oneself and re-establishing clean patterns of living, the marriage may still not be salvageable. This is because the victim may not be able to forgive and forget. Bringing up the subject day after day for months or years on end is not the way to allow healing. It is a difficult path to take, but if the couple can't move past the adultery, the marriage will fail. A reasonable period of time should be given to discussing and venting, but then the partners should discuss the event with the counselor only. They should permit the marriage to heal. We all understand that this act was a violation on many levels, but to permit the adulterer to live in constant punishment is not right, either. Habits must be changed. Accountability should be established. There should be a line drawn where we must assume the lesson is learned. After that, it is up to the victim to forgive and forget, or not.

TRAUMA COUNSELING

In the months following the 9/11 terrorist attack on the United States, trauma counselors descended on New York City with the aim of helping the victims cope with the horrible tragedy. The loss of safety, life, security, and loved ones sent many into sleepless, unfocused despair. Others went through their daily lives trying to make sense of the life-altering destruction. One of the recurring descriptions of trauma victims is a feeling of being in a dream, as if they would awaken any moment and things would be normal.

For days after an emotional or physical disruption, victims reported trying over and over to rouse themselves from the nightmare they believed they were in. In a sense, this is the same "denial" stage encountered by those facing a terminal disease. Days or weeks later, when the victims accepted the "realness" of the event, the work of repairing the psyche began.

Prior to the event, the commonly held view lent itself to the establishment of group sessions where each person could tell his story and work through the pain by commiserating with others in similar pain. The belief was simplistic and across the board. Soon, data began to appear that showed some who received counseling were deteriorating at rates faster than those who had received no counseling at all. Some, who received no counseling, were coping better than those who met in group counseling sessions. Since the results were spread across the board, it was obvious the conditions were not tied to particular counselors or companies.

Psychologists began to investigate. The findings were interesting and weighty enough to be covered here.

As we will see in the chapters explaining personality types, there are those who process information as introverts and those who experience the world as extroverts. In trauma, and the counseling that follows, these two types of people had opposite reactions to group counseling.

For some, the sharing of traumatic experiences off-loads the stress. As grief is shared by the group their stories are told, the pain is vented and emotional pressures are relieved. The knowledge that others have experienced the same trauma gives strength and hope as this type sees the group moving together toward healing. Strength is found in numbers. Stability is found in leaning on others. Healing comes in the telling and sharing of the story. Listening to the stories of others allows this type to identify and emotionally bond, yielding a sense of community and comfort.

However, those who keep their feelings in and process their grief over time were adversely affected by group sessions. Internalization of emotions does not allow for the venting of grief for the introvert. There is no "sharing" of their feelings. If the event is not processed and understood, the telling of the story only adds to the internal chaos. The group sessions become only a story told without the benefit of any emotional relief. This forces the introvert to relive a small part of the trauma, thereby further enhancing or renewing the prior pain.

Furthermore, hearing others tell of the nightmare added to the pain of the experience, as the patients were carrying their own burdens as well as the grief absorbed from empathizing with those in the group. Plainly stated, hearing stories of the suffering of others made this type of individual very uncomfortable. The despair and feeling of loss as well as feelings of hopelessness intensified.

After data was released and coordinated with the types of patients, the results became clear. Different people require different therapies. Those who tend to hold feelings in and not talk about the events should share on a one-on-one level with a counselor who is prepared to listen as time allows the patient time to process, organize, and articulate feelings.

Those who function in an outgoing and more communicative manner should join the group sessions. The patients who process information and feelings in a more introverted or internal way should be allowed time to come to grips with all that has taken place. The story must be told in the proper time. That time depends on the person. Some hold feelings in. They brood over events. They take things apart, categorize, analyze, and internalize as part of their healing process. This is normal for them, but not for all.

Other data reflected higher occurrences of post traumatic stress symptoms from those whose counselors openly discussed a list of possible symptoms. If the counselors listed sleeplessness, lack of ability to concentrate, loss of short term memory, to name a few, the patients were much more likely to exhibit these conditions.

People who have experienced trauma or cataclysmic events are more susceptible to suggestion; however, this can be used to the benefit of the suffering patient, if counselors were to remain on message. The message should be one of encouragement, healing, and continued improvement over time. Know your patient before you begin leading the healing journey.

First – Do No Harm. That could mean giving the psyche time to heal. Generally, post traumatic stress disorder should not be considered until at least six months have passed since the event. It's normal to be distressed immediately after a disaster. Many people have difficulty sleeping and concentrating. Some have nightmares.

Most symptoms subsided after a few months passed. A couple of months after 9/11 only 7.5 percent of victims had P.T.S.D. Six months after 9/11 less than one percent had P.T.S.D. The question remains; why do some people develop P.T.S.D. and others do not?

As counselors of post 9/11 interviewed their patients, many of those with P.T.S.D. had trouble remembering the day in full. Memories were jumbled, scrambled, disjointed, and spotty. The lack of continuity of memories did not allow the patients to organize, understand, or process the glut of negative information. As the counselors led the patients through the events to fill in gaps and help them make sense of the flow of events, some patients began to improve.

Both fear and the memory of frightening events are essential for survival. But researchers say that in people with P.T.S.D. the fear system seems to get stuck in the "on" position. Sufferers feel a sense of anxiety as if the event is happening now or will happen again. They avoid any situation that reminds them of the event. At times, the only way to treat the condition is with anti-anxiety medication. At this point patients should be referred to a doctor. The counselor must know his limitations.

PAIN AND SUFFERING

When times are good and we believe we are in control, most of us can be sweet and adorable. Let times get bad or let us experience pain for any length of time and we can take it out on everyone around us. Pain draws our focus to ourselves. It forces the mind into a selfish mode and we can become brats, lashing out at all those around us.

This is not to make light of suffering or pain. The pain of terminal patients, cancer patients, or the torment of burn victims, rivals being slowly boiled in oil. This is not a matter to be brushed aside. It is, however, something the counselor will have to deal with and understand. When ministering to the elderly, infirmed, and those in pain, there will be issues of hostility and anger. Lashing out is a defense response for some. Pain lets us know we are not in control and we are not the center of the universe.

From the mature patient we will see dignity and grace in suffering. There will be kindness and appreciation for those serving and ministering to the person in pain. For others, however, there will be inner turmoil as they come to grips with the fact they are not in control and their wishes do not matter to the condition or disease. Through anger and irritability, they will speak out in harshness, as if someone or everyone is to blame for their condition. They may even try to drive all caregivers away. There is resentment at what has happened to them. They are too immature to contain their feelings.

We all have negative feelings and pain, but maturity allows us to have these feelings without need to inflict them on others. Feelings are not facts. They are, at times, a temporary sensation, which if vented, will leave a permanent emotional scar on others.

It is not that the minister or counselor should play the bad guy or add insult to injury, but there will be times when one person in pain and self-pity will drain the family dry through constant demands and emotional abuse. This is a very selfish tactic and it will be up to the minister to remind the person of the alternatives of not being cared for.

As a family, we are expected to love, care, and extend ourselves to accommodate those who are suffering. However, the good of the one should not be allowed to compromise the good of the many. There must be a line where one can say, "Your condition does not give you the right to treat others with spite, anger, or hatred."

After checking with the attending physician, normally a plan can be put in place to aid in the correction of the emotional outbursts and how they affect others. The plan may have components of mood elevators, sedatives, and means for providing care of a more "as needed" basis with less unnecessary contact until the patient understands that even though they are in pain, their actions have consequences.

We are told to let our suffering be as a testimony to our faith. Love in good times is easy. Love and grace in bad times are a window into the real person. As we grow older we may become a burden. If we become injured we may need the help of others. Let us set our minds and hearts to be thankful that we have sown the seeds of love and respect in others, which would call them to love us enough to help us. Appreciation is the proper emotion toward those serving us.

Appreciation is the acknowledgement of grace (unearned favor) and is the tie that binds our heart to the heart of God.

As the anger abates and exhausts itself into reason, the question will be asked, "Why has this happened to me?" The rain falls on the just as well as on the unjust. The sun shines on the just and the unjust. Good things have happened to those who are not good people. Bad things happen to those who we call good, but the Bible says no one is good but God. The question has no answer that will satisfy our sense of justice, as justice is a matter of perspective. Certainly, we have all sinned and fallen short. We have all done or considered evil deeds. We all suffer the consequences of our actions and decisions. Smoking brings cancer. Gluttony brings heart attacks. Gossip brings guilt and mistrust, which in turn bring problems of the heart and mind. But, there is no good answer to disease visited upon the innocent. What does one tell the parent of a two year-old dying of injury or disease?

Our actions affect each other and we are held accountable before God. Hopefully, we are also held accountable by law. Many diseases are caused by man's interference. Strains of drug resistant diseases are brought into existence by the choice not to complete a round of antibiotics. Factories spew out toxins causing tumors and leukemia in children. AIDS patients cultivate tuberculosis, pneumonia, and cancer within bodies that serve as the perfect walking Petri dishes. The result of a man drinking to excess can be the death of an innocent child. Thus one man's freedom of choice is another person's death sentence.

Even God steps aside for the sake of free will…for us it is impossible to know where to draw the line. Therefore, in a world with billions of people, why bad things happen to good people can many times be traced back years previously in the actions of those we never knew. It is not a satisfying answer. There is no one left to blame.

It simply is what it is.

STRESS

Headaches, high blood pressure, acid reflux, problems with digestion, explosive temper, the feeling of not being able to do enough are all signs of stress. Stress management is the ability to maintain control when situations, people, work, or events make excessive demands. Below are simple techniques to manage stress in daily life.

Pray

Yes, this may sound simplistic but it is one of the most important tools in managing stress. It is the kind and technique of prayer that makes this a very effective measure.

Sitting in the presence of God, quietly, silently, and patiently, without word or discourse is a salve for our souls. The procedure and techniques used for this kind of prayer will be covered later in this chapter.

Change the Situation

Can you change or control the situation that is making you feel stress? Can you remove yourself or diminish time or involvement? Give yourself a break if only for a few moments.

Get Real

Set realistic goals for yourself. Don't get caught up in the demands of work or family if they are not realistic. Your boss, spouse, or family may wish to push you beyond what is reasonable. It is up to you to set goals and decide what is important and what is necessary.

Push Back

Reduce the number of events going on in your life. Make a list of the major concerns in your life. Take care of those things first and don't sweat the small stuff. Many times they will take care of themselves. You may be surprised that others will pick up the slack if you let them. Prioritize and let the little things slide. Don't be a detail driven person.

Don't Borrow Trouble

"Sufficient unto the day is the evil thereof." Handle each task as it comes. Focus on one thing at a time. Don't worry about what might happen tomorrow. Plan ahead as best you can and let the chips fall where they may. Deal with things only when the problem has arisen.

Rest and Sleep

The more stress you are under the more rest you need. If fatigue sets in there will be a sense of hopelessness or helplessness to compound the stress. As with a person fighting addiction, the rules for fighting stress are: do not become too lonely, too hungry, or too tired. Stress can cause the mind to race at night so sleep won't come. There will be times it is best to seek help in breaking the stress/sleepless cycle. Try teas and mild sleep aids, meditation, hot baths, and extra time to get a deeper sleep.

Exercise

Work out your stress and frustrations with exercise. Spend at least half an hour in hard, aerobic exercise to allow the body to reach the needed state.

Change Your State Of Mind

Get happy. Part of the problem is what we do to ourselves in our own thought process. Focus on positive and hopeful aspects.

Techniques of Christian Meditation

Let the remembrance of Jesus be present with your every breath. Then indeed you will appreciate the value of stillness.   John Climacus

As we begin our time of meditation and prayer we must be careful. We must first still and focus the mind. This first stage, called centering, is somewhat like techniques used in Eastern mysticism. However, objects or words used in our Christian technique should be kept completely Christ-centered in their representation.

As we sit in meditation and prayer, many times we find our minds in turmoil, with thoughts chasing themselves like a pack of monkeys. We must first have a way of clearing the mind of such thrashing.

Before we can pray clearly we must be able to think clearly. Before we can think clearly we must stop the mind from running amok. Even in this preliminary stage of centering it takes about twenty minutes to still the mind. Before we begin the first steps of meditation we must find a comfortable and undisturbed place. Sit quietly. Close your eyes and relax. Find in your heart a sacred word. In your heart and soul it must have a direct connection with Christ. Let the word be something special to you. Let it be grace, peace, love, hope, charity, or some word that connects you with Christ himself. Or, you may pick out some sacred object such as a cross or painting which you know will draw your heart to Him. Focus your mind and your heart upon this sacred word or object. Do not let it waiver and do not let it go.

It is common that after only a matter of moments your mind will start to wander. You'll find your focus lost, and your mind chasing itself and swirling like a storm. Your thoughts will become scattered and chaotic. Do not fret and do not worry, this is very common. It is the first obstacle to overcome in order to fully pray and meditate upon Him. God waits on the other side of chaos in our minds and hearts. This is the first step in the process of stripping away all of those things that stand in the way between our Lord and ourselves.

The mind will protest and complain. It is like a stubborn mule which strains and complains against the bridle. But bridle our minds we must. It will take infinite time and patience simply to learn to quiet and control our minds so that we can pray and meditate wholly on Him.

There are only two things in existence, the creator and created. As our minds become more still and quiet we must continually push out all of the things that try to enter in. We must allow room only for God in our hearts and minds. Whether it is height, depth, blackness, emptiness, or nothingness itself, all things but God must be pushed out of the mind and heart.

These two things exist -- God and His creation are all there is in the universe. Everything that is not God is creation. If we empty our minds and hearts of everything created what is left will be God.

DEPRESSION

FROM THE NATIONAL INSTITUTE OF MENTAL HEALTH

In any given 1-year period, 9.5 percent of the population, or about 18.8 million American adults, suffer from a depressive illness. The economic cost for this disorder is high, but the cost in human suffering cannot be estimated. Depressive illnesses often interfere with normal functioning and cause pain and suffering not only to those who have a disorder, but also to those who care about them. Serious depression can destroy family life as well as the life of the ill person. But much of this suffering is unnecessary.

Most people with a depressive illness do not seek treatment, although the great majority – even those whose depression is extremely severe – can be helped. Thanks to years of fruitful research, there are now medications and psychosocial therapies such as cognitive/behavioral, "talk" or interpersonal sessions that ease the pain of depression.

Unfortunately, many people do not recognize that depression is a treatable illness. If you feel that you or someone you care about is one of the many undiagnosed depressed people in this country, the information presented here may help you take the steps that may save your own or someone else's life.

Depression

- *Persistent sad, anxious, or "empty" mood*
- *Feelings of hopelessness, pessimism*
- *Feelings of guilt, worthlessness, helplessness*
- *Loss of interest or pleasure in hobbies and activities that were once enjoyed, including sex*
- *Decreased energy, fatigue, being "slowed down"*
- *Difficulty concentrating, remembering, making decisions*

- *Insomnia, early-morning awakening, or oversleeping*
- *Appetite and/or weight loss or overeating and weight gain*
- *Thoughts of death or suicide; suicide attempts*
- *Restlessness, irritability*
- *Persistent physical symptoms that do not respond to treatment, such as headaches, digestive disorders, and chronic pain.*

Causes of Depression

Some types of depression run in families, suggesting that a biological vulnerability can be inherited. This seems to be the case with bipolar disorder. Studies of families in which members of each generation develop bipolar disorder found that those with the illness have a somewhat different genetic makeup than those who do not get ill. However, the reverse is not true: Not everybody with the genetic makeup that causes vulnerability to bipolar disorder will have the illness. Apparently additional factors, possibly stresses at home, work, or school, are involved in its onset.

In some families, major depression also seems to occur generation after generation. However, it can also occur in people who have no family history of depression. Whether inherited or not, major depressive disorder is often associated with changes in brain structures or brain function.

People who have low self-esteem, who consistently view themselves and the world with pessimism or who are readily overwhelmed by stress, are prone to depression. Whether this represents a psychological predisposition or an early form of the illness is not clear.

In recent years, researchers have shown that physical changes in the body can be accompanied by mental changes as well. Medical illnesses such as stroke, a heart attack, cancer, Parkinson's disease, and hormonal disorders can cause depressive illness, making the sick person apathetic and unwilling to care for his or her physical needs, thus prolonging the recovery period. Also, a serious loss, difficult relationship, financial problem, or any stressful (unwelcome or even desired) change in life patterns can trigger a depressive episode. Very often, a combination of genetic, psychological, and environmental factors is involved in the onset of a depressive disorder. Later episodes of illness typically are precipitated by only mild stresses, or none at all.

Depression in Women

Women experience depression about twice as often as men. Many hormonal factors may contribute to the increased rate of depression in women – particularly such factors as menstrual cycle changes, pregnancy, miscarriage, postpartum period, pre-menopause, and menopause. Many women also face additional stresses such as responsibilities both at work and home, single parenthood, and caring for children and for aging parents.

A recent NIMH study showed that in the case of severe premenstrual syndrome (PMS), women with a preexisting vulnerability to PMS experienced relief from mood and physical symptoms when their sex hormones were suppressed. Shortly after the hormones were re-introduced, they again developed symptoms of PMS. Women without a history of PMS reported no effects of the hormonal manipulation.

Many women are also particularly vulnerable after the birth of a baby. The hormonal and physical changes, as well as the added responsibility of a new life, can be factors that lead to postpartum depression in some women. While transient "blues" are common in new mothers, a full-blown depressive episode is not a normal occurrence and requires active intervention. Treatment by a sympathetic physician and the family's emotional support for the new mother are prime considerations in aiding her to recover her physical and mental well-being and her ability to care for and enjoy the infant.

Depression in Men

Although men are less likely to suffer from depression than women, 3 to 4 million men in the United States are affected by the illness. Men are less likely to admit to depression, and doctors are less likely to suspect it. The rate of suicide in men is four times that of women, though more women attempt it. In fact, after age 70, the rate of men's suicide rises, reaching a peak after age 85.

Depression can also affect the physical health in men differently from women. A new study shows that, although depression is associated with an increased risk of coronary heart disease in both men and women, only men suffer a high death rate.

Men's depression is often masked by alcohol or drugs, or by the socially acceptable habit of working excessively long hours. Depression typically shows up in men not as feeling hopeless and helpless, but as being irritable, angry, and discouraged; hence, depression may be difficult to recognize as such in men. Even if a man realizes that he is depressed, he may be less willing than a woman to seek help. Encouragement and support from concerned family members can make a difference. In the workplace, employee assistance professionals or worksite mental health programs can be of assistance in helping men understand and accept depression as a real illness that needs treatment.

Depression in the Elderly

Some people have the mistaken idea that it is normal for the elderly to feel depressed. On the contrary, most older people feel satisfied with their lives. Sometimes, though, when depression develops, it may be dismissed as a normal part of aging. Depression in the elderly, undiagnosed and untreated, causes needless suffering for the family and for the individual who could otherwise live a fruitful life. When he or she does go to the doctor, the symptoms described are usually physical, for the older person is often reluctant to discuss feelings of hopelessness, sadness, loss of interest in normally pleasurable activities, or extremely prolonged grief after a loss.

Recognizing how depressive symptoms in older people are often missed, many health care professionals are learning to identify and treat the underlying depression. They recognize that some symptoms may be side effects of medication the older person is taking for a physical problem, or they may be caused by a co-occurring illness. If a diagnosis of depression is made, treatment with medication and/or psychotherapy will help the depressed person return to a happier, more fulfilling life. Recent research suggests that brief psychotherapy (talk therapies that help a person in day-to-day relationships or in learning to counter the distorted negative thinking that commonly accompanies depression) is effective in reducing symptoms in short-term depression in older persons who are medically ill. Psychotherapy is also useful in older patients who cannot or will not take medication. Efficacy studies show that late-life depression can be treated with psychotherapy.

Improved recognition and treatment of depression in late life will make those years more enjoyable and fulfilling for the depressed elderly person, the family, and caretakers.

Depression in Children

Only in the past two decades has depression in children been taken very seriously. The depressed child may pretend to be sick, refuse to go to school, cling to a parent, or worry that the parent may die. Older children may sulk, get into trouble at school, be negative, grouchy, and feel misunderstood. Because normal behaviors vary from one childhood stage to another, it can be difficult to tell whether a child is just going through a temporary "phase" or is suffering from depression. Sometimes the parents become worried about how the child's behavior has changed, or a teacher mentions that "your child doesn't seem to be himself." In such a case, if a visit to the child's pediatrician rules out physical symptoms, the doctor will probably suggest that the child be evaluated, preferably by a psychiatrist who specializes in the treatment of children. If treatment is needed, the doctor may suggest that another therapist, usually a social worker or a psychologist, provide therapy while the psychiatrist will oversee medication if it is needed. Parents should not be afraid to ask questions: What are the therapist's qualifications? What kind of therapy will the child have? Will the family as a whole participate in therapy? Will my child's therapy include an antidepressant? If so, what might the side effects be?

The National Institute of Mental Health (NIMH) has identified the use of medications for depression in children as an important area for research. The NIMH-supported Research Units on Pediatric Psychopharmacology (RUPPs) form a network of seven research sites where clinical studies on the effects of medications for mental disorders can be conducted in children and adolescents. Among the medications being studied are antidepressants, some of which have been found to be effective in treating children with depression, if properly monitored by the child's physician. Many forms of psychotherapy, including some short-term (10-20 week) therapies, can help depressed individuals. "Talking" therapies help patients gain insight into and resolve their problems through verbal exchange with the therapist, sometimes combined with "homework" assignments between sessions. "Behavioral" therapists help patients learn how to obtain more satisfaction and rewards through their own actions and how to unlearn the behavioral patterns that contribute to or result from their depression.

Two of the short-term psychotherapies that research has shown helpful for some forms of depression are interpersonal and cognitive/behavioral therapies. Interpersonal therapists focus on the patient's disturbed personal relationships that both cause and exacerbate (or increase) the depression. Cognitive/behavioral therapists help patients change the negative styles of thinking and behaving often associated with depression.

Psychodynamic therapies, which are sometimes used to treat depressed persons, focus on resolving the patient's conflicted feelings. These therapies are often reserved until the depressive symptoms are significantly improved. In general, severe depressive illnesses, particularly those that are recurrent, will require medication (or ECT under special conditions) along with, or preceding, psychotherapy for the best outcome.

How To Help Yourself If You Are Depressed

Depressive disorders make one feel exhausted, worthless, helpless, and hopeless. Such negative thoughts and feelings make some people feel like giving up. It is important to realize that these negative views are part of the depression and typically do not accurately reflect the actual circumstances. Negative thinking fades as treatment begins to take effect. In the meantime:

- *Set realistic goals in light of the depression and assume a reasonable amount of responsibility.*
- *Break large tasks into small ones, set some priorities, and do what you can as you can.*
- *Try to be with other people and to confide in someone; it is usually better than being alone and secretive.*
- *Participate in activities that may make you feel better.*
- *Mild exercise, going to a movie, a ballgame, or participating in religious, social, or other activities may help.*
- *Expect your mood to improve gradually, not immediately. Feeling better takes time.*
- *It is advisable to postpone important decisions until the depression has lifted. Before deciding to make a significant transition – change jobs, get married or divorced – discuss it with others who know you well and have a more objective view of your situation.*
- *People rarely "snap out of" a depression. But they can feel a little better day-by-day.*
- *Remember, positive thinking will replace the negative thinking that is part of the depression and will disappear as your depression responds to treatment.*
- *Let your family and friends help you.*

How Family and Friends Can Help the Depressed Person

The most important thing anyone can do for the depressed person is to help him or her get an appropriate diagnosis and treatment. This may involve encouraging the individual to stay with treatment until symptoms begin to abate (several weeks), or to seek different treatment if no improvement occurs. On occasion, it may require making an appointment and accompanying the depressed person to the doctor. It may also mean monitoring whether the depressed person is taking medication. The depressed person should be encouraged to obey the doctor's orders about the use of alcoholic products while on medication.

The second most important thing is to offer emotional support. This involves understanding, patience, affection, and encouragement. Engage the depressed person in conversation and listen carefully. Do not disparage feelings expressed, but point out realities and offer hope. Do not ignore remarks about suicide. Report them to the depressed person's therapist. Invite the depressed person for walks, outings, to the movies, and other activities. Be gently insistent if your invitation is refused. Encourage participation in some activities that once gave pleasure, such as hobbies, sports, religious or cultural activities, but do not push the depressed person to undertake too much too soon. The depressed person needs diversion and company, but too many demands can increase feelings of failure.

Do not accuse the depressed person of faking illness or of laziness, or expect him or her "to snap out of it." Eventually, with treatment, most people do get better. Keep that in mind, and keep reassuring the depressed person that, with time and help, he or she will feel better. (end of article.)

Many of the ways we can deal with depression are identical to the treatments for stress. We need sleep, but not too much sleep. We need activity and exercise. We know that exercise helps alter levels of certain chemicals in the brain. However, in the case of clinical depression there is a cycle that must be broken. Depression both causes and is caused by chemicals produced by the brain and body. If the depression causes inappropriate levels of these chemicals to be produced, then the depression becomes a result of the chemicals caused by the condition itself. Medical assistance is needed to break the cycle. Don't hesitate to send the patient to a doctor.

On a more practical note, it is often said that depression is anger turned inward. Although that sounds like a "pat and lightweight" answer, it is often true.

Depression comes in part from the lack of ability to express or change one's feelings in a negative environment. When expression becomes counter-productive or is not permitted, and change seems unlikely, the only outlets left are to abandon the situation, become angry, and rebel against the situation, or feel hopeless and depressed about the situation.

Notice that the first two reactions are active, while depression is a passive reaction. This is the seat and cause of the problem. Depression is echoed in the words, "I can't." "I can't change him." "I can't leave." "I can't take this." When opposing expressions become deadlocked without obvious resolution there will be depression.

Many times depression is caused by fatigue or sleeplessness. Chemical changes or interruptions in sleep cycle, time, or depth can lead to depression. This is why stress can be a factor, since it is known to change sleep patterns. If one sees life's obstacles as too much to bear, depression is soon to follow. Being tired, fatigued, or highly stressed can cause everyday life to seem mountainous.

To look at situations logically from a fresh and rested perspective often helps. To make plain and articulated choices to endure or not, to leave or stay, or how much of a situation to take, may help. We must impress upon the person that all situations in life come down to their choice; however, all choices come with a price and an elimination of other pathways. To choose one way is to reject another. Once clear decisions are made and settled, some cases of depression resolve themselves.

Find the cause of the anger or frustration. Examine the cause of hopelessness or lack of clear direction. Give schedules and suggestions of rest, breaks, help, and clear decisions. Give an ear for the person to vent and express. Help resolve anger and stalemate. If depression does not abate, recommend a visit to a physician.

DRUG AND ALCOHOL ABUSE

The following information was taken directly from the National Institute on Drug Abuse Fact Sheet as posted in October of 2005. The data covers trends in 2002-2003. This data is already outdated. In 2005 an epidemic of methamphetamine was declared and drug taskforces were being formed in small, rural towns throughout the South to slow the spread of drug abuse and the crime that follows.

> This fact sheet highlights information from the latest published proceedings of NIDA's Community Epidemiology Work Group* (CEWG). The information covers current and emerging trends in drug abuse for 21 major U.S. metropolitan areas, as shared at CEWG's June 2003 meeting.
>
> The findings are intended to alert the general public, policymakers, and authorities at the local, State, regional, and national levels to the latest trends in drug abuse.** The CEWG is a network of researchers from Atlanta, Baltimore, Boston, Chicago, Denver, Detroit, Honolulu, Los Angeles, Miami, Minneapolis/St. Paul, Newark, New Orleans, New York, Philadelphia, Phoenix, St. Louis, San Diego, San Francisco, Seattle, Texas, and Washington, DC.
>
> CEWG members (epidemiologists and researchers) assess drug abuse patterns and trends from the health and other drug abuse indicator sources below. These data are enhanced with qualitative information from ethnographic research, focus groups, and other community-based sources:
>
> * the Treatment Episode Data Set (data from treatment facilities) and the Drug Abuse Warning Network (emergency department – ED – mentions and medical examiner death mentions involving illicit drugs), both funded by the Substance Abuse and Mental Health Services Administration;

* the Arrestee Drug Abuse Monitoring program, funded by the National Institute of Justice;

* the System to Retrieve Information on Drug Evidence and other information on drug seizures, price, and purity, from the Drug Enforcement Administration;

* drug seizure data from the United States Customs Service; and

* the Uniform Crime Reports, maintained by the Federal Bureau of Investigation.

Trends of Use
Cocaine/Crack

Cocaine/crack abuse was endemic in almost all CEWG areas in 2002. Rates of ED mentions per 100,000 population were higher for cocaine than for any other drug in 17 CEWG areas. Rates increased significantly between the second half of 2001 and the first half of 2002 in Baltimore, Denver, Newark, and San Diego, while decreasing in San Francisco and Seattle. ED rates were highest in Chicago, Philadelphia, Atlanta, Baltimore, and Miami in the first half of 2002. Rates for cocaine were much higher than those for methamphetamine in west coast areas. Trends in treatment admissions from 2000 to 2002 showed little change in most CEWG areas. Primary cocaine admissions constituted more than 40 percent of illicit drug admissions (excluding alcohol) in seven areas, with the majority being for crack. Additionally, polydrug use was common among powder and crack cocaine abusers. Cocaine was reported frequently as a secondary drug by heroin abusers admitted to treatment. Between 27 and 49 percent of male arrestees tested positive for cocaine in 14 CEWG areas. Nationwide in 2002, 61,594 kilograms of cocaine were seized by the DEA – 3.6 percent more than in 2001 and 35.9 percent more than in 1995.

Heroin

Heroin indicators were relatively stable in 2002, but continued at high levels in Boston, Chicago, Detroit, Newark, Philadelphia, and San Francisco. Primary heroin treatment admissions ranged from 62 to 82 percent of all illicit drug admissions (excluding alcohol) in Baltimore, Boston, and Newark. Rates of heroin ED mentions exceeded 100 per 100,000 population in Chicago and Newark, and heroin/morphine-involved death mentions reported by DAWN ranged from 195 to 352 in Boston, Baltimore, and Chicago. Conversely, significant decreases in ED rates were observed between the first half of 2001 and the first half of 2002 in six CEWG areas: Baltimore, Dallas, Detroit, Phoenix, San Diego, and Washington, DC. Of the eight CEWG areas reporting local medical examiner data on heroin/morphine-related drug mortality in 2002, figures were highest in Detroit, Philadelphia, southern Florida counties, and Phoenix. DEA data showed that heroin purity in 2001 was highest in Philadelphia (73 percent pure), and ranged from 56 to 68 percent in New York, Boston, and Newark—all areas where South American and Southwest Asian heroin are widely available.

Misuse of Prescription Opiates

Opiates/narcotics (excluding heroin) appear increasingly in drug indicator data, particularly hydrocodone and oxycodone products. Increases in oxycodone ED mentions were reported in 12 CEWG areas from the first half of 2001 to the first half of 2002, and 7 of these were statistically significant. In San Francisco, oxycodone ED mentions increased 110 percent during the same time period. Other CEWG members reported an increase in oxycodone medical sales, diversion of the drug from clinics, and increased arrests. Hydrocodone, which is often used in combination with alcohol and other drugs, was cited as a problem in several CEWG areas including Phoenix, Texas, Minneapolis/St. Paul, and South Florida. Preliminary ED data for the first half of 2002 show that the rate of narcotic analgesics/combinations mentions per 100,000 population was 2 to 7 times higher in Baltimore than other CEWG areas. In 11 of the 20 CEWG areas included in the DAWN mortality system in 2001, the number of narcotic analgesic-related death mentions exceeded those for cocaine, heroin/morphine, marijuana, and methamphetamine.

Marijuana

Marijuana is the most frequently used illicit drug in CEWG areas, and levels of use and abuse are high among adolescents and young adults. Rates of marijuana ED mentions per 100,000 population increased significantly between the first half of 2001 and the first half of 2002 in Miami, Newark, Phoenix, and San Diego, but decreased in Chicago, San Francisco, and Seattle. Primary marijuana admissions (excluding alcohol) accounted for approximately one-quarter to one-half of admissions for illicit drug use in 12 of the 20 CEWG areas reporting 2002 treatment data. The proportions were highest in Minneapolis/St. Paul, Miami, Colorado, New Orleans, and Seattle. The percentages of adult male arrestees testing marijuana-positive in 2002 exceeded the percentages testing positive for other drugs in 12 of 16 CEWG areas. The same was true of female arrestees in only three of nine CEWG sites. The DEA reported seizures of 195,644 kilograms of marijuana in 2002, the lowest amount since 1996.

Methamphetamine

Methamphetamine abuse continues to spread geographically and to different populations. In addition to the large "super labs" in California and trafficking from Mexico, there has been a proliferation of small "mom and pop" laboratories throughout the country, especially in rural areas. Methamphetamine abuse and production continue at high levels in Hawaii, west coast areas, and some southwestern areas, and abuse and manufacture continues to move eastward. Several CEWG areas report new populations of methamphetamine users, including Hispanics and young people in Denver, club goers in Boston, and African-Americans in Texas. Primary admissions for amphetamines/methamphetamine (excluding alcohol) represented a sizable minority of treatment admissions in eight CEWG areas in 2002. Most admissions were primary methamphetamine users. The percentages of adult male arrestees testing positive for methamphetamine use trended upward in nine CEWG areas between 2000 and 2002. Additionally, one-half of adult female arrestees in Honolulu tested positive in 2002, as did nearly 42 percent in Phoenix and 37 percent in San Diego. Not only methamphetamine users, but also children exposed to and agencies that seize and clean up methamphetamine labs are also in danger of serious health consequences.

MDMA

MDMA (methylenedioxymethamphetamine; often called ecstasy) indicators suggest that use of this drug has spread to populations outside the club scene. MDMA is often used in combination with alcohol and other drugs, and pills sold in clubs as ecstasy often contain substances other than, or in addition to, MDMA. The number of MDMA ED mentions decreased in 11 CEWG areas from the first and/or second half of 2001 to the first half of 2002, with a significant increase reported only in New Orleans. The highest numbers of ED mentions in 2002 were in Philadelphia, Miami, San Francisco, Atlanta, Los Angeles, and New York. Two CEWG members reported statewide treatment admissions data for 2002: for Illinois, 2002 was the first year that "club drug" treatment admissions were tracked and a majority of those admitted were male (68 percent) and White (75 percent); in Texas, treatment admissions with a primary, secondary, or tertiary MDMA problem rose from 63 in 1998 to 521 in 2002.

Emerging Drugs: PCP

PCP indicators increased in five CEWG areas—Los Angeles, Philadelphia, Phoenix, Washington, DC, and Texas—and remained steady in Chicago communities. Los Angeles reported an 11 percent increase in PCP-related arrests since 2001. In Phoenix, PCP ED mentions increased significantly between the first half of 2001 and the first half of 2002— from 27 to 42 mentions. In Texas, ED mentions increased significantly from 46 to 74 during the same time period. In the first half of 2001, 6 CEWG areas had more than 73 PCP ED mentions, ranging from 74 in Dallas to 542 in Philadelphia. In 2002, both primary PCP treatment admissions and ED mentions were highest in Washington, DC. DC also reported increases in both adult and juvenile arrestees who tested positive for PCP. (end of article.)

One of the most tragic and destructive conditions facing the U.S. is drug abuse. Of all drugs, methamphetamine is the fastest growing plague above all other plagues. Meth, crack, speed, upper, or crystal, as it is called, is a looming scourge and scar on our nation today. Generations are growing up addicted and giving birth to children who seem to contract their addiction through exposure to this diabolical drug. Grandparents, parents, and children are being arrested together in drug busts taking place across the nation. In many cases, mothers are neglecting children or mercifully abandoning them at hospitals and police departments. It is all done in the search for the next buy, the next hit, and the next high.

Recipes have been developed that allow the manufacture of the drug with readily available components in spaces as small as the trunk of a car. As the drug infiltrates the body, it changes brain chemistries and alters the level of serotonin. When the euphoric high subsides, a depression as deep and black as one could imagine descends. In order to avoid the crushing low, the addict chases the next high.

Days run into days and those who have not slept begin to break with reality as drug induced psychosis rules the mind. Sleeplessness, irritability, rage, mood swings, rapid weight changes are all indications of meth abuse. What can be done?

Of all the rules of counseling, the one that rings most true is: "If they don't ask the question, they are not ready for the answers." In other words, if they don't want to end the addiction and if they are not fully committed to the journey, they will return to the drug and the counselor will have wasted time better spent on others more willing to heal. Until they seek help, they are not likely to respond to help.

Even if the addict wishes to escape, the drug will call to them through the altered brain chemistry. However, there are ways to help and to, as much as possible, avoid recidivism. All things that permit access to the drug must be removed from life. Friends who do or have done drugs should be avoided. Places where drugs were bought, sold, acquired, or used should be off limits. Items that relate to use as well as things that remind the addict of the high should be eradicated.

The addict must change their playpen, playmates, and play things. The basic human needs of the addict must be provided. These needs are broader and deeper than one may first assume. All people have the same basic needs. Food, clothing, shelter, companionship, love, purpose, and self-expression are all basic needs. If any of these are lacking for too long, the person will seek them in whatever venue is available. This is where most counselors fail and the reason most addicts return to the drug scene. It is in the fundamental misunderstanding of what is needed and the inability to provide or guide the addict toward finding those things that eventually forces him back into the drug world.

We must ask ourselves, would we wish to live without companionship, love, purpose of life, or the ability to constructively express ourselves? Why would we expect others to do so? These needs or the opportunity to find these needs outside the former circle of friends must be provided. If one grows lonely, friendships will be sought. Let it be with a newly developed circle of Christian, drug-free friends.

Even assuming this is done, we must be clear about the condition of the addict. One of the side effects of amphetamine addiction is possible secondary addiction to sex. The drug increases energy across the board and much of the increase goes into sexual energy.

Other drugs may also be used to counteract the effects of meth in order to allow the user to sleep. This opens the door to alcohol and barbiturate abuse.

Once the addict has been away from drugs for about 2 weeks, the body has purged most of the drug. However, what remains is to deal with habit, conditioning, and the brain chemistry which draws them back. To keep the condition from recurring, we must determine why it has happened. What brought the person to this condition? Why does a person choose addiction? Is it not obvious that when one chooses to take an addictive substance, one becomes its slave?

From talking with hundreds of addicts over the last ten years, two reasons people choose addition stand out: self-medication and self-destruction.

In the case of self-medication we should look to underlying problems such as clinical depression, and bi-polar or manic/depressive disorders. The subject experiencing these types of conditions will seek ways to equalize moods and may turn to drugs and alcohol to assuage the internal pain. As the person cycles toward a low point, the happy, euphoric feeling obtained from the drug offsets the swing and stalls the coming darkness. Drugs and alcohol numb and counter the impending cloud. Often, once the underlying condition is treated properly, it becomes much easier to break the addiction.

A related condition is self-destructive behavior. Abuse, mistreatment, and pernicious neglect can fracture a child's psyche. The child grows up believing he is worthless. They may come to a point of believing they are unlovable. The child grows into an adult incapable of receiving love, forming close bonds, or feeling worthy of life. They want to die. Playing hard and fast with life sometimes is a sign that life isn't worth living.

Imagine living with the shame of believing you were not wanted or deserving of life. Alcohol or drugs can be used to numb the internal pain, to turn down the self-eviscerating voices of shame or guilt, and to hide from disappointment in life. The counselor must ascertain the underlying motive. In this case it may be the scars left by defective parents. This does not excuse antisocial actions, but it may be an explanation of the source of pain, anger, or self-destruction. The source of torment must be addressed before the addiction can be broken. Trust must be established. Within a trusting environment, love must be planted and nurtured. The heart of the suffering must be opened and past abuses need to be addressed before healing can begin. But, remember, when you begin to address family issues you must treat the family, not just the addict. This may prove difficult as family members may balk at the suggestion they need counseling.

Sexual abuse and extended emotional or physical abuse yields damage in the child that grows into open wounds of self-contempt as an adult.

Of course, peer pressure often comes into play in the teenage years. If an impressionable individual comes under the influence of a drug abuser they can fall prey to addiction. However, with the idea of immortality so prevalent in youth, the belief that they are stronger than the drugs, could be to blame. They happily take the drugs knowing they are in control, stronger than the drug, and will never become addicted. This is narcissism, and whether related to the folly of youth or a mental condition, it yields the same result; a life lost to drugs. Convincing the person they are not in control and they need help may be more difficult than it would first appear. It would mean giving up the illusion of control and superiority, which some find more comforting than reality.

Even looking into a mirror at their own sunken eyes and soulless face will not convince them they need help. Death is preferable to admitting you are wrong to this type of person. "I am sorry, "I was wrong", and "Please help me" are foreign words to them. First the counselor must convince them they have a problem that is bigger than they are.

Whatever the addiction is, the steps to recovery are always the same: recognize the problem, admit the problem, seek help for the problem, free yourself of the problem, and live like the problem is a beast that is always stalking you.

ACTING IT OUT OR WORKING IT OUT

All of us are either "acting out" or "working out" our problems. As we go through the day and receive different triggers relating to our youth or bringing up past emotions, we must, in some way, dissipate them. This is done by working them out in such a way which releases us from their effects.   On the other hand, we may act them out in a way to relieve pressures while not addressing the true issue causing the pain. In working out a problem, there must be a conscious understanding and evaluation that takes care of the immediate feelings of anger or hurt and also works toward a healthy emotional equilibrium concerning the basic problem.

In acting out, a person feels a stress brought about by the same mechanism, but there is no conscious understanding or healing which occurs. Instead, the person's emotions are repressed; anger and hurt are "swallowed down" and are harbored on some level until such time as the psyche is full. The unconscious overflow of this anger and hurt comes out in attitudes and actions aimed at making a statement that their fear or repression has kept them from making consciously.

These statements are almost always designed to go in two directions. The first is regarding the self and is self-worthlessness, self-destructiveness, or self-protection. The second is fear, anger, and hurt caused by the people or situations which brought about the first feelings.

We must ask ourselves: Are we working things out, or are we acting things out? If we are working things out, we will not keep repeating past mistakes. We will come to understand and take responsibility for our lives and all of the things in it. Like a pendulum that seeks its center, we will find ourselves off balance less and less, and mistakes will occur less frequently.

If we are acting things out, we will find it hard to take responsibility for our lives. It will always be the other person's fault. We will find ourselves consumed with anger, or fear, or pain. We strike out or act without thought. Sometimes, even before we realize it, we will say, "Look what you made me do." We will repeat patterns and mistakes over and over without getting any closer to having it right. Worst of all, we won't think about it, or if we do, it will seem hopeless because we will not admit we have control, and therefore responsibility, over our own actions.

There are always choices. Either change yourself, or change your situation. It is never an option to try to change another person. That's not your place. It can only cause another to have negative emotions toward you. And those, too, will either have to be worked out or acted out.

It is a logical but bizarre twist that can compel us to act out in a manner that seems opposite to what is our normal behavior. This same reflex will make the personality types swing from extreme to extreme. They will be mirror images contained within the same person.

Let us consider the many priests and clergy who are being uncovered today as con men, pedophiles, homosexuals, and abusers. When we sense a problem in our personality, we are faced with the question of what to do about it. We could face the problem head on, seek the counsel of others, start into therapy, and work through the pain until we are healed. This is the most difficult, but it is also the most rewarding choice. On the other hand, we could deny the existence of any problem and continue to act overtly. This is the worst choice.

We can decide to put ourselves in a situation that we believe will defuse the bomb within us. We believe, if we make it very difficult to act on any of our imbalanced impulses, that we have fixed the problem. So we lock ourselves away in an environment which is the antithesis of the nature of the problem, as a shield between it and us.

Truth is like cream; it will always rise to the top. As the stratification occurs, we start to act out again. We do so this time, in an environment chosen for its purity and piety. In this environment we preach to ourselves, pray for ourselves, even do penance for what we are fighting within ourselves. We cloister ourselves away, and symbolically we cloister the sickness away inside of us. Day after day we beat it back, but like the dragon in the basement, it is always there, waiting, promising to one day break through. In spite of our walls, denials, or whips we use to control it, we never deal with the problem. Problems that are not solved will forever recur.

The difference between a balanced person and a criminal is the wholeness of the person; this wholeness is the integration of those levels in ourselves we consider anathema. These hidden pockets must be faced, conquered, and integrated back into the personality. While the "disintegration" is in progress, we can expect it to cause the affected types to appear as opposites. It must be remembered they will usually swing within the extremes of the same type. Remembering there are twelve types of people, a type five could be either a communicator or a con-artist. A type six could be priest or a pervert. A type eight could be a fair judge or ruthless dictator.

When typing personalities or examining our own personality, we have to remember not to be deceived or to deceive ourselves. If these blind and deaf areas of ours could be opened to us, and we could learn to hear and recognize the voices and feelings of our three parts (the child, the parent, and the adult), we could allow the adult to make our choices in its logical way. We would not have to be driven and blinded by the barely recognizable voices and feelings from our past. Our lives would be ours. While we would not get rid of the feelings and voices, we would learn to identify them in order to quantify, compensate, and mute their effects in our lives.

We are like children trying to escape a dragon. To do so we must run from the danger. So as not to leave a trace, we must change our playthings, playmates, and playpens. Sometimes saying, "get thee behind me, Satan," is not as effective as turning our backs on him and running.

VOICES

Inside each of us there is a trio. The three voices in the trio are hardly ever in harmony. The voice of the child can be heard during the times of escapism and other more emotional behaviors. It is based in need or fear. It is selfish.

The voice of the parent is usually associated with restrictive, more sterile, behavior. It is that voice of self criticism, and unbalanced or negative self image. The parent is also part of our conscience, but it is the "learned" and distorted part.

The third part of the trio is the adult. It represents a reasonable, moderate point of balance. It is the only part of us that has the ability to act with forethought and logic. The adult voice is the thoughtful voice of reason. It is capable of seeing the outcome for us and others and making a mature decision.

The below is a list of common actions and attitudes. It gives a general idea of the voice that we are listening to and by what we are being driven, based on the outward manifestation of our problem. The adult is the side of us that is reasonable, logical, understanding, moderate, and balanced. Here are two quick checks to see how in touch with the adult you are:

1. Ask yourself how immature and selfish you really are. The honesty of this answer will reveal volumes.
2. Remember the last time that you made a serious mistake in a relationship. Weren't you aware that it was a foolish choice when you made it?

These answers will add insights into yourself. If you have arrived at the point which puts you in touch with your own behavior, it is only a short step to being in control of it. If you are confused between what is right and wrong simply examine the intent.

If you work on your mind with your mind, how can you avoid the immense confusion?

Child	Parent
Sex addiction	Prudishness
Alcoholism	Abstinence
Drug abuse	Self-condemnation
Being late	Extremely punctual
Not keeping appointments	Stickler for details
Not accepting responsibility	Blaming self
Passive/aggressive	Disciplinarian
Passive/indecisive	Stern
Being silly	Always serious
Abused	Abuser
Sloppy	Obsessively clean
Chaotic	An order addict
Emotional	Repressed
Food addiction	Eating disorders
Hypochondria	Stoicism

LET IT GO

In those times of our lives when we are being eaten alive by an emotional issue, we can easily lose our self-control. We may know we should "let the situation go," but our hearts won't listen. Obsession results. Dwelling on a painful or traumatic event is not uncommon, but when we lose the capacity to direct our minds away from it, the event can become the focal point of our "thought-lives." The trauma starts a cycle that can render us incapacitated. It can come from an event in the present. It can be brought back to the foreground from the past by a seemingly unrelated issue. Damage can be as obvious as abuse, or as insidious as simply not being celebrated as a person.

What happens when our world becomes more and more subjective? It becomes smaller and smaller, and we become more and more dysfunctional, even immobilized. The way out of this self-imposed trap is a very simple but obscure one. We must take that which is subjective and bring it out of ourselves. We must take what haunts us within and make it objective. In Alcoholics Anonymous it is called "turning the problem over to your higher force." In Christian circles it is called "letting go and letting God have it." These terms seem easy enough to understand, but how do we do it? Before we realize what has happened to us, we have jumped on the treadmill that makes this a formidable issue.

The cycle is a simple one. We are shocked, hurt, or traumatized by an event or situation. If it is sudden or dramatic enough, we usually pass through a stage of denial. This is marked by feelings that it is not real, possibly only a dream. Inside, we may even try to force ourselves to wake up from what we may feel to be a bad dream. Our senses seem to tell us we are awake, but a part of our mind refuses to accept the reality of what has happened. We may even try to live our lives as though the event never happened in the hope that would make it so. If it is a continuing action or if it is a part of our childhood, we may repress the event. Either way, we may simply not want to deal with it.

The next step for some is to splinter. A part of their psyche is shattered and a piece is left at the time and place of the trauma. This part of our mind and emotions keeps repeating the situation over and over, trying to figure a way out, and trying to stop the event or get out of it. We must keep in mind that our emotions have no past, only the present. So the part of us left in the past keeps drawing the whole persona back to it, as it continues to search for an answer and a way to stop the pain which, emotionally, is still happening.

Obsession occurs when the pain and cries of that piece of us left behind, outweigh the ability of the remaining persona to concentrate or function. At this point, the primary unit in us is drawn back to the shard and emotionally re-experiences the trauma. Each time this happens there is more left behind, and less of us remaining in the present. We feel as if we are being split in two. That instrument which we used to avoid and solve the problem has itself become the problem. "If you work on your mind with your mind how can you avoid the imminent confusion?"

Thoughts give way to actions, and obsessions give way to compulsions, as the thing your mind is locked on creates emotions which are acted out. You may struggle against the thought, but by this point you're fighting yourself.

How can you win? By having a force driving you that is at least as strong as the one haunting you. The obsession can be counteracted by understanding…each time you are drawn into the obsessive thoughts, you are creating a habit that is entrenching itself more and more deeply.

One of the most insidious of all injuries is to simply not be celebrated as a person. If a child grows up not being thought of as a unique and special person, or if he is made to endure a childhood that was never a time of playfulness and love, he will forever miss a sense of having a special place in the world. A type of insecurity will result, based in a feeling of insignificance. Part of him will be looking for an identity. We must all have a feeling that we are unique and fill a special place in the world.

Whether it happens as a spontaneous act of the psyche, or by the sovereign grace of God, when that which is so entrenched within the mind is revealed in the objective light of day, it leaves the mind free to settle and become still. It is the stillness that is so needed and so lacking in a state of obsession.

Whether it is a childhood injury or a sudden trauma, when the mind gets stuck on something long enough or deeply enough to form a habit of thought, that person is in trouble. We can start the healing process by re-training our minds with another thought habit, or we can face the dragon head-on, and with it defeat the scenario that frightens us; or we can choose to do both.

For the following example, let us assume the trauma has been caused by adultery, divorce, or death, since they all fall in the same category of loss. Your mind has been fixated on the missing person, and you may think you cannot go on living without him. However, you must realize you lived without him before he came into your life. The deeper this sinks in, the better you will become at combating the feelings of hopelessness. You were happy before, and you can be happy again.

Secondly, you should choose a focal point. This should be the strongest and most compelling point for your healing. Always, the best reason to keep going is to keep evolving into a better individual; however, in times of crisis it is difficult to be motivated by an intangible. Most of the time it is better to concentrate on a situation, thing, or person that makes your life worth living.

You must take into account in times of depression, you will feel as if you have nothing worth living for; but feelings are not facts. They just seem that way. You must suspend your feelings as much as possible for a short time and use only reason and logic to come to an adult realization. This must be used to reprogram your mind. Each time the obsession rears its ugly head, you must plug in the focus you have chosen. Dwell on this thought as much as possible.

Lastly, and most importantly, you must face the nemesis head on. You do this by asking yourself what the worst thing that could happen would be. This will effectively take an internal issue and allow you to face it out in the open. The fact will always be the same. No matter how you may feel, the fact remains that before you met the person whose loss you mourn, there was life, and after him there will still be life. We must grieve our losses. There will be pain and anger, and feelings of abandonment. These things are real, natural, and necessary, but after this, there is life. Do not be afraid to ask your doctor for help. When deep sorrow occurs, there can be chemical reactions inside the brain that cause a condition leading to depression. The depression can cause chemicals to be released which cause hopelessness, tiredness, and more depression. The cycle feeds on itself and cannot be broken without medical help.

APPLIED PHYSICS

If a man in despair walks to the roof's edge and jumps; then on the way down he repents, asks to be forgiven, and is saved, he will hit the ground a saved man, but he will most certainly hit the ground. This is a lesson in "Spiritual Inertia." That which is put in motion will stay in motion until acted on by an outside force.

If we come to God and receive salvation, the sins of the past will still catch up to us. They will come. We will have to pay the bill, but we will have the Lord to help us through the hard times. We will have the hope of a cleaner, more peaceful life. We will not fear the knock at the door. However, the bills of sin are paid by all men.

Sin always takes you farther than you wanted to go, makes you pay more than you wanted to pay, and makes you stay longer than you wanted to stay.

These lessons must be taught to those in our counsel. Salvation will lead to a better and eternal life; a life with Jesus, but it will not stop the inertia of the sins from the past and they will have to be dealt with here on earth. To be forgiven of your sins by God does not answer the needs of the law or the physics of life. Life rolls on. This is the law of "Spiritual Inertia."

TAKE A LOAD OFF ANNIE

The gauge of your maturity is the honesty of your own selfishness.
Richard Bach

One of the gauges of mental health is our ability to view situations objectively and place responsibility accordingly. We should never try to thrust the blame for our actions or reactions on another person, nor should we ever accept blame for actions or reactions which are not our own. It is a common human condition to want to be right, but it is not healthy to want it enough to blame someone when it is not his fault. This lets us off the hook so we do not have to deal with the problem. It may make us feel better not to be held responsible for our actions, but it guarantees we will have to deal with the same problem again and again. If a person is abused and then is blamed for the abuse, he is doubly abused and the guilty go free, never having to correct the problem and will certainly abuse again.

More than a solution, this is an explanation and a plea to those emotional abusers to stop. The heart aches for a way out of the prison of the abusive relationship. The person who feels trapped will try anything to keep it from happening again. This often includes throwing away one's objectivity and self-image to the point of taking to heart the convoluted accusations of the abuser – those cutting tones and words of blame which push the responsibility of the abuse back again onto the person who has already been injured physically or emotionally.

You can always identify the act by its preamble: "If you hadn't…" or "If you just wouldn't…" or "You made me…" The person just attacked convinces himself this must be true. He tells himself he knows how this person is when he loses his temper, or drinks too much, or takes drugs, or is under pressure from work, and if the abused person had acted accordingly the pain would not have happened.

The tragic thing about this condition is it offers the person receiving the abuse a sick form of hope. The hope is if he can be good enough, it might not happen again. If he could only love enough, care enough, empathize enough, he might be able to stop the cycle. Buying the blame is buying the illusion of control and the hope that it brings. But what are we trading for this hope? We are trading the feeling of being such a bad person that we can cause someone to abuse us. We are accepting the feeling of being worthless enough to deserve being beaten. It is not a good trade.

To those who have been the abuser and have allowed this shifting of blame, I plead with you to correct it. To falsely cause a person to feel responsible for his own destruction is a load no one should have to bear. Once you have seen the abuser in yourself, it is your responsibility to free your mate or child from the prison you have built for him. Go to that injured little child and make him understand. Only a child would try so hard to make you love him.

Whether you are hurting the child within the adult or the literal child in the family, you have injured him and now is the time to free him. If he is an adult, you may find all through his childhood he has tried to get his parent to love him, and the child inside of him is still functioning in that time. Now you have become the image of the abusive parent, and his prison continues. Perhaps by your actions you are now creating that abused child in your own family. Take the responsibility and stop the abuse. Take your load off him.

DEATH AND DYING

In her 1969 book, <u>On Death and Dying</u>, Swiss-born psychiatrist Elizabeth Kubler-Ross outlined the five stages of grief felt by someone who is dying. These stages represent a path taken by a majority of individuals facing certain and approaching death. Terminal cancer patients and others with life-taking diseases may walk this path. However, it should always be remembered that there will be those who will not "go quiet into that good night," but will instead, rage – rage against the close of day. Some will be in two or three stages at once, passing from one to the other or vacillating between stages. The job of the counselor is to act as a guide toward the completion of life's journey.

- **Denial and isolation:** "This is not happening." The person may believe they are actually in a nightmare. There is a feeling that if they could just wake up they would be well and things would be as they were before. Reality is refused. This means they may also distance themselves from loved ones.

- **Anger:** "God can't do this." Reality begins to sink in and the result is defiance. If handled constructively, this can be a positive phase. Anger must be directed away from God and focused on the clear circumstances. They have a disease and they can fight it with all the defiance they have within them. Those who take a stand here in a constructive way are the people who last longer or go down fighting.

- **Bargaining:** "God, if you let me live I will change." This can be a negative stage. The person can take on a false hope and fall back into denial, believing God has agreed to the deal and death is cheated for a while. This stage can also incorrectly limit the length of time the patient expects to live. Having made a bargain to live until a milestone is reached, such as the birth of a grandchild, when the birth occurs, death may be anticipated.

- **Depression**: "I can't bear waiting–I can't bear another day." Any number of issues drive the person toward depression. The pain or debilitation of sickness, the waiting for death to overtake them, the torture their family must endure in care-giving and monetary outlay all contribute to depression. Yet, hope must spring eternal and the love of the family makes the connection deeper through serving. If the patient was well and someone in the family was ill, the patient would serve them as they are now being served. It is what love calls us to do. Depression can be treated by developing a sense of gratitude for the love and devotion that drives those who serve. Pain and mood swings must be treated with medication.

- **Acceptance**: "I have made my peace. I am ready to go home." This stage may come quickly to those whose loved ones have died before them. The elderly whose mate is already dead and those with no loved ones left, often embrace this phase freely. Death comes easily for those with faith they will see their loved ones again. "I am homesick for a place I have never been," my grandfather said, "where I will see my mom and dad, sisters and brothers again." Acceptance of death in the elderly is a weariness of life and a feeling of wishing to shed this mortal coil and be free of all the trouble and pain the body holds. In the younger patient, it is a resignation and preparation of the soul.

GRIEF AND GRIEVING

Grieving does not have to be initiated through death. It can begin through divorce, estrangement, or separation. Any emotional loss can throw a person headlong into grief. Children experience grief when parents separate or divorce. Spouses feel grief and anger when spouses leave. The grieving process can take as long as five years to complete. After the journey there will still be scars and memories. These we will learn to live with. We will function and live again, but we will not forget.

As with death and dying, Dr. Elisabeth Kubler-Ross named five stages of grief people commonly go through after a serious loss. Some stages are common between both dying and grieving. The perspective may change but to leave or to be left, frequently evokes the same feelings.

- **Denial and Isolation:** Like the first stage listed in death and dying, this is a stage of withdrawal from reality and other people. It is a temporary defense mechanism to allow the mind time to come to grips with the global personal changes. Denial allows one to develop strategies to work through the upcoming stages.
- **Anger and Resentment**: This stage is characterized by anger and even rage at whatever caused the loss. Children may be angry at the loss of a parent, blaming them for leaving and being angry and the parent. Divorce brings blame. The counselor should allow the outpouring of anger. It is part of the process of grief. If the grieving person has been part of an accident there may be guilt attached to the anger. The question may be simply, "Why not me?"
- **Bargaining**: Often people attempt to bargain with God. This is seen in divorce at times when one will bargain to reunite with the person who has left. There may also be threats in this stage where the person will cry out to God or those around them, even to the ex-spouse in cases of divorce. They will declare an intention to kill themselves if the pain

doesn't stop. It is emotional blackmail and should not be rewarded; however, the pain or loss is real.

- **Depression**: When bargaining doesn't work, and the person realizes there is nothing they can do to change the situation, depression sets in. It is due to a feeling of helplessness. The realization that what has occurred is out of one's control is a difficult step to take. This is the time when one admits what has happened and is mindful of his or her grief.
- **Acceptance**: When anger, sadness, and depression have decreased, acceptance starts to come. Unlike death and dying, where defiance and anger can result in a healthy fight for life; in grieving there is already loss. Life has changed. Something has died, but life continues. God gave us life. It is a gift to be treasured. It would be a shame not to live it to the fullest. Growth and triumph are not only possible but also inevitable if you do not give up.

Life is about grieving. In a way we are programmed for it. If we had a good childhood we will grieve for those days when life was sweet and carefree. We grieve the loss of innocence.

If we had a bad childhood with abuse or neglect we will grieve when good times come. They have always come at a horrible price. When happiness comes we grieve the impending cost.

The only solution is to live in the moment, and in each atom of happiness, drink it in for all it is worth. The past in gone and cannot be changed. The future has not yet come. The present is real, here, and now. If God offers you a gift in this present time, take it. A thankful heart sings to God, and He hears it.

CO-DEPENDENT NO MORE

...IF YOU SAY SO

The tongue-in-cheek chapter title says it all. Over the years the definition of "co-dependence" has changed. At one time the meaning was restricted to those who needed to be needed, to the extent they chose to live with those who were controlling personalities or needy personalities such as addicts or alcoholics. However, over the years, co-dependency has expanded into a definition which describes a dysfunctional pattern of living and problem solving, developed during childhood years and by family rules.

The co-dependent person takes his cues from others. Co-dependency is a loss of personal identity. Will and self-governance are traded for security and approval. It is an extension of a passive personality type.

As adults, co-dependent people have a greater tendency to become involved in relationships with people who are aggressive, unreliable, emotionally unavailable, or needy. The co-dependent person tries to provide and control everything within the relationship without addressing their own needs or desires; setting themselves up for continued lack of fulfillment.

There are two types of co-dependent conditions. The first involves the broken pieces of a personality fitting within the other person's personality, like a puzzle. This is observed when an aggressive person is coupled with a passive person. An aggressive person is one who attempts to impose their wishes on others. A passive person has lost individuality and self-motivation. The aggressive person demands that the passive or co-dependent person follow his or her orders, even to the point of thinking as the aggressive person wishes them to think. The co-dependent person acquiesces; needing acceptance, approval, and love. They address the wishes of the other person and ignore their own.

The other type of co-dependent person seeks out needy mates in the form of addicts, alcoholics, "rage-aholics", or emotionally distant and cold people. They then set themselves the task of fulfilling the needs or desires of the other person to the exclusion of their own needs or wishes.

The signs of co-dependency are:

- Your self-esteem and good feelings about yourself depend upon receiving appreciation or approval from your partner.

- You find yourself saying "Yes" to things when you want to say "NO!"

- You sacrifice your own interests and wishes to accommodate your partner.

- Your fear of rejection determines what you say or do.

- You dislike or fear being alone.

Counselors must be aware of the co-dependent's tendency to become dependent on counseling. We as counselors generally invite people to rely on us. We tell people what to do in order to guide them out of various traps in their psyche or society. This can develop into a situation where others become dependent on us. Thus, a co-dependent relationship is born.

Assertiveness training and the setting of proper personal boundaries are the tools to overcome co-dependence. The patient must be shown the difference between aggressiveness and assertiveness. Not only should they identify the difference when demonstrated by their partner but they should seek to achieve a healthy assertiveness in their own life.

Self-determination and self-respect should be cultivated. The rules of the co-dependent relationship will change when the passive person begins to define his boundaries, needs, wants, and desires. As the relationship changes, the aggressive or controlling person may resist by increasing domination of the more passive person. Screaming matches and physical violence is possible, as one struggles for control and the other struggles for freedom.

In most co-dependent relationships there is an element of manipulation. There does not have to be a passive person in a co-dependent relationship. If one person is needy and the other is desperate to be loved and needed, instances occur where there is sabotage of personalities. For example, if a woman marries an alcoholic because she is driven to take care of him out of her own fear of abandonment, thinking that the alcoholic will always need her; she may manipulate situations in order to ensure he continues to drink. This can include sabotaging his attempts to quit. This is seen many times when one person marries an obese person and the obese person attempts to lose weight. Sabotage of the diet by the mate ensures the obese person will remain fat and unattractive to others, ensuring the emotional security of the saboteur. The act of encouraging or enabling unhealthy acts to continue is call "enabling." In this kind of co-dependent relationship, it is the person who serves and enables who is in control.

It is difficult to help in this situation as the addict (whether addicted to food, drugs, alcohol, or even sex) does not wish to quit and the enabler is fearful the person he or she is serving could begin healing, therefore making the enabler no longer needed.

The relationship must be built on love and not on need. Both must learn to trust in love and God to sustain the relationship and not some mutual need.

ANGER

Ask your patient these questions:

Do people avoid you because you are angry? Does you family walk in wide circles around you? Do you and your partner fight? Have you lost friends or estranged loved ones due to anger, temper, yelling, fighting, or striking? Do holidays bring out the worst in you? Are you angry, sarcastic, mean-spirited, moody, crabby, grumpy, or generally seething? Do you have trouble with authority figures? Have you lost a job due to attitude?

If the answer to any of these questions is yes... even a qualified yes, they have a problem with anger.

Usually angry people come from angry families. Families that yell and fight produce children who do the same. It is not only a learned response but it may have actually developed as a survival mechanism. It may seem like no one listens in an angry family, but the children listen. In the passion of yelling and screaming at the child, imprints are made through statements that should never be uttered to a child: "you are an idiot," "you are stupid," "you are dumb." These are internalized and believed by the child. The anger is stored and cultivated within. The evidence of the damage is a person who, when they make a mistake will hit themselves on the head and say to themselves "stupid" or "dumb."

Physical, mental, or sexual abuse causes a huge amount of anger. There is fear mixed with rage, and it is a time bomb. The message from the abuser is loud and clear and is screamed into the child's soul. You are not worth a happy life. Your purpose is to be treated like this. How could this not cause rage?

But if the abuse or family situations are in the past, why continue the anger? Reasons vary, but the main ones are control, manipulation, redirecting blame, to keep people from getting too close, choosing to misunderstand to give reason for anger, and habitual response.

Control and manipulation: If I get angry enough I can make you do what I want. If I brow-beat you I can make your will weaken and get my way. Winning through intimidation.

Redirecting blame: If I get angry first it will hide the fact I was wrong. I will attack first to cover my mistake.

Closeness issues: If I let people close they may hurt me. I will use anger to keep the relationship in flux and not let anyone get close.

Mistrust: People are out to get me. People are against me. I perceive that it has happened so often that I will get angry even before it actually happens, simply because I believe it is coming.

Choosing to misunderstand: I am actually very angry and I am looking for a way to vent it at you. I will choose to misunderstand and pick a fight. What we fight about will not be the real issue so you will not be able to defend against my attack.

Habitual response: I have no reason to react as I do, but I have been reacting like this all my life. It is how I have always been. I like the feeling that anger gives me.

Most of us identify yelling, screaming, swearing, striking, pounding fists, punching walls or people, pushing, grabbing, spitting, kicking or choking as signs of anger. There are many ways to show anger that are just as destructive but are not easily identifiable. Forgetting important assignments, not performing up to par, being late or making others late, or procrastinating, ignoring or shunning, withholding affection, pouting, or whining, to name a few. All of these can be mechanisms of control. Most issues regarding control come from either fear or selfishness.

Breaking the cycle is not easy. It takes forethought and planning. One of the most difficult but rewarding accomplishments in life is to learn controlled detachment. In this case, detachment does not mean you do not care. It means you have let go of the ego involvement. The outcome is not taken personally. There are steps to accomplish a more anger-free lifestyle.

Step one: Monitor physical precursors. Shallowness of breath, rapid breathing, tense muscles, clenched fists, tightened jaw, and glaring eyes are all signs of an impending explosion of anger.

Step two: Control and reverse the physical responses. Breathe deeply and slowly. Relax jaw, eyes, fists, chest and stomach muscles.

Step Three: Most issues are not that important. In the overall scheme of things, either way an argument may be resolved will not change life significantly. Evaluate the issues being discussed and ask yourself if it is important enough to risk your relationship. No one has to get their way all the time.

Step four: Watch yourself and the situation from an emotionally detached perspective. See it play out before you as in a movie. You are the director. You can choose your reaction. You can have anger or understanding. The choice is yours. What is the relationship worth to you?

Most angry outbursts are actually temper tantrums. Many times, anger is a signpost of a childish, spoiled approach to life. This is not to discount the fact that abuse could have occurred in the past that gives rise to anger, but anger of this type is almost always vented on the wrong person.

Common types of anger can also be caused by a childhood filled with good things. A child that is allowed their way too often will grow up assuming that life is easy. A child that is protected from the consequences of his actions does not learn that life is about fairness and justice. A child not subjected to work will grow up thinking the world owes them something. Life's disappointments and compromises seem like a slight against these childish attitudes, thus a tantrum occurs. We would spank a child having a tantrum or striking out. When it is an adult having the tantrum our choices are narrowed to leaving, staying, or having him jailed.

As counselors, we are concerned about maintaining the integrity of the family. Let us keep in mind the extraordinarily high percentages of hospitalizations and murders that arise from domestic violence. We can work on assisting anger management only after the person being attacked is safe.

Monitoring physical responses, as covered in the chapters before, will help only so much. The training takes time. An honest reality check is the best medicine. The world owes us nothing. We are sinners saved by grace. We have no right to harm others. If there was abuse that was an injustice, but it is a worse injustice to take it out on those that had nothing to do with it. Every action carries a consequence. If violence continues the consequence will be a damaged relationship and jail time for the abuser.

WORRY

Some psychologists think that excessive worrying is rooted in personality types. Others believe it can be traced back to negative childhood events. More serious anxiety disorders can be due to a disturbance of chemicals in the brain. Many times, worry is a response brought about by an attempt to control a situation that is difficult or impossible to control.

Thinking through problems and challenges is a healthy way to regain control of life's pressures and challenges. It is probably a natural reflex that prompts us to seek answers to issues we anticipate but have not yet encountered. If there are no clear answers to the anticipated problems we can become caught up with unresolved concerns. At this stage, planning turns into worry. Worry can prevent us from enjoying life. Worrying, if habitual, can become "anxiety disorder." When this happens, we need professional help.

The Bible tells us how to avoid many worries. Sufficient unto the day is the evil thereof. In other words, don't worry about tomorrow. Today, this very moment, has enough for us to think about. To stop worrying, live fully in the moment.

Worry causes health and energy depletion. It can also lead to depression. A thing or situation is only worth so much time and worry. Decide what it is worth and alot only that much time and concern to it.

To reduce worry, handle issues one piece at a time. Break problems down into components so the main problem is not so overwhelming. Having closure or resolution of small issues will relieve the pressure of the main problem in increments.

Ask yourself what the worst outcome could be. Face the worst possible scenario, then work toward a better conclusion. After the worst is faced anything else will be a blessing.

Much of the worry that people subject themselves to arises from attempting to make decisions based on insufficient data. If you don't have enough information to make a decision you should wait until you gather more information.

Revisiting decisions causes unnecessary and repetitive worry. Once a conclusion has been carefully and prayerfully reached do not second-guess yourself. The matter is closed and you have done the best you can do. Work to implement your decision. After the matter is resolved, let it go.

Although people react differently, here is a list of symptoms indicating excess worry.

- rapid pulse
- a feeling of breathlessness
- trembling
- sweaty palms
- dry mouth
- chest pains
- nausea/ loss of appetite/ stomach ache
- headache
- sleeplessness

- feelings of helplessness
- difficulty with making decisions
- a lack of self-confidence
- difficulty concentrating
- panic attacks
- obsessive behavior

Worry about nothing, but pray about everything. Trust that God has a plan He is working out. Let the Holy Spirit guide you. Trust He will guide you even through your quandary. If God is not powerful enough to work in spite of your worry, you should re-examine your idea of God.

MIMIC, OPPOSE, COMPENSATE

Mimic, oppose, compensate – these are the only ways to deal with the voices in our heads. To mimic implies approval or agreement. To oppose implies disagreement to such a degree that a middle ground cannot be found. To compensate implies partial agreement, with some modifications in those areas of dispute to make them acceptable. Therefore, as in politics, whether it be the politics of nations, or of the psyche: we agree, disagree, or reach a compromise with the voices from within or without.

Generally speaking, in childhood we mimic the parental voice since children always assume the parental voice is correct. In adolescence we attempt to establish our own identity so we oppose our parental voice. This is why many experience rebellion in the teen years. In adulthood we attempt to find ways to compensate and find a balance in order to live in peace, somewhere between the parental voice and the voice of our own established self-identity.

DOMESTIC ABUSE

Domestic abuse is a universal problem. No one is exempt. Although abuse is more common in low-income households, it is widespread across all divides of race, income, and sexual orientation.

The most common form of abuse is that of men against women, however, there are a growing number of cases in which women are the abusers. The homosexual community is also affected.

Husbands murder almost half of all women killed in the U.S. Women are abused at the rate of one every 15 seconds, 24 hours a day, leading to almost 4 million murders a year. In Texas, a study revealed that 75 percent of murder victims had called the domestic violence hotline at least 5 times. In another study it was found that in the two years prior to the occurrence of a domestic homicide, 85 percent of the victims had called the police once and 50 percent had called 5 times or more.

The abusers tend to follow a pattern of behavior. Starting with a first date, he is usually very nice and attentive. Attentiveness turns to jealousy. Jealousy becomes control. Control leads to violence. First they will be yelling, then pushing, slapping, and finally beating. The abuse wears the victim down by making them feel worthless. The abusers demean their victims, verbally and emotionally. The victims are somehow blamed for the abuse and made to feel like they deserve being beaten. After the abuse the perpetrator may feel guilty. Abuse may turn to loving attention and promises of never doing it again. But soon the cycle begins to repeat and the abuse recurs. Many times drugs or alcohol are involved and the abuser may blame the incident on the fact they were impaired.

Why do those abused stay? The answers vary, but here is a chilling statistic for us to consider. Many women say they stay because they are afraid the husband will take custody of the children. On the surface it does not seem reasonable that the courts would award primary custody to an abusive parent. However, in Massachusetts a study documented that 70 percent of the cases where fathers attempted to get custody of the children, they were successful. Why? In many cases, the father had the most money and could hire the best attorney.

Other abused women stay because they feel they are without resources to make it on their own. They feel vulnerable. They know instinctively that the violence increases as control increases and if they attempt to leave, the ultimate control may be imposed – that of death. Thus, more abuse victims are killed as they attempt to escape.

Although many will say they stay for the sake of the children, the statistics tell a different story. Suicide rates of teenagers involved in abusive households are soaring. Drug abuse occurs at a much higher rate. The majority of runaways and pregnant teens grow up witnessing violence in the home.

What causes a person to become an abuser? There is a component of learned behavior where the abuser witnessed continual abuse growing up, or was an abused child. However, most abusers have narcissism personality disorder.

The Diagnostic and Statistical Manual of Mental Disorders (DSM) defines narcissism personality disorder (NPD) as an all-pervasive pattern of grandiosity (in fantasy or behavior), need for admiration or adulation and lack of empathy, usually beginning by early adulthood and present in various contexts.

A narcissistic person is someone who almost obsessively seeks self-gratification, domination, and control. They may be frustrated that the world has not noticed them for what they believe they are. They believe they are entitled, privileged, and above or exempt from rules, laws, or social restraints. They tend to exaggerate their abilities and importance, exaggerating to the point of lying. Around 70 percent are men and most have other symptoms such as reckless behavior, the inability to consider the consequences of their actions, and many abuse drugs or alcohol.

The disorder begins to present itself in adolescence when the pre-teen or early teen begins to exert control and self-determination. Because many times the disorder is linked to peer abuse, authority images, or parental images, it is thought that narcissism is a control issue resulting from feelings of anger, rage, fear, and inadequacy.

To an average person, a narcissist may seem to be quite self-confident but the narcissist suffers from a great deficit in self-esteem and needs an outside supply of adulation, admiration, fame, and greatness to fill an inner lack of self- acceptance.

According to Sam Vaknin PhD, a leading authority on the topic of narcissism, you may recognize that someone you love suffers from narcissistic personality disorder by identifying 5 or more traits from the list below.

1. Has a grandiose sense of self-importance, exaggerates achievements and talents, and expects to be recognized as superior without commensurate achievements.

2. Is preoccupied with fantasies of success, power, brilliance, beauty, or ideal love, control, or domination.

3. Believes that he or she is "special" and unique and can only be understood by, or should associate with, other special or high-status people or institutions.

4. Requires excessive admiration.

5. Has a sense of entitlement, i.e., unreasonable expectations of especially favorable treatment, an exemption to the rule, above law or rules, or expects automatic compliance with his or her expectations.

6. Is interpersonally exploitative, takes advantage of others to

achieve personal ends and seems to be without remorse or regret at doing so.

7.   Lacks empathy: is unwilling to recognize or identify with the feelings and needs of others.

8.   Is often envious of others or believes that others are envious of him or her.

9.   Shows arrogant, haughty behaviors or attitudes.

Anger and indignation are the by-products and results of narcissism. Most mental disorders that are not based in passivity are prone to excessive and explosive anger, although underlying reasons and triggers may vary. Healthy people experience anger as a transitory state. The person with narcissistic personality disorder may seem to carry a grudge, resentment, and anger all the time, as if they have a chip on their shoulders. In many cases anger was justified due to exposure to abuse in youth, but the ability to vent and express the anger was not permitted because of the fear of retaliation. Now, they live with a profound sense of injustice and the rage it has caused. They believe the world now owes them and no one should get in their way.   There are two elements firing the rage: the feelings of inadequacy, leading to a fear of abandonment, and the feelings of injustice leading to a sense of being owed something.

The abusive person may claim the outbursts of anger and violence are spontaneous. They are not. They are control mechanisms activated because they have not gotten their way in life. The cause of the underlying anger may not even be the person they are beating, but the simple fact they have been angry most of their life at the world in general.

Anger, by its nature, diminishes empathy. The abuser never thinks of the one they are abusing as a "person" with feelings. Indeed, after the cycle begins, the abuser spends time demeaning and dehumanizing the victim, which causes a "counter empathy reaction" as the violence increases.

Now, here is the "rub." If control is the issue, then we must watch for a reverse phenomenon wherein the abused person is exerting an odd and twisted ability to control the abuser by "pushing the right buttons" and inciting the person to violence. This is not to dismiss or excuse the abuser of the violent actions, but to warn the counselor that it is not always a clear-cut case of abuse without cause. Personal interactions must always be considered. Since men are usually the abusers, we should watch for passive/ aggressive control behavior on the part of the women. If one must have control and the only way is to incite to violence, then we have two issues to consider. First, as in the case of some sexual interaction of domination and submission, the true control is in the hands of the submissive person. They can simply stop playing the part and the relationship will cease. In cases of control issues, where there is an obvious co-dependent reinforcement of violence, separation while being counseled may be the safest way to proceed.

The counselor must begin by addressing the rage and feelings of entitlement and control. Dig into the childhood of the abuser. Find the cause of the anger. Address free will as being the cornerstone of God's plan and how that must also apply to the marriage. Love must be given and received freely, otherwise, it is servitude.

Beating someone because of fear of abandonment is counter-productive, to say the least. Fear will not make them stay forever.

Forming a separation and distinction between the parent, who abused or abandoned the abuser, and the spouse, who is innocent, is necessary for the relationship to heal.

Feelings and expectations caused by an exaggerated sense of importance and empowerment result in anger when they do not line up with how others treat the abuser. The idea that we have all sinned and deserve death and nothing more should be drilled into the abuser's heart. He may have an inner feeling that he is worthless. This is a true statement.

He is worthless. But, he is worth the same as you or I, because we have all sinned and become worthless. Then, there is grace, which was shed abroad for all who would receive it.

THERE IS NO SUCH THING AS MARRIAGE COUNSELING

Most of a counselor's time may be spent in the counseling of couples. Marriage counseling usually occurs when one partner drags the other into the office of the counselor for the purpose of having the counselor confirm how wrong the "draggee" is. There is usually disbelief and resistance when the "dragger" who demanded the session finds he or she also has issues to work on.

In truth, it takes two healthy people to have one healthy relationship. This is why we will not discuss marriage counseling in any depth. We must first work on the individual, then we can work on interactions. To do otherwise treats the symptoms and not the ailment.

Damage inflicted between the partners must be halted before healing can begin. Toxic habits must be broken. The counselor may suggest time apart or restricted communication in order to contain the ongoing damage. When the pain has been contained, the mind is free to consider a path of restoration.

As with most dysfunction, one must dig deep to find the underlying motives and problems. Journaling is a valuable tool in this situation as well as other situations involving self-discovery. Past events that may have been repressed or forgotten, but still may have strongly influenced our formative years, are written down and verbalized.

Have the patient start by keeping two journals. One will go forward in time. The patient will record events and feelings on a daily basis. The other will go back in time. As the journal of the past works itself back, the patient will start with major memories and fill in the details as they are linked like a chain to the bigger events. The picture of the past will become clearer. Events will emerge that were forgotten. What you have become will be explained by what you have experienced.

To understand why we do what we do is the easy part. Changing is more difficult. It will take self-control and discipline. We must want to change. Knowing we are prone to fear or anger in certain conditions will allow us to compensate by disciplining ourselves against the excess reactions in those areas. We can begin to form new habits in the handling of the problems.

After change begins, the marriage will have to be renegotiated under new rules. It cannot be the same marriage since the people in it will not be the same.

STAGES AND JOURNEYS OF LIFE

EXO 8:27 We will go three days' journey into the wilderness, and sacrifice to the LORD our God, as he shall command us.

NUM 10:12 And the children of Israel took their journeys out of the wilderness of Sinai; and the cloud rested in the wilderness of Paran. 13 And they first took their journey according to the commandment of the LORD by the hand of Moses.

DEU 2:24 Rise ye up, take your journey, and pass over the river Arnon: behold, I have given into thine hand Sihon the Amorite, king of Heshbon, and his land: begin to possess it, and contend with him in battle.

DEU 10:11 And the LORD said unto me, Arise, take thy journey before the people, that they may go in and possess the land, which I sware unto their fathers to give unto them.

The journey is your teacher, and the road, he is your friend, and you know they will never harm you or turn on you in the end; the teacher or the friend.
From a song by the gospel group, Lazarus.

There are three distinct journeys in life. They are for separate purposes, but they can occur at the same time.

The first journey starts as we venture out on our own to conquer the world. As we struggle to make our mark, gain a place, and make a statement of independence, we are making the first journey. The first journey is made externally, in the physical world, and is related to acquisitions, conquests, and the establishment of self-identity and territory. Because of the nature of this sojourn, its signs are more easily identified and understood, unlike the second journey, which is made from deep within.

The second journey is not of ego, but of the very soul. As we battle our way through the first journey, we encounter situations in which we recognize basic spiritual truths, and as a wise man once said, "Most times, men trip over the truth and then pick themselves up, rushing off as if nothing has happened."

The memory of the enlightening thought, idea, or realization fades within hours. These are everyday awakenings, but they dissolve into vague recognitions. Memories wash out like the traces of a quickly fading dream. We know the lesson was there only moments ago, but the epiphany thrust upon us does not last. The spiritual inertia that entraps us is not broken, and we continue to be held in bondage. Pray for the deeper awakenings. So begins the second journey.

Deeper awakenings pierce the soul with intractable barbs, injecting their lessons. This makes the two, lesson and soul, not a mixture as before, but a compound, inseparable and demanding of a reaction. These cause the second journey; the journey through our own personal growth, maturity, and curse. It is the time to do battle with the dragons we have kept chained in the high tower of our subconscious, the dragons we have been working so hard to forget throughout the first journey. We work furiously in the first journey to outrun and forget the dragons of hurt and fear seeded in our youth, those habits and patterns which hold us back. So we turn our sights outward and we work, drink, eat, and love to excess, trying to become so concentrated on the outside world we can ignore that nagging emptiness on the inside. That was the first journey, and it did not work.

While at times, during the first journey, honor and decorum may have been pushed aside in order to achieve a goal or conquest, in the second journey the aim itself forces an unwavering devotion to the truth as we learn we only lie to ourselves. Therefore, in the first journey the battle cry tends to be, "Whatever it takes" or "Nothus non vexatio" – don't let them get you down.

As we proceed along the second journey, the motto and banner change to "Dulce et decorum est veritas" (truthfulness is pleasant and sweet), or on a higher level, "Semper fidelis" (honor or trustworthiness first). The second journey is about the understanding and honesty of self. It is about being the real and authentic you. The second journey is the act of becoming our own hero or simply our own real person. On the most basic level, it is about discovering who we are and becoming our true selves.

The change of direction, importance, and purpose of life, which marks the transition between the first and second journeys, is only the beginning. For those who pursue the journey to its end, there will be other changes. As the juxtaposition between the outer concerns of the first journey and the inner concerns of the second come into sharper contrast, we will be drawn more deeply toward the path of the spiritual pilgrim and mystic. The experiences and maturity collected along the way will drastically alter the way we view the world and our relationship to it. This will change the way we act in the world and to others, which will in turn, alter the way the world responds to us. To those well on their way in the journey, the world will give the title of hero or heretic, priest, sage, shaman, reader, soothsayer, holy man, warrior, saint, mystic, martyr, or madman. The world will set you apart. Many will not understand you. There will be those who will revere you, and those who will revile you. There will be few in between, but you will be changed forever, so be prepared.

Driven by a divine discontent, we are urged on to new destinations and into new directions of knowledge and discovery. Often, we do not know what direction to take. We say we cannot hear the voice of God, but He is here and He is not silent. His voice is heard as much in the feelings of trepidation and angst warning us away from people and paths, as it is heard in the feelings of contentment and peace which come from being on the path where we ought to be, even though it may not be an easy one to walk. God is steering us, driving us, speaking to us in voices of peace and anxiety that go beyond our selfishness. We could hear Him clearly if we were to step beyond our fears and need. Many times, a misdirected second journey is called a mid-life crisis, while a God-directed one is called maturity and wisdom. The same divine discontent drives both, but one is divinely guided.

For those who are guided by God there is a divine peace when facing the third and last journey. When preparing for one's own death there is a grace and poise that is remarkable to observe. Only those who have passed the tests and trials of the second journey fair well in third and final journey – facing the end of life. Death, for them, is the last great frontier. Crossing the unknown desert leads to eternity in the presence of the Lord. To be absent from the body is to be present with the Lord. Knowing this, those who understand that life is about caring and love will themselves be loved forever.

ROM 8:18 For I reckon that the sufferings of this present time are not worthy to be compared with the glory which shall be revealed in us.

THE UNASKED QUESTION

We journey to find answers to unarticulated questions of the soul. The questions are asked without words and are only answered through feelings. Feelings of a vague uncertainty open the senses within and allow a spiritual pathway to form between the inner and outer person. One would think growth should be an everyday theme, but it is not; at least this type of growth isn't.

Like Cerberus, the three-headed dog who guards the gates of hell from those attempting rescue or escape, our egos and stubborn habits shield us from initiating a profoundly new viewpoint. As with the three heads which see into the past, present, and future – guarding against those coming, those who are here, and those who attempt to leave: our minds assimilate information from the past, present, and future based on how we view life. All that has happened, is happening, and will happen, is cropped, cut, and modified to fit our ongoing view. Some event must slip past the ego gate and into our souls to start the internal shift. We otherwise live out our lives precariously perched between Scylla and Charybdis, knowing if we waiver an inch too far in one direction or another, we will be rejected by our peers, or worse yet, lose some superficially defining part of our identity.

So we wait, hoping we will have an experience like the apostle Paul. We go on blindly with our injustices to ourselves and those around us waiting to have a lightning bolt hit us and knock us off our high horses. In an instant we expect insights and revelation so deep we are immediately changed and have no desire to return to our former selves. This is an easy way out. For most of us, we will struggle through the birth and maturing of the change, afraid to go forward, and afraid to go back. But this is the hero's second journey, and the difficult, internal journeys make for strong, compassionate heroes. This is the type of hero whom others need to help them through their journeys.

It is difficult to put objective and physical labels on subjective, emotional terrain. Myth and scripture do so in story form as spiritual metaphors. In these myths, the last stage is for the hero who has made it through the journey and out the other side to act as a beacon, road map, or lighthouse for others. I am sure this is what is meant in the Bible by the injunction for Christians to be the "light of the world." Salvation, however, is not the journey, as so many choose to think. It is just the starting point of the journey. Becoming Christ-like…that is the journey.

Truths can only be taught by metaphor. It is impossible to address something that is not tangible, let alone a spiritual state that cannot be comprehended by the "everyday" mind. We can only point toward it and describe what we see from different viewpoints. In the words of the Zen master, "It is like a finger pointing toward heaven. If you concentrate on the finger, you will miss all of the heavenly glory." The person making the journey cannot afford to concentrate too much on the person who has made the journey or is pointing the way. The journey is a personal one. He is likely to miss a great part of his own journey by trying to make it conform to another's path. We, who attempt to speak of the journey, should help by speaking in general terms.

There is a saying in fundamental Christian circles: "If someone gets saved in a briar patch, he tends to drag everyone to the briar patch to get saved." Let us not fall into this egocentric assumption by thinking we have traveled "the path." We have traveled only in "that direction," and there are infinite paths leading from here in "that direction." If there are many reasons to begin the journey, it only makes sense there will be at least as many starting points and paths. All roads lead to where we are, but not all roads are the same.

There is another very stereotypical mistake made within the journey, that of thinking we have made the sojourn in the first steps. It is a common human assumption which, in the moment we notice a change of internal landscape, we believe we have made the full journey. Since there are few road signs and no mile markers, nor is there a clear point of destination, there is no way to know how far we have come or how much further there is to go. Sailing on the ocean or traveling in the desert, the only way to know is to look at the stars. Within us there is little room for a sextant. In this void of information, those with egos so inclined will tend to believe they have made the full leap. It is never true.

An old friend of mine epitomized this point. He was a follower of Guru Maharaji. One of the goals of this teaching, according to my friend, was an objective state of mind brought about by a condition of "no ego." One day he knocked on my door and announced he had achieved a state of no ego and was darned proud of it. I believe that, in his inch of progress, he missed the fact the journey was light-years long. The journey is long and there are many stages. The complete cycle of human spiritual pilgrimage can be divided into three separate journeys. The first journey is that of conquering the environment and outside world, the second journey is about conquering the world within and is a spiritual journey, and the third journey, being just as spiritual, is about our mortality and death itself.

In the second journey there are several stages. On the first stage of the journey we, in the words of a poet, "have fitful dreams of the greater awakenings." These fitful dreams can cause problems if not understood. As we struggle to escape the inertia that has held us in chains for so long, one of the first events which show progress is a claiming of our own identity and self-expression. In the first journey, many times the self is stifled to make room for the jobs at hand and the acquisitions we need. At the same time in the first journey, we struggle to free ourselves from the baggage of our parents. This makes for a confusing series of events as we strive for independence (from ages eighteen to thirty), and at the same time sell out for job and money (from age twenty-five to forty-five).

In the second journey we must come to grips with ourselves. Part of the journey is to shed the old societal concepts of "male" and "female" bias. In a myth told by Plato, men and women were once one complete being of both sexes. Now we wonder through life looking for our "split-apart". This may or may not be true in marriage or dating, but it is very true when it comes to the search for balance within. In the second journey, men must embrace their soft and giving side and women must embrace their strong and self-reliant side. To be healthy we must be fully integrated beings. We must find and incorporate our "split-apart" nature in ourselves. We must be whole. **Peace is no longer enthetic.**

In the face of expression repressed for years due to job, friends, or parents, the unleashing of the feelings is usually random at first. This means things can be said or done without much forethought or discretion. Damage can be done by envenomed words. The feeling of release which comes from abandoning the old fears and inhibitions is nearly as intoxicating, and we wrongly assume what feels right must be right. The abrasive words, if they are to be spoken at all, need to be directed to those who formerly squelched them, not at those who supported us. It is easier to speak to friends defiantly; however they are not the enemy. Friends will be more likely to take the abuse. Nevertheless, it is a useless and easy way out, as the problem of stifled self-expression came from others, assuming we have chosen our friends wisely. We must look objectively for the ones who have kept us from being ourselves and address the problem to them.

IS THIS ALL THERE IS?
A MIDLIFE CRISIS

"Do not go gentle into that good night, old age should burn and rave at close of day; rage, rage against the dying of the light." (Thomas)

Have I done anything of importance? Have I left the world a better place? Have I squandered all the years God has given me? Who will remember me when I am gone? Will I be remembered as a good or kind person? What lives have I touched? Have I left them better by knowing me? Is this all there is? Why am I here? I feel like I haven't accomplished anything of importance. I have so many regrets. What good could make up for all of my mistakes?

Welcome to the big crisis. At the age of 36 I had reached my goals. I owned a nice house, a nice car, and had no debts. I had a wife, a daughter, and good friends. My job was respected and secure. I had published my first book. My life was storybook perfect, and I was a man most miserable. I had reached my goals, looked around, and decided Solomon was correct. It was all empty and meaningless. Counselors and friends told me I had reached my life goals and did not have any other goals set. This is why I reacted as I did. I needed to set new goals, they told me. This was some of the most pervasive and unanimous advice I had received. Everyone agreed, and EVERYONE WAS WRONG! It was not the goal that was missing. It was the heart that was missing.

I set new goals, and each time I reached the goal I would be more unhappy. Why? Because we think that by reaching a goal we will be better, different, changed somehow. I am now over 50 and have reached several new goals. I am the same basic creature I was at 35. Maybe wisdom has been gained along the way. Maybe I have learned more about me as I placed myself in new situations. Maybe I am better by some small amount, but it is only a little and it is only superficial improvement. My soul still longs for the answer to the questions first posed.

In western society, and especially in the United States, we are goal oriented. We are extroverts. Our minds and hearts are turned outward. Setting goals plays to this audience. It keeps our minds and hearts occupied from the questions at hand. Accomplishments do not make us happy. They take our minds off of the questions and thus dull the pain of not knowing. We chase the younger woman or faster car to remind us of the youth so quickly fleeing us. We strain at the bits of our lives and sometimes we break the reins, escaping home and marriage only to fall victim to our own fears in the end. We give up those who loved us through thick and thin and trade years of marriage for an illusion of being younger for only a while. As we tire of trying to outrun our dragons, they catch us unaware.

Looking back, it is possible the advice of the counselor to set more goals caused me to miss my best vehicle for inner growth. Pain can focus and direct us on. If I had let the pain boil I could have found it would have made me a better person years ago.

If I worry about my legacy I will work toward the greater good. If I worry about the name I will leave after my death, I will be sure to treat people with love and dignity. If I believe all accomplishments are empty and meaningless, I will seek out what matters in life. It is the good we do for others. It is the life touched by Christ through us. It is the food put in the hungry mouth or a shirt on the back of the poor. It is comfort and support that allows those who are about to give up to push on and succeed in life. This carries our memories beyond the grave.

GROUPING AND CLASSIFYING PEOPLE

Before you are introduced to the Twelve Tribes or types of personalities, I thought I would remind you of some of the ways psychologists have classified us in the past. I also hope this will give you a comparison so you can see how much more informative and easy the Twelve Tribes' method is. The means by which psychologists grouped and typed people in the past was varied. One personality typing system is the MBTI, which was based on the work of Carl Jung.

According to Carl Jung, there are two "archetypes": extrovert and introvert, and four planes, or ways of perception: mental or thinking; physical; emotional or feeling; and intuitive. These labels refer to the way information is processed. They do not necessarily indicate how a person acts directly, although action must be a by-product of thought. Each type can be classified into this matrix of archetypes and planes. The information adds insight into the ways a person thinks and perceives. Keep in mind these are simply ways to group certain types of personalities together according to a common mode or function. Use this information to gain insight into how the personalities function, how they are alike, and how they differ.

Although the basic typing system was conceived by Carl Jung the data was adapted years later by Myers and Briggs.

Myers-Briggs Type Indicator (MBTI) is an instrument for measuring a person's preferences, using four basic scales with opposite poles. The four scales are:

(1) extraversion/introversion

Do you like to: have action, variety, talk to people, spontaneity, be part of the crowd? Then you are an extravert.

Do you like to: have things quiet, have time to think things out, set your own standards, work alone, move with caution or consideration? Then you are an introvert.

(2) sensate/intuitive

Do you like to: experience things as they happen, use your senses to take in the environment, stick with standard problems, stay away from new problems or issues, keep things simple, approach things in a down-to-earth way? Then you are a sensate.

Do you like to: pay attention to patterns and how things fit together, hidden meanings of words or phrases, figuring out new or better ways of doing things, not staying in the old ruts, viewing things from a big picture level? Then you are an intuitive.

(3) thinking/feeling

Do you like to: have things logical, black and white, fair and just, straightforward and to the point? Then you are a thinking type.

Do you like to: decide things by your heart, take people's feelings into consideration, predict how others would feel about things, keep harmony and shun conflict? Then you are a feeling type,

(4) judging/perceiving

Do you like to: have a plan of action, decide things ahead of time, have your mind made up, live by the rules, have things come out so that the good guys win? Then you are a judging type.

Do you like to: handle things as they come up, go with the flow, have a lot of irons in the fire, be exposed to new information, be in the action and not miss anything? Then you are a perceiving type.

The combinations of preferences result in 16 personality types. The MBTI is "the most widely used personality inventory in history." A profile for each of the sixteen types has been developed. Each profile consists of a list of characteristics frequently associated with your type, such as:

- Insightful, conceptual, and creative

- Rational, detached, and objectively critical

- Likely to have a clear vision of future possibilities

- Apt to enjoy complex challenges

- Likely to value knowledge and competence

- Apt to apply high standards to themselves and others

- Independent, trusting their own judgments and perceptions more than those of others

- Seen by others as reserved and hard to know

The MBTI is based upon Carl Jung's notions of psychological types. The MBTI was first developed by Isabel Briggs Myers (1897-1979) and her mother, Katharine Cook Briggs. Myers had a bachelor's degree in political science from Swarthmore College and no academic affiliation. Brigg's father was on the faculty of Michigan Agricultural College (now Michigan State University). Her husband was a research physicist and became Director of the Bureau of Standards in Washington.

According to Jung, some of us are extraverts and some are introverts. (McGuire and Hull 1997: The spelling of "extravert" is Jung's preference. All citations are to McGuire and Hull.) Extraverts are more influenced by their surroundings than by their own intentions. The extravert is the person who goes by the influence of the external world, other people, society, or sense perceptions. Jung also claims that the world in general, particularly America, is extraverted as hell, the introvert has no place, because he doesn't know that he beholds the world from within. The introvert goes by the subjective factor. He bases himself on the world from within and is always afraid of the external world. He always has resentment.

Jung also claimed that there is no such thing as a pure extravert or a pure introvert. Such a man would be in the lunatic asylum. They are only terms to designate a certain penchant or a certain tendency. The tendency to be more influenced by environmental factors, or more influenced by the subjective factor defines the introvert or extravert. The line between the two is a gray area and depends on the circumstance at the time. There are people who are fairly well balanced and are just as much influenced from within as from without, or just as little. Jung's intuition turns out to be correct here and should be a warning to those who have created a typology out of his preference categories. A typology should have a distribution and be viewed as a range or percentile of functionality because most people fall between the two extremes of introversion and extraversion. Thus, "although one person may score as an E, his or her test results may be very similar to those of another person's, who scores as an I" (Pittenger 1993).

Jung claimed that thinking/feeling is another dichotomy to be used in psychological typing. "Thinking, roughly speaking, tells you what [something] is. Feeling tells you whether it is agreeable or not, to be accepted or rejected." The final dichotomy, according to Jung, is the sensation/intuition dichotomy. "Sensation tells you that there is something....and intuition is a perception via the unconscious."

Jung spoke about the extravert and the introvert as types. He also spoke about the thinking type, the feeling type, the sensation type, and the intuition type.

Jung seems to have realized the limitations of his work. He noted that it is only a scheme of orientation. There is such a factor as introversion, there is such a factor as extraversion. The classification of individuals means nothing, nothing at all. It is only the instrumentation for the practical psychologist to explain for instance, the husband to a wife or vice versa. A good typing systems is the only way to systematically minimize self-deception or to identify causes or areas of imbalance where there are unknowns.

Myers-Briggs instrument generates sixteen distinct personality profiles based on which side of the four scales one tends toward. Several studies have shown that when retested, even after intervals as short as five weeks, as many as 50 percent will be classified into a different type. This may be due to having personality types so close to the midpoint that a situation or mood swing places the person on the other side of the line.

Since there are 16 possibilities in the Myers-Briggs matrix and there are only 12 basic tribes, one can assume that several of the tribes will have the possibility of functioning in more than one MBTI group. Although the MBTI tendency for each tribe is listed, these are only tendencies. Each tribe has a strong propensity toward a set of MBTI types but each and every tribe can function in at least two MBTI groups.

In the explanations that follow the general definitions of the MBTI is explained.

EXTROVERTS are very comfortable in the outer world, with objects, people, and situations. Their attitude is romantic, and can seem flighty or shallow, and adventurous. They are ill at ease with subjective and subconscious matters. They are likely to jump into things without a lot of forethought.

If they make a mistake, it doesn't affect them as deeply as the introvert, and since it doesn't sink in, they are likely to get caught in the same situation more than once. Their contact with others is immediate. If unchecked they can become compulsive, infantile, or egocentric. Because the body, soul, and mind communicate with their owner in a kind of subjective way, the extrovert can neglect them; therefore, they can push them too far at times. They may spread themselves too thin, work too hard, or suffer from physical or emotional stress.

They view the world and things that happen from the outside in; that is, they see the world influencing them, more than they influence the world. This was the way Freud looked at things. He saw the person as being molded mostly by what was experienced as a child. Privacy is not a big issue for extroverts. They may tend to be superficial and take words quite literally; for example, "You must come to tea one day," which wasn't what was meant at all.

INTROVERTS take choosing friends very seriously. They usually have fewer but deeper relationships than extroverts. They value self-knowledge and understanding. They insist on privacy and they respect others' privacy. The energy of perception flows away from the object to the subject. They see the interaction of people and things. They understand their internal view of the world matters and influences comprehension of it. Jung viewed the world in this way. He understood the personality saw things from an individual standpoint and this subjective approach greatly influences one's interpretation of the world.

Introverts' subjective reactions to the outside world are the most important things to them. They may deal in abstracts. They are uncomfortable in the outside, objective world. Peace and quiet are important.

The four planes can be understood by saying that a person can see things with his sensations, can classify things with his thinking, evaluate things with his feelings, and estimate possibilities with his intuition. We know all people have all types within them; it's just a matter of emphasis.

It is important to note there are inferior and superior functions. The superior function is the one you function with. It is the function you can control and focus. The inferior function is the one which controls you. If you get hurt in a relationship, it is usually in the area of the inferior function.

The inferior and the superior are opposites. You are more likely to marry people of your inferior type. The thinking type is vulnerable on his feeling side, while the feeling type is vulnerable on his thinking side. When a person is hit on his inferior side, he can get emotional and out of control. Sensation is the opposite of intuition. Thinking is the opposite of feeling. Next we view the four Planes of Expression.

MENTAL or THINKING Plane:

Mind, reason, thought, leadership, a picture of reality, what we perceive, objectivity, directed mentality, and highly resentful of criticism. Logical, analytical, principled, critical.

PHYSICAL or JUDGING Plane:

Tenacity, responsibility, conformity, patience, senses, practicality, common sense, observation via the senses, experience driven, realistic, and able to remember facts. Structured, efficient, organized, decisive.

EMOTIONAL or FEELING Plane:

Feeling, imagination, emotion, sympathy, harmonious, supportive, creativity, likes and dislikes based on feelings; this means they are likely to be strong-willed and arbitrary at times. Social, can be generous.

INTUITIVE or SUBCONSCIENCE Plane:

Driven through inner guidance, imaginative, analytical with an inner sense, insightful, feeling about where things will lead, may not relate to the physical world or their body very well, apt to jump from point to point in a conversation because they tend to forget people aren't following their inner thoughts. When they speak their minds, it may be in the middle of a thought.

Others have tried to group us into other categories. They include:

- Caring: intelligent, desirous of higher education, compassionate, teaching, counseling, ministering, and doctoring.
- Driven: passionate, convicted, intense, strong-willed.
- Dexterous: affectionate, demonstrative, possessing manual dexterity, clever, skillful.
- Mental: becoming absorbed in their own thoughts, verbal, creative, moody if stifled.
- Persistent: resolute, stubborn, obstinate, possessing endurance, and persevering in difficult situations in order to reach a goal.

- Active: possessing great amounts of physical and mental energy, reckless, fidgety, nervous, aggressive at times, more likely to be allergic or hyperactive.
- Discerning: mental penetration, insight, music or science as strong points.
- Enterprising: determined, purposeful, having a natural incentive to accomplish things.

MORE INFORMATION ON THE PLANES OF EXPRESSION

As the archetypes of Introvert and Extrovert are combined with the sub-types of the planes of expression the combinations and number of classifications increase dramatically.

EXTROVERTED SENSING: Realists. Able to retain facts, they experience the concrete world, but they don't assimilate it into themselves. They love new experiences and sensations, being physical, and are given to materialism or pleasure seeking. These can over-exert themselves. They are likely to get bogged down by facts and details.

INTROVERTED SENSING: Highly attuned and spiritual. They have an inner physical attitude. They can sense the unseen. They take the information coming in, and then go away to boil it down to abstracts, file their findings away, and do it again. They may spin their wheels if they dwell too much on details.

INTUITIVE EXTROVERT: They use intuition, an unconscious perception. For the extrovert, this perception is directed outwardly. It appears to be an attitude of expectation. It is concerned with seeing possibilities and hunches, great for pioneers since it works best when there is nothing to go on. In conversations they leap from point to point, much to the confusion of any sensation people that may be listening, who must fill in the gaps. They live in the future or the past and are most uncomfortable in the present. This means they react in retrospect or anticipation, but draw a blank on the immediate experience. They hate repetition. Since they are weak on the sensation side they tend to neglect their bodies and end up with fatigue or ulcers. Their thinking is speculative. They can see the potential in people. They make good educators, teachers, counselors, and psychologists.

INTUITIVE INTROVERT: They draw from deep levels of the unconscious. This is good for pioneers and dealing with the intangible. They have vision, and don't get bogged down in facts and details. If their other sides are neglected, they will have their heads in the clouds.

THINKING EXTROVERT: These are people who can intellectually reconstruct concrete actuality and accepted ideas. Engineers are the thinking extrovert type. Things must relate to objective facts and scientific data. They try to condition and construct their whole lives and the lives of those around them by formulas constructed from objective data. They try to work in absolutes; this can make them rigid. They must beware of critical, domineering, disgruntled mind-sets. If they ignore their feelings, they can take up a particular belief, even a religious one, and become ruthless tyrants. The normal, balanced extroverted thinker strives to replace old ideas with correct new ones. Darwin is a good example.

THINKING INTROVERT: Unlike the extroverted thinker, the introverted thinker's thoughts are aimed more within. They are the philosophical types. They often have trouble finding the right words because they are trying to present images coming from the unconscious. They do not directly relate to objective facts. They may seem distant, naive, or detached, but they are trying to remain separate in order to understand others. They hold you at arm's length to placate you. If they are exposed to objective situations they can become timid, anxious, even aggressive. They are likely to throw their ideas out to others as is, not realizing they might not be clear to others. If they aren't perceived clearly, they can get annoyed and think less of others for not understanding. They don't make good teachers. They take their theories apart and examine every detail, even thinking of objections and opposing thoughts. Twelve is an example of this type.

FEELING EXTROVERT: These people are likely to have traditional social standards, not to upset the feeling situation. It is an act of accommodation. Fashion, culture, and social abilities are the thrust. More women than men fall into this category. If they are unbalanced, they can become vicious, cold, untrustworthy, and materialistic. They do this by putting people down while trying to make themselves look good. This is done with subtlety, in a socially acceptable way (knife in the back while smiling). This is a kind of passive-aggressive action whose anger, aggression, and intentions are hidden behind a socially acceptable facade. You must judge their intentions. They have definite likes and dislikes, and the ability to appraise things and people. This rational function can be applied to ministry, counseling, social work, and/or manipulating people, especially the intellectual types who are vulnerable to the games of their opposite type. Because men are stereotyped as thinking types, the feeling man is in for a socially rough ride with this one.

FEELING INTROVERT: Feelings are derived from an inner premise. They may be hostile to an object or person with which they are dealing. They may seem inaccessible and silent. They protect themselves from the outside world by removing themselves from it and belittling it. They retreat into themselves or some place to feel safe. They have an insecurity about their environment, and at times present a child-like appearance, hiding their real personality. They are in a world of their own. Their feelings are not extensive but are intensive.

There are general, but not specific, correlations between the Twelve Tribes of types of personalities and the Myers-Briggs profile. The major similarity is a parallel between the inferior functions of the types and those of the Myers-Briggs categories. (The inferior function of a type is that area of personality in which he or she functions least well.) As the types are described the Myers-Briggs classifications will be noted.

VIEWS AND TERMS

In recent years, the mental health community has come up with a primary list of disorders and/or expressions of personalities. Most people, including myself, will have some degree of one or more of these anomalies. Here is a partial list along with overly-simplified explanations. Any type can exhibit these traits, certain types are far more likely to show certain dispositions.

Passive – Repressed feelings or preferences. Resigning decisions and preferences to the whims of others. Not acknowledging one's own viewpoints, likes, dislikes, or ideas. Emotionally hiding. A need to become inconspicuous or "invisible." A fear of self-expression.

Aggressive – A direct attempt to control and influence others and situations by threatening words, posture, innuendos, anger, or bullying. An invasion of the personal space of others.

Passive/aggressive - A resistance to expectations or demands made in an indirect way so the person cannot be directly blamed. Manipulation through procrastination, dawdling, stubbornness, intentional inefficiency, and forgetfulness. Indirect attacks made by vague or intentionally misunderstood comments. Attempts to indirectly control others and situations.

Borderline – Mood and self-image problems resulting in depression, inappropriate amounts of anger, problems in coping with being alone, feelings of emptiness or boredom. This type can become enraged and violent. They are dangerous to those who live with them.

Narcissistic – A grandiose sense of self-importance or success. Self-centered behavior and a feeling the rules do not apply to them. Preoccupation and an exaggerated view of their beauty, wealth, status, power, or achievements. Fantasies involving unrealistic goals. A sense of entitlement and self-importance leading to a lack of empathy, exploitation of relationships, and devaluing others.

Antisocial - Violating the rights of others. Lying, cheating, stealing, fighting, truancy, aggressive sexual behavior, abuse of children and/or spouse, drug abuse, drunkenness, inability to hold down a job, and/or the inability to keep a meaningful personal relationship. Feeling that others are against them…they are probably correct as no one in their right mind would like these guys. Sociopaths have no clear sense of conscience. They have no immediate sense of right and wrong; no moral compass. Normally they are so self-absorbed in the moment that the feelings or rights of others are not considered.

Sociopath – Having no moral compass. Having no empathy. Unable to feel for or with others. Having no conscience. Most sociopaths are outgoing, friendly, manipulative, and very self-concerned. Many counselors feel this is one of the two incurable conditions, pedophilia being the other. On the other hand, many politicians fall into this category.

Assertive – Usually considered a healthy stance in which a person asserts and protects the right to have ideas, opinions, and personal space that does not violate the rights of others.

TWELVE TYPES OF PEOPLE

Now, it is time to introduce you to the Twelve Tribes or types. Let me remind you that you will see yourself in more than one type, so you must decide exactly what motivates you. The thing that drives you is the most important identifier. It could be fear of rejection, or greed; it could be positive or negative, but you must be totally honest in your assessment.

Up to now, we have examined society, the effects of society on the individual, and general issues of psychology. Let us narrow our view further and look closely at the personality.

SHADOWS A SOUL WOULD CAST

What is a "Type" or "Tribe"?

Simply put, classifying people into types or tribes is a method of placing people into groups based on their differences. For "typing" to work, the categories must be broken into areas with the greatest number of mutually exclusive attributes. For example, a shy person will not be compelled to go to parties to meet new people. An extrovert will not want to sit at home alone for days. The value and accuracy of typing will depend on the organization of various types of people into different groups having as little as possible in common with other groups and as much as possible in common with those in the same group. These groups or types will have the same motivations and the same expressions of those motivations.

Why place people into categories?

There are six billion people on our little planet. Those six billion people need someone to talk to, someone to understand them, and someone to help them. In my small organization alone there are 14,000 people spread through 40 countries. I will come to know only a few dozen of these good people well enough to offer advice. Typing will allow us to quickly categorize, understand, and minister to a vast variety of people.

This gives us a huge advantage in being able to help and counsel many in their times of need. Any good minister will have turned this spotlight on himself before using it on others. After all, wouldn't you want the person you ask to counsel you to have more stability and deeper personal insight than you do?

In the following pages there is a brief outline of basic personality types, their strengths, weaknesses, and motives a person is driven by through fear or desire. It is presented here, not in order to make this a book on psychology (it is not intended to be), but to allow the person to gain insight into the personality so he or she will cease to be their own worst enemy and become better prepared for the journey ahead.

Interior happenings mark the path further into the journey of the development of the inferior function. According to Jungian psychology, each of us has a superior and inferior function of our personality. The superior function is the way that our minds normally process information. The inferior function is foreign to us. It is the opposite of the way we usually think. In general, we are in control of our superior function, whereas the inferior function controls us. The inferior side sneaks up on us and hits us with an emotional blow. When triggered, the inferior function causes us to react with emotion and without thinking.

As mentioned previously, the two archetypes in Jung's system are called introverts and extroverts. I will go out on a limb and say much of the superior function is mostly "hard wired" and is the way the mind naturally functions. The inferior function is a process which has to be learned if balance and greater understanding are to be accomplished. If, by reading this list or doing research on your own, your type can be identified, then you can look to the opposite type to see what part is to be stressed, tested, or likely to be a downfall during the journey.

ISRAEL AND THE TWELVE SONS

GEN 49:2 Gather yourselves together, and hear, ye sons of Jacob; and hearken unto Israel your father.

Reuben, thou art my firstborn, my might, and the beginning of my strength, the excellency of dignity, and the excellency of power: Unstable as water, thou shalt not excel; because thou wentest up to thy father's bed; then defilest thou it: he went up to my couch.

Simeon and Levi are brethren; instruments of cruelty are in their habitations. O my soul, come not thou into their secret; unto their assembly, mine honour, be not thou united: for in their anger they slew a man, and in their self-will they digged down a wall. Cursed be their anger, for it was fierce; and their wrath, for it was cruel: I will divide them in Jacob, and scatter them in Israel.

Judah, thou art he whom thy brethren shall praise: thy hand shall be in the neck of thine enemies; thy father's children shall bow down before thee. Judah is a lion's whelp: from the prey, my son, thou art gone up: he stooped down, he couched as a lion, and as an old lion; who shall rouse him up? The scepter shall not depart from Judah, nor a lawgiver from between his feet, until Shiloh come; and unto him shall the gathering of the people be. Binding his foal unto the vine, and his ass's colt unto the choice vine; he washed his garments in wine, and his clothes in the blood of grapes: His eyes shall be red with wine, and his teeth white with milk.

Zebulun shall dwell at the haven of the sea; and he shall be for a haven of ships; and his border shall be unto Zidon.

Issachar is a strong ass couching down between two burdens: And he saw that rest was good, and the land that it was pleasant; and bowed his shoulder to bear, and became a servant unto tribute.

Dan shall judge his people, as one of the tribes of Israel. Dan shall be a serpent by the way, an adder in the path that biteth the horse heels, so that his rider shall fall backward. I have waited for thy salvation, O LORD.

Gad, a troop shall overcome him: but he shall overcome at the last.

Out of Asher his bread shall be fat, and he shall yield royal dainties.

Naphtali is a hind let loose: he giveth goodly words. Joseph is a fruitful bough, even a fruitful bough by a well; whose branches run over the wall: The archers have sorely grieved him, and shot at him, and hated him: But his bow abode in strength, and the arms of his hands were made strong by the hands of the mighty God of Jacob; (from thence is the shepherd, the stone of Israel:)

Even by the God of thy father, who shall help thee; and by the Almighty, who shall bless thee with blessings of heaven above, blessings of the deep that lieth under, blessings of the breasts, and of the womb: The blessings of thy father have prevailed above the blessings of my progenitors unto the utmost bound of the everlasting hills: they shall be on the head of Joseph, and on the crown of the head of him that was separate from his brethren.

Benjamin shall ravin as a wolf: in the morning he shall devour the prey, and at night he shall divide the spoil. All these are the twelve tribes of Israel: and this is it that their father spake unto them, and blessed them; every one according to his blessing he blessed them.

GEN 49:29 And he charged them, and said unto them, I am to be gathered unto my people: bury me with my fathers in the cave that is in the field of Ephron the Hittite...

A VIEW OF THE SONS AND THE PERSONALITIES

As was the custom in the days of Jacob, his sons were born of several different women. Both wives and handmaidens were mothers to the twelve sons of Jacob. Some sons made a direct and immediate impact on the world. Others raised sons and daughters who, in turn, grew into tribes which produced men and woman of historical impact. The deeds, actions, and personalities of these men, along with the insights and blessings Jacob gave to each son at the time of Jacob's death, announce the kind of men they were and the traits of the tribes the sons would produce.

As you read through this book, you will continually find references to "numbers and types" with the numbers one through twelve assigned to them. These numbers do NOT designate any order of importance or priority. They are only used to classify a type of person and serve ONLY as a name for the type as assigned in the Holy Bible for the birth order of the sons of Jacob.

REUBEN, THE FIRST SON

Reuben, the first son, was a leader. He was headstrong, selfish, and rash. Although his rashness and selfishness made him unstable, he was considered a force of strength and might. Many times he would act on impulse, only to regret his actions. Because he was a leader, others suffered from his decisions. Reuben would rather be a cowboy in the wilderness than a soldier for a cause. In its worst state, this rebellious individuality led Lucifer to decide it was better to reign in hell than to serve in heaven. To Reuben, it was more important to do what he wanted than to obey and do what was right.

GEN 29:32 And Leah conceived, and bare a son, and she called his name Reuben: for she said, Surely the LORD hath looked upon my affliction; now therefore my husband will love me.

GEN 35:22 And it came to pass, when Israel dwelt in that land, that Reuben went and lay with Bilhah his father's concubine: and Israel heard it. Now the sons of Jacob were twelve:

GEN 49:2 Gather yourselves together, and hear, ye sons of Jacob; and hearken unto Israel your father. Reuben, thou art my firstborn, my might, and the beginning of my strength, the excellency of dignity, and the excellency of power: Unstable as water, thou shalt not excel; because thou wentest up to thy father's bed; then defilest thou it: he went up to my couch.

GEN 37:17 And the man said, They are departed hence; for I heard them say, Let us go to Dothan. And Joseph went after his brethren, and found them in Dothan. And when they saw him afar off, even before he came near unto them, they conspired against him to slay him. And they said one to another, Behold, this dreamer cometh. Come now therefore, and let us slay him, and cast him into some pit, and we will say, Some evil beast hath devoured him: and we shall see what will become of his dreams. And

Reuben heard it, and he delivered him out of their hands; and said, Let us not kill him. And Reuben said unto them, Shed no blood, but cast him into this pit that is in the wilderness, and lay no hand upon him; that he might rid him out of their hands, to deliver him to his father again.

GEN 37:28 *Then there passed by Midianites merchantmen; and they drew and lifted up Joseph out of the pit, and sold Joseph to the Ishmaelites for twenty pieces of silver: and they brought Joseph into Egypt. And Reuben returned unto the pit; and, behold, Joseph was not in the pit; and he rent his clothes. And he returned unto his brethren, and said, The child is not; and I, whither shall I go?*

SIMEON, THE SECOND SON

Simeon was a politician. He was a diplomat with an agenda. He was able to persuade others that he had their best interest at heart, all the while planning their downfall. He did not fight head to head, but would set up emotional and political scenarios to manipulate and entrap others. He used subterfuge to get his way. This personality type must choose between diplomacy and duplicity.

GEN 29:33 And she conceived again, and bare a son; and said, Because the LORD hath heard I was hated, he hath therefore given me this son also: and she called his name Simeon.

GEN 34:1 And Dinah the daughter of Leah, which she bare unto Jacob, went out to see the daughters of the land. And when Shechem the son of Hamor the Hivite, prince of the country, saw her, he took her, and lay with her, and defiled her. And his soul clave unto Dinah the daughter of Jacob, and he loved the damsel, and spake kindly unto the damsel. And Shechem spake unto his father Hamor, saying, Get me this damsel to wife. And Jacob heard that he had defiled Dinah his daughter: now his sons were with his cattle in the field: and Jacob held his peace until they were come. And Hamor the father of Shechem went out unto Jacob to commune with him. And the sons of Jacob came out of the field when they heard it: and the men were grieved, and they were very wroth, because he had wrought folly in Israel in lying with Jacob's daughter: which thing ought not to be done.

GEN 34:8 And Hamor communed with them, saying, The soul of my son Shechem longeth for your daughter: I pray you give her him to wife. And make ye marriages with us, and give your daughters unto us, and take our daughters unto you. And ye shall dwell with us: and the land shall be before you; dwell and trade ye therein, and get you possessions therein. And Shechem said unto her father and unto her brethren, Let me find grace in your eyes, and what ye shall say unto me I will give. Ask me never so much dowry and gift, and I will give according as ye shall say unto me: but give me the damsel to wife. And the sons of Jacob answered Shechem and Hamor his father deceitfully, and said, because he had defiled Dinah their sister:

And they said unto them, We cannot do this thing, to give our sister to one that is uncircumcised; for that were a reproach unto us: But in this will we consent unto you: If ye will be as we be, that every male of you be circumcised; Then will we give our daughters unto you, and we will take your daughters to us, and we will dwell with you, and we will become one people. But if ye will not hearken unto us, to be circumcised; then will we take our daughter, and we will be gone. And their words pleased Hamor, and Shechem Hamor's son. And the young man deferred not to do the thing, because he had delight in Jacob's daughter: and he was more honorable than all the house of his father.

And Hamor and Shechem his son came unto the gate of their city, and communed with the men of their city, saying, These men are peaceable with us; therefore let them dwell in the land, and trade therein; for the land, behold, it is large enough for them; let us take their daughters to us for wives, and let us give them our daughters. Only herein will the men consent unto us for to dwell with us, to be one people, if every male among us be circumcised, as they are circumcised. Shall not their cattle and their substance and every beast of theirs be ours? only let us consent unto them, and they will dwell with us.

GEN 34:24 And unto Hamor and unto Shechem his son hearkened all that went out of the gate of his city; and every male was circumcised, all that went out of the gate of his city. And it came to pass on the third day, when they were sore, that two of the sons of Jacob, Simeon and Levi, Dinah's brethren, took each man his sword, and came upon the city boldly, and slew all the males. And they slew Hamor and Shechem his son with the edge of the sword, and took Dinah out of Shechem's house, and went out. The sons of Jacob came upon the slain, and spoiled the city, because they had defiled their sister. 28 They took their sheep, and their oxen, and their asses, and that which was in the city, and that which was in the field, And all their wealth, and all their little ones, and their wives took they captive, and spoiled even all that was in the house.

GEN 49:5 Simeon and Levi are brethren; instruments of cruelty are in their habitations. O my soul, come not thou into their secret; unto their assembly, mine honour, be not thou united: for in their anger they slew a man, and in their self-will they digged down a wall. Cursed be their anger, for it was fierce; and their wrath, for it was cruel: I will divide them in Jacob, and scatter them in Israel.

LEVI, THE THIRD SON

Levi had a choice. He could follow the crowd as he followed Simeon, or he could be the divine communicator. Levi was called out to be the voice of the people to God and the voice of God to the people.

From the tribe of Levi, Moses was chosen to communicate between God and Israel. In turn, Moses asked God to choose a man to speak to the Pharaoh for Moses. God called Aaron, brother of Moses, another Levite. Levites are showmen and at the center of attention at the ceremonies of the Lord. Levites were the arrayed in "show garments," robes, and ephods. They were taken care of by the tithes of the people. Levites owned no land and were not counted in the census. Of all numbers, 3 and 7 are used most as holy numbers. It is no wonder that the third son is chosen to serve the Lord.

GEN 29:34 And she conceived again, and bare a son; and said, Now this time will my husband be joined unto me, because I have born him three sons: therefore was his name called Levi.

EXO 2:1 And there went a man of the house of Levi, and took to wife a daughter of Levi. And the woman conceived, and bare a son: and when she saw him that he was a goodly child, she hid him three months. And when she could not longer hide him, she took for him an ark of bulrushes, and daubed it with slime and with pitch, and put the child therein; and she laid it in the flags by the river's brink. And his sister stood afar off, to wit what would be done to him. And the daughter of Pharaoh came down to wash herself at the river; and her maidens walked along by the river's side; and when she saw the ark among the flags, she sent her maid to fetch it. And when she had opened it, she saw the child: and, behold, the babe wept. And she had compassion on him, and said, This is one of the Hebrews' children.

Then said his sister to Pharaoh's daughter, Shall I go and call to thee a nurse of the Hebrew women, that she may nurse the child for thee? And Pharaoh's daughter said to her, Go. And the maid went and called the child's mother. And Pharaoh's daughter said unto her, Take this child away, and nurse it for me, and I will give thee thy wages. And the woman took the child, and nursed it. And the child grew, and she brought him unto Pharaoh's daughter, and he became her son. And she called his name Moses: and she said, Because I drew him out of the water.

NUM 1:49 Only thou shalt not number the tribe of Levi, neither take the sum of them among the children of Israel: But thou shalt appoint the Levites over the tabernacle of testimony, and over all the vessels thereof, and over all things that belong to it: they shall bear the tabernacle, and all the vessels thereof; and they shall minister unto it, and shall encamp round about the tabernacle.

NUM 17:8 And it came to pass, that on the morrow Moses went into the tabernacle of witness; and, behold, the rod of Aaron for the house of Levi was budded, and brought forth buds, and bloomed blossoms, and yielded almonds.

DEU 31:9 And Moses wrote this law, and delivered it unto the priests the sons of Levi, which bare the ark of the covenant of the LORD, and unto all the elders of Israel.

JUDAH, THE FOURTH SON

Judah was stubborn and driven. He was fundamental in his judgment and quick to forgive. He was "earthy" and genuine as a person. He saw his faults when they were pointed out. Judah is the foundation and root from which our Christian faith springs. Jesus is called the Lion of Judah. This tribe was given the promise of the Law and Scepter. God considered them solid and reliable.

GEN 29:35 And she conceived again, and bare a son: and she said, Now will I praise the LORD: therefore she called his name Judah; and left bearing. Judah, thou art he whom thy brethren shall praise: thy hand shall be in the neck of thine enemies; thy father's children shall bow down before thee. Judah is a lion's whelp: from the prey, my son, thou art gone up: he stooped down, he couched as a lion, and as an old lion; who shall rouse him up? The scepter shall not depart from Judah, nor a lawgiver from between his feet, until Shiloh come; and unto him shall the gathering of the people be. Binding his foal unto the vine, and his ass's colt unto the choice vine; he washed his garments in wine, and his clothes in the blood of grapes: His eyes shall be red with wine, and his teeth white with milk.

GEN 37:26 And Judah said unto his brethren, What profit is it if we slay our brother, and conceal his blood? Come, and let us sell him to the Ishmaelites, and let not our hand be upon him; for he is our brother and our flesh. And his brethren were content.

GEN 38:13 And it was told Tamar, saying, Behold thy father in law goeth up to Timnath to shear his sheep. And she put her widow's garments off from her, and covered her with a veil, and wrapped herself, and sat in an open place, which is by the way to Timnath; for she saw that Shelah was grown, and she was not given unto him to wife. When Judah saw her, he thought her to be an harlot; because she had covered her face. And he turned unto her by the way, and said, Go to, I pray thee, let me come in unto thee; (for he knew not that she was his daughter in law.) And she said,

What wilt thou give me, that thou mayest come in unto me? And he said, I will send thee a kid from the flock. And she said, Wilt thou give me a pledge, till thou send it? And he said, What pledge shall I give thee? And she said, Thy signet, and thy bracelets, and thy staff that is in thine hand. And he gave it her, and came in unto her, and she conceived by him. And she arose, and went away, and laid by her veil from her, and put on the garments of her widowhood.

And Judah sent the kid by the hand of his friend the Adullamite, to receive his pledge from the woman's hand: but he found her not. Then he asked the men of that place, saying, Where is the harlot, that was openly by the way side? And they said, There was no harlot in this place. And he returned to Judah, and said, I cannot find her; and also the men of the place said, that there was no harlot in this place. And Judah said, Let her take it to her, lest we be shamed: behold, I sent this kid, and thou hast not found her. And it came to pass about three months after, that it was told Judah, saying, Tamar thy daughter in law hath played the harlot; and also, behold, she is with child by whoredom. And Judah said, Bring her forth, and let her be burnt. When she was brought forth, she sent to her father in law, saying, By the man, whose these are, am I with child: and she said, Discern, I pray thee, whose are these, the signet, and bracelets, and staff. And Judah acknowledged them, and said, She hath been more righteous than I; because that I gave her not to Shelah my son. And he knew her again no more.

DAN, THE FIFTH SON

Quixotic and reckless, Dan was quick to turn and quick to strike. The tribe turned to idols and gold. They turned to the sea and stayed in ships. They were spies and artisans; idol worshippers, and warriors. They sought earthly wisdom and pleasure, and turned away from God. They were seduced by the things of this world.

GEN 30:6 And Rachel said, God hath judged me, and hath also heard my voice, and hath given me a son: therefore called she his name Dan.

GEN 49:16 Dan shall judge his people, as one of the tribes of Israel. Dan shall be a serpent by the way, an adder in the path that biteth the horse heels, so that his rider shall fall backward. I have waited for thy salvation, O LORD.

DEU 33:22 And of Dan he said, Dan is a lion's whelp: he shall leap from Bashan.

EXO 38:23 And with him was Aholiab, son of Ahisamach, of the tribe of Dan, an engraver, and a cunning workman, and an embroiderer in blue, and in purple, and in scarlet, and fine linen. All the gold that was occupied for the work in all the work of the holy place, even the gold of the offering, was twenty and nine talents, and seven hundred and thirty shekels, after the shekel of the sanctuary.

JOS 19:47 And the coast of the children of Dan went out too little for them: therefore the children of Dan went up to fight against Leshem, and took it, and smote it with the edge of the sword, and possessed it, and dwelt therein, and called Leshem, Dan, after the name of Dan their father.

JDG 5:17 Gilead abode beyond Jordan: and why did Dan remain in ships? Asher continued on the sea shore, and abode in his breaches.

NAPHTALI, THE SIXTH SON

Naphtali was a servant and a worker. He was a good man, blessed of God. He was a family man who took care of his widowed mother and cared for his family and king.

GEN 30:8 And Rachel said, With great wrestlings have I wrestled with my sister, and I have prevailed: and she called his name Naphtali.

GEN 49:21 Naphtali is a hind let loose: he giveth goodly words.

DEU 33:23 And of Naphtali he said, O Naphtali, satisfied with favor, and full with the blessing of the LORD: possess thou the west and the south.

JDG 5:18 Zebulun and Naphtali were a people that jeoparded their lives unto the death in the high places of the field.

1KI 7:14 He was a widow's son of the tribe of Naphtali, and his father was a man of Tyre, a worker in brass: and he was filled with wisdom, and understanding, and cunning to work all works in brass. And he came to king Solomon, and wrought all his work.

GAD, THE SEVENTH SON

In the day of Gad, the lawgiver was the man of letters who knew the scripture and the law. He was a man of learning. He was part priest and part judge. These men were held in high esteem because of their knowledge of the laws of God. Gad was wealthy, polished, and learned. Yet there was a place where all of the teachings failed him and he turned from God. In the long run, knowledge never became wisdom. Gad, a troop shall overcome him: but he shall overcome at the last.

GEN 30:9 When Leah saw that she had left bearing, she took Zilpah her maid, and gave her Jacob to wife. And Zilpah Leah's maid bare Jacob a son. And Leah said, A troop cometh: and she called his name Gad.

NUM 32:1 Now the children of Reuben and the children of Gad had a very great multitude of cattle: and when they saw the land of Jazer, and the land of Gilead, that, behold, the place was a place for cattle;

DEU 33:20 And of Gad he said, Blessed be he that enlargeth Gad: he dwelleth as a lion, and teareth the arm with the crown of the head. And he provided the first part for himself, because there, in a portion of the lawgiver, was he seated; and he came with the heads of the people, he executed the justice of the LORD, and his judgments with Israel.

JOS 22:25 For the LORD hath made Jordan a border between us and you, ye children of Reuben and children of Gad; ye have no part in the LORD: so shall your children make our children cease from fearing the LORD.

ASHER, THE EIGHTH SON

Asher enjoyed the finer things of life; royal dainties and rich bread. He dwelt on the seashores. We can speculate that trading and mercantile, wealth, and the things money can bring were the reason for his decision. Out of Asher his bread shall be fat, and he shall yield royal dainties.

GEN 30:13 And Leah said, Happy am I, for the daughters will call me blessed: and she called his name Asher.

DEU 33:24 And of Asher he said, Let Asher be blessed with children; let him be acceptable to his brethren, and let him dip his foot in oil.

JDG 5:17 Gilead abode beyond Jordan: and why did Dan remain in ships? Asher continued on the sea shore, and abode in his breaches.

ISSACHAR, THE NINTH SON

In Issachar we have the first mention of servitude. The land was good enough. His life was tolerable, so he remained in place… in a day to day existence. Issachar is a symbol of how we pay for our life in the energy, time, or simple endurance of a daily burden. If we do not take note, we will have lived out our lives in servitude to conditions that are only tolerable, and seldom wonderful. Omri is mentioned as a son of Issachar. It bears noting that Omri was the king in Samaria at the time of the ten tribes in the split kingdoms of Judah and Israel. The ten tribes were in the second best place, serving in a secondary temple, worshipping an idol set up by a king not descended from David. They remained in this condition until taken captive. Many times life takes us captive without us realizing it until it is too late.

Issachar is a strong ass couching down between two burdens: And he saw that rest was good, and the land that it was pleasant; and bowed his shoulder to bear, and became a servant unto tribute.

GEN 30:17 And God hearkened unto Leah, and she conceived, and bare Jacob the fifth son.

18 And Leah said, God hath given me my hire, because I have given my maiden to my husband: and she called his name Issachar.

1CH 12:32 And of the children of Issachar, which were men that had understanding of the times, to know what Israel ought to do; the heads of them were two hundred; and all their brethren were at their commandment.

1CH 27:18 Of Judah, Elihu, one of the brethren of David: of Issachar, Omri the son of Michael:

ZEBULUN, THE TENTH SON

The tribe of Zebulun was a strong and directed people. They were not afraid. They were writers and scholars. To write and handle the pen put one in a superior position at the time. Scribes were in high positions in ancient societies. Books were copied and knowledge was a means to influence, persuasion, and control. Scriptures were checked and rechecked. The number of letters in a line were counted and verified. Each page was proofread. All scriptures were copied word for word. Scribes were perfectionists. The faithfulness of the transmission of the word of God depended on the precision of the scribe. Letters were drawn in a codified but artistic fashion. Their work was respected and admired.

GEN 30:20 *And Leah said, God hath endued me with a good dowry; now will my husband dwell with me, because I have born him six sons: and she called his name Zebulun. Zebulun shall dwell at the haven of the sea; and he shall be for an haven of ships; and his border shall be unto Zidon.*

DEU 33:17 *His glory is like the firstling of his bullock, and his horns are like the horns of unicorns: with them he shall push the people together to the ends of the earth: and they are the ten thousands of Ephraim, and they are the thousands of Manasseh.*

18 And of Zebulun he said, Rejoice, Zebulun, in thy going out; and, Issachar, in thy tents.

JDG 5:14 *Out of Ephraim was there a root of them against Amalek; after thee, Benjamin, among thy people; out of Machir came down governors, and out of Zebulun they that handle the pen of the writer.*

1CH 12:33 Of Zebulun, such as went forth to battle, expert in war, with all instruments of war, fifty thousand, which could keep rank: they were not of double heart.

DEU 33:18 And of Zebulun he said, Rejoice, Zebulun, in thy going out; and, Issachar, in thy tents.

19 They shall call the people unto the mountain; there they shall offer sacrifices of righteousness: for they shall suck of the abundance of the seas, and of treasures hid in the sand.

JOSEPH, THE ELEVENTH SON

A vision is called a dream by those who do not see. The name "Joseph" means "to add." To add to this world takes vision and determination. Joseph saw and believed. He never wavered from his vision. Thus, he believed in his God and his destiny. He rose through the ranks as a politician, statesman, and leader. Even when tempted to do the wrong thing, Joseph held to his ideals and vision.

GEN 49:26 Even by the God of thy father, who shall help thee; and by the Almighty, who shall bless thee with blessings of heaven above, blessings of the deep that lieth under, blessings of the breasts, and of the womb: The blessings of thy father have prevailed above the blessings of my progenitors unto the utmost bound of the everlasting hills: they shall be on the head of Joseph, and on the crown of the head of him that was separate from his brethren. And when they saw him afar off, even before he came near unto them, they conspired against him to slay him. And they said one to another, Behold, this dreamer cometh. Come now therefore, and let us slay him, and cast him into some pit, and we will say, Some evil beast hath devoured him: and we shall see what will become of his dreams.

GEN 39:1 And Joseph was brought down to Egypt; and Potiphar, an officer of Pharaoh, captain of the guard, an Egyptian, bought him of the hands of the Ishmaelites, which had brought him down thither. And the LORD was with Joseph, and he was a prosperous man; and he was in the house of his master the Egyptian. And his master saw that the LORD was with him, and that the LORD made all that he did to prosper in his hand. And Joseph found grace in his sight, and he served him: and he made him overseer over his house, and all that he had he put into his hand. 5 And it came to pass from the time that he had made him overseer in his house, and over all that he had, that the LORD blessed the Egyptian's house for Joseph's sake; and the blessing of the LORD was upon all that he had in the house, and in the field.6 And he left all that he had in Joseph's hand; and he knew not ought he had, save the bread which he did eat. And Joseph was a goodly person, and well favored.

DEU 33:13 And of Joseph he said, Blessed of the LORD be his land, for the precious things of heaven, for the dew, and for the deep that coucheth beneath. And for the precious fruits brought forth by the sun, and for the precious things put forth by the moon, And for the chief things of the ancient mountains, and for the precious things of the lasting hills, And for the precious things of the earth and fullness thereof, and for the good will of him that dwelt in the bush: let the blessing come upon the head of Joseph, and upon the top of the head of him that was separated from his brethren.

BENJAMIN, THE TWELFTH SON

When it came to training and warfare, the tribe of Benjamin was more machine than man. They were left-handed and could fight equally well with both left and right. They were perfection in motion. Seven hundred chosen men of Benjamin were left-handed and every one could sling stones at a "hair breadth," and not miss. They looked at training as formula, system, and science. The tribe of Benjamin spawned King Saul. The king was appointed by God, anointed by a priest, and was insane in the end. This type has the ability to be leader and king, but struggles with the ability to contain and express conflicting emotions. Benjamin's people were prophesied to be powerful and successful, if they could temper their tendency to "ravin" – "be violent, greedy, or to devour greedily." Benjamin represents the highest and lowest that man alone can achieve. King or lunatic, conqueror or madman, scientist or fanatic, it is all decided in the spiritual balance.

Gen 49:27 Benjamin shall ravin as a wolf: in the morning he shall devour the prey, and at night he shall divide the spoil. All these are the twelve tribes of Israel: and this is it that their father spake unto them, and blessed them; every one according to his blessing he blessed them.

DEU 33:12 And of Benjamin he said, The beloved of the LORD shall dwell in safety by him; and the Lord shall cover him all the day long, and he shall dwell between his shoulders.

JDG 20: 14 But the children of Benjamin gathered themselves together out of the cities unto Gibeah, to go out to battle against the children of Israel. And the children of Benjamin were numbered at that time out of the cities twenty and six thousand men that drew sword, beside the inhabitants of

Gibeah, which were numbered seven hundred chosen men. Among all this people there were seven hundred chosen men left-handed; every one could sling stones at an hair breadth, and not miss. And the men of Israel, beside Benjamin, were numbered four hundred thousand men that drew sword: all these were men of war.

2CH 34:32 And he caused all that were present in Jerusalem and Benjamin to stand to it. And the inhabitants of Jerusalem did according to the covenant of God, the God of their fathers. And Josiah took away all the abominations out of all the countries that pertained to the children of Israel, and made all that were present in Israel to serve, even to serve the LORD their God. And all his days they departed not from following the LORD, the God of their fathers.

1SA 11:15 And all the people went to Gilgal; and there they made Saul But now thy kingdom shall not continue: the LORD hath sought him a man after his own heart, and the LORD hath commanded him to be captain over his people, because thou hast not kept that which the LORD commanded thee.

THE BLESSINGS OF MOSES ON THE TWELVE TRIBES OF ISRAEL

1   DEU 33:1 And this is the blessing, wherewith Moses the man of God blessed the children of Israel before his death.

2   And he said, The LORD came from Sinai, and rose up from Seir unto them; he shined forth from mount Paran, and he came with ten thousands of saints: from his right hand went a fiery law for them.

3 Yea, he loved the people; all his saints are in thy hand: and they sat down at thy feet; every one shall receive of thy words.

4 Moses commanded us a law, even the inheritance of the congregation of Jacob.

5 And he was king in Jeshurun, when the heads of the people and the tribes of Israel were gathered together.

6 Let Reuben live, and not die; and let not his men be few.

7   And this is the blessing of Judah: and he said, Hear, LORD, the voice of Judah, and bring him unto his people: let his hands be sufficient for him; and be thou an help to him from his enemies.

8   And of Levi he said, Let thy Thummim and thy Urim be with thy holy one, whom thou didst prove at Massah, and with whom thou didst strive at the waters of Meribah;

9 Who said unto his father and to his mother, I have not seen him; neither did he acknowledge his brethren, nor knew his own children: for they have observed thy word, and kept thy covenant.

10 They shall teach Jacob thy judgments, and Israel thy law: they shall put incense before thee, and whole burnt sacrifice upon thine altar.

11 Bless, LORD, his substance, and accept the work of his hands; smite through the loins of them that rise against him, and of them that hate him, that they rise not again.

12 And of Benjamin he said, The beloved of the LORD shall dwell in safety by him; and the Lord shall cover him all the day long, and he shall dwell between his shoulders.

13 And of Joseph he said, Blessed of the LORD be his land, for the precious things of heaven, for the dew, and for the deep that coucheth beneath, DEU 33:14 And for the precious fruits brought forth by the sun, and for the precious things put forth by the moon,

15 And for the chief things of the ancient mountains, and for the precious things of the lasting hills,

16 And for the precious things of the earth and fullness thereof, and for the good will of him that dwelt in the bush: let the blessing come upon the head of Joseph, and upon the top of the head of him that was separated from his brethren.

17 His glory is like the firstling of his bullock, and his horns are like the horns of unicorns: with them he shall push the people together to the ends of the earth: and they are the ten thousands of Ephraim, and they are the thousands of Manasseh.

18 And of Zebulun he said, Rejoice, Zebulun, in thy going out; and, Issachar, in thy tents.

19 They shall call the people unto the mountain; there they shall offer sacrifices of righteousness: for they shall suck of the abundance of the seas, and of treasures hid in the sand.

20 DEU 33:20 And of Gad he said, Blessed be he that enlargeth Gad: he dwelleth as a lion, and teareth the arm with the crown of the head.

21 And he provided the first part for himself, because there, in a portion of the lawgiver, was he seated; and he came with the heads of the people, he executed the justice of the LORD, and his judgments with Israel.

22 And of Dan he said, Dan is a lion's whelp: he shall leap from Bashan.

23 And of Naphtali he said, O Naphtali, satisfied with favour, and full with the blessing of the LORD: possess thou the west and the south.

24 And of Asher he said, Let Asher be blessed with children; let him be acceptable to his brethren, and let him dip his foot in oil.

25 Thy shoes shall be iron and brass; and as thy days, so shall thy strength be.

26 There is none like unto the God of Jeshurun, who rideth upon the heaven in thy help, and in his excellency on the sky.

27 DEU 33:27 The eternal God is thy refuge, and underneath are the everlasting arms: and he shall thrust out the enemy from before thee; and shall say, Destroy them.

28 Israel then shall dwell in safety alone: the fountain of Jacob shall be upon a land of corn and wine; also his heavens shall drop down dew.

29 Happy art thou, O Israel: who is like unto thee, O people saved by the LORD, the shield of thy help, and who is the sword of thy excellency! And thine enemies shall be found liars unto thee; and thou shalt tread upon their high places.

34:1 And Moses went up from the plains of Moab unto the mountain of Nebo, to the top of Pisgah, that is over against Jericho. And the LORD shewed him all the land of Gilead, unto Dan,

2 And all Naphtali, and the land of Ephraim, and Manasseh, and all the land of Judah, unto the utmost sea,

3 And the south, and the plain of the valley of Jericho, the city of palm trees, unto Zoar.

4 And the LORD said unto him, This is the land which I sware unto Abraham, unto Isaac, and unto Jacob, saying, I will give it unto thy seed: I have caused thee to see it with thine eyes, but thou shalt not go over thither.

5 So Moses the servant of the LORD died there in the land of Moab, according to the word of the LORD.

6 And he buried him in a valley in the land of Moab, over against Bethpeor: but no man knoweth of his sepulcher unto this day.

TWELVE TRIBES

Twelve tribes. Twelve types of people. Some destined for land, some for sea, and some destined for the mountains. Some are physically strong and some are spiritual warriors. Each tribe has traits and personalities of its own. These characteristics are gifts from God. Each person in the tribe shares the traits of the tribe. There are twelve types of people. There are twelve different personalities. There are twelve precious gifts that are strengths given by God to be used by man to commune, and conquer. Let us examine each one.

Here is the crux of the matter. Here are the central questions. What tribe are you from? What type of person are you? What are your gifts? What are your strengths? What weaknesses haunt you? How do you overcome your weaknesses and show forth your strengths? How can you best use the gifts God has given you?

Most of us are blind to our own weaknesses. Are we ready to face ourselves so we may learn and grow? Are we ready to study and learn the twelve patterns so we may help others?

A human personality cannot be summed up in a few lines or even a few pages. We are much too complex for that. When typing yourself or others, do not try to match every trait with those listed. Some traits will not apply. Each type is presented as a list of traits, motives, and descriptions. All traits will not apply to everyone in that type. The traits and descriptions form a general and overall view of the type. When typing, go with the overall fit. When searching your own heart or counseling others, if confusion regarding motives occurs, it is best to rely on the **S.P.A.M.** theory. All sins can be traced back to **SPAM. Sex, Pride, Authority, or Money**.

- **Sex** – Sexual encounters, conquest, pornography, sexual addictions, perversions, gratification.
- **Pride** - Self aggrandizement, ego, self-image
- **Authority** – The ability to force others to do their will. The ability to do as they wish. Power over others.
- **Money** – Possessions, acquisitions.

Each of the twelve types or tribes is described in the following manner:

- **Gift**: Part of our personality is hard-wired. It is given to us at birth. It is a gift from God. In the purest form it is the ultimate strength. If used, it will allow us to conquer, first ourselves and then our world. What are your gifts?
- **Motive**: What needs, addictions, or weaknesses are driving the person?
- **Spouse/Lover**: What are the traits exhibited as a partner?
- **Parent**: How is the type likely to act as a parent?
- **Person**: What are the general, overall traits?
- **Complete Story**: All of the details and background of the personality.
- **Ascent/Descent**: When the person becomes more healthy or unhealthy, what are the signs of change?
- **Fault Line**: If the person comes under stress and begins to suffer emotionally, what areas are likely to be affected?

JER 17:9 The heart is deceitful above all things, and desperately wicked: who can know it? I the LORD search the heart, I try the reins, even to give every man according to his ways, and according to the fruit of his doings.

The following descriptions offered for the Twelve Tribes and their associated types of people, are written in the most concise way, using adjectives and adverbs in somewhat incomplete sentences. The information is condensed and compact. It is explanatory and easy to remember. It is not meant to be a narrative.

TYPE ONE – THE TRIBE OF REUBEN

Gift: Boldness, Leadership, Aspirations

Motives: Achievement, leadership, determination, striving for perfection, judging what is right and wrong in a situation or person, trying to do things to perfection, led by an internal judging voice. Thinking they see the correct way for themselves and for others. Fear of being wrong, judged, or challenged.

As a Spouse/Lover: A pioneer, strong individual, given of new direction, a leader. Willful, persuasive, able to sell people on an idea.

As a Parent: Must guard against being critical or hard to please. Watch for setting unreasonable standards for yourself and your children. You could have felt like you didn't fit into the family, but don't make others feel likewise. The lack of balance is in the area of acceptance, will, and being self-centered. Be careful not to be blind to your own conflicting and arbitrary ways or ideas.

As a Person: Ones have ambition, drive, strength of will, self-concern and are not easily swayed by the opinions of others. Their temper shows when they are disagreed with. Domineering, they dislike being directed or bossed around. Ones are individualistic and nonconformist. They are loners, self-reliant, argumentative, and must be heard. They are quick-witted and can become sarcastic if angered.

This type is best for salesmen or persons who must put ideas across. They may proclaim their love too quickly. Ones may have an interest in teaching, law, writing, preaching, selling, collections, or owning a business of their own, needing to direct, and spearhead. One brings out a more individualistic and willful nature in the given person. They believe in and stick by their own judgments and ideas. If healthy, the One is capable of persisting and enduring to the point of success. This is a blessing. If they become convinced of the moral rightness of their stance, they will not relent. Ones have musical talent, executive ability (director, department head, group leader, etc).

Ones may be self-centered. They must take care not to be arrogant, selfish, or stubborn. They must learn to consider others first. They usually don't think about others since they assume others function as they do and will take care of themselves. Ones need to remember they could be wrong. They may need to learn to control their tempers. They may choose a mate based on status, outward appearance, or what he or she could provide them.

Ones may come across as strong and certain, yet most times they are insecure and more uncertain than they appear. It is their nature to be capable of delivering a convincing, strong, or persuasive point, not even knowing if they are correct. Often they begin to believe their self-image. This will bring them to a place of egocentric stubbornness.

TYPE ONE - THE COMPLETE STORY

Ones see themselves and the world around them as always needing improvement, since they compare everything to some imagined "ideal". The One strives and drives toward their aim of making things perfect. Because of this, they can become pushy and meddlesome as they tell everyone how to make things better.

Ones do not like to be told what to do. They have ego, drive, and are impatient with slow minds. They may seek praise or try to prove themselves. They may think of people as an extension of their own will. They are decisive and creative, usually in writing. They may be critical, but unable to take criticism because they get their feelings hurt. They are opinionated. They are individualistic. Ones are resilient in love and will not be dominated. They have a need to direct. They are usually the heads of the household. They have a gift for art, writing, and usually music. Many can play by ear.

They are good at conveying an individualistic opinion. Many do favors with the idea of what they can get back in return. They are happiest when they're in control. The One seeks praise or leadership positions. They may want to own their own business. Beware of a lack of consideration of others, or lack of compassion because of selfishness. If not harmonious, Ones are stubborn and tend to procrastinate. They won't admit mistakes or change their minds. Because of their self-centered viewpoint, they may take money, status, or outward show into account when they marry.

It matters not how strait the gate,
How charged with punishments the scroll;
I am the master of my fate. I am the captain of my soul.
   Invictus by William E. Henley

How can this lone wolf be described except to say that the paradox of the phrase is description enough? Like the wolf, the One is perceived as a loner, but is, in fact, a social creature in search of belonging. The One is strong-willed and independent but not without the need to be loved as he is. They hate criticism and would do almost anything to avoid it, and it is this strain between the need of approval and the sensitivity to criticism that forms the first protective layer of the One. The pain caused by criticism is interpreted as a lack of acceptance. The reaction is to pull away and put on the appearance of a loner. This loner persona may be hostile or unconcerned, but always somewhat stubborn and resistant to correction. In the search to do their best they tend to be frugal and even stingy at times. They will, however, splurge and spend freely on themselves.

One is the type of the leader or reformer. They want to be right, to strive to improve others, to justify their position, and to be beyond criticism so as not to face condemnation. The ego looks strong, but has been damaged in childhood. They aim for the ideal, not content to be as they are. They keenly feel the struggle between good and evil, head and heart, irrationality and their own rational minds. They are sure of themselves, less because they are perfect and more because they are sure of their ideals. They see themselves as less than the ideals for which they strive. They subordinate themselves to an abstract ideal such as truth or justice. They embrace a work-oriented theology and ethic, thinking that one must work and strive toward an ideal. They may seem confused and disbelieving when they see effort and hard work sometimes doesn't pay off.

Whether it is because of fate or personal failure, Ones don't consider it fair when a return for effort isn't forthcoming. They feel uplifted and set apart from the norm by striving to reach their goal. So as not to be condemned, they act as if they are perfect and right. They constantly measure the distance between themselves and the ideal and how far they have come. They are caught between having these ideals and implementing them in the world. They repress many emotions and impulses, riding herd over them to keep them in check and live up to their idealistic aims. Despite their apparent strength of will and character, this repression and striving (which may be to seek the father image's approval), can cause obsessive/compulsive behavior.

Although Ones are liked and accepted, they still get very lonely at times inside of their self-sufficient facade. Ones are the extroverted thinking type. They elevate objective reality and formula to the ruling principle for themselves and their environment. By these criteria all abstracts are measured (good or evil, beauty or ugliness...).

Everything that agrees with the formula is right, and the rest is wrong. People must also conform to it. All who don't are immoral, wrong, and are going against the universal laws. As we can see, if this law is broad enough, it may serve a sociological purpose; however, it seldom is, and provides nothing more than a whipping post by which he forces himself and others into his mold. Ones will get angry with others when they are really angry at themselves for not being perfect.

Ones tend to be introverts. The superior function of the One is mental or thinking; the inferior function is emotional or feeling. In childhood the One identified negatively with the father image. The father may have been critical. In some way the child got the message he was not acceptable. He tried to become blameless by shifting blame, avoiding blame, and trying to be perfect. The message, "you must be better," drove him to repress many emotions and impulses. The condition was reinforced by a parent who punished them if they let an impulse slip or told them they were bad, wrong, or unacceptable. The parent had few kind words for the One. The father could have been stern, abusive, missing, critical, cold, or alcoholic. The child was forced to be an adult and not to do or say anything wrong for fear of being punished. The child was not able to be a child, especially in the sense of needed emotional freedoms. They may have been called on to help raise younger siblings or to keep the household running in some way. This can truncate a childhood and stop growth. At first they did not rebel; instead they felt guilty for not performing up to some expected level and they felt frustrated.

The feeling of failure for not being good enough and the pressure of the critical environment begat anger, both at the parent and themselves. They tried to internalize the anger. The anger increases when they see others do not have to conform to the same perfection that was laid upon them. The super-ego of the One now is imprinted with the values and critical inner voice of the parent. The voice we all have that talks to us, critiques us, encourages us, and gives us the running commentary comes partly from the superego. It is our internal parent.

Ones push themselves toward perfection, just as they felt in their childhood. At worst, they repress their wants and desires in exchange for doing only what is right and correct, in order to silence the inner voice. Isn't it odd from the time we are old enough to identify with those in authority over us to the time we die, we strive to please them or rebel against them? This is the choice the One type will make. They will either be hard, egocentric, willful, and defiant, or they will be perfectionists, driving themselves to the point of exhaustion, probably remembering words from their past such as, "you are lazy" or "you are stupid."

They don't understand others are not driven as they are. They usually don't really understand what drives them until they are stopped by some situation which forces them to take time enough to look inside. They can come to resent those who can do as they wish without the interference of an inner voice. As Ones go to the limits, they may forsake trying to quiet the voice, and rebel against all social rules. They may even form a kind of split in which they perform as adults when seen by those they know and as a child at other times. The child within them is forced into a defensive attitude due to the discomfort of being wrong "all of the time," even though by now the majority of the insufficiency they feel is from within therefore, they have a hard time admitting they are wrong.

They become opinionated and loud to keep from being challenged. They become critical of others as a defense against being criticized. At this point, they usually show signs of stress and nervousness, having repressed much anger and fear from their past. The aim is to silence the critic within, so they may turn to excesses of drink, drugs, or sex. They may have crying spells or spells of rage that temporarily reduce the pressures.

Ones have to realize their way is comfortable to them, but it is not the only way. Others have different stresses driving them. There is more than one right way. They also need to see that when they were young, love was a reward for being good, but that is not the way it should be. True love asks nothing but its own expression. They must break with the old ways and old voices within and come to accept themselves and others without fear of rejection. We are all imperfect, yet we all should be loved. We have to forgive all of the cuts, criticisms, and demands placed on us in the past, and to allow ourselves to be less than perfect. We should see ourselves as the people we are, better than some, worse than some, just people who are trying; if we could be satisfied with that, we could feel a release from our self-imposed prisons.

One's deepest need is to feel loved even though imperfectly. The sad thing is, they can't love themselves because the inner voice of their parents is judging them all of the time. This view allows us to see a vulnerable, needy side of the One type. The child within has braced his small frame against the next cut, and waits with defiant tears for the one who will accept them as they are. The defiance is what shows, not the child. They are very concerned with how others view them, although they may not admit it. They judge situations against a view of potential perfection (how perfect it could be versus how far it falls short). Those are old ways that did not serve us well. Let us seek a release from them now.

Healthy Ones are wise, discerning, and tolerant; realistic and balanced in judgment, rational, moderate, principled, objective, ethical, with high integrity; teachers, and leaders. They try not to let their feelings get in the way of good judgment. They allow their emotions to surface and they discover they are not as chaotic as they had been led to believe. They lay aside the rules to try simply to become complete people. They have a moral vision and are sought for guidance. They can understand and tolerate different points of view without having to agree or enforce them.

They are passionate about righteousness and justice. They live their convictions, even if it means going against civil law. Their goodness is deeply satisfying to them. Original, creative, progressive, determined, optimistic, having willpower, and leadership. They are individualistic, direct, to the point, self-starters, courageous, and pioneering.

Average Ones are high-minded idealists, striving for excellence; reformers, crusaders, advocates. Orderly, efficient, and impersonal, they are too emotionally controlled. Critical, judgmental, opinionated, perfectionists, moralizing, indignant, angry, abrasive. They can exhort themselves and others to improve. They find it hard to allow others their views. They are elitists with a noble, lofty sense of self. They take on the challenge of righting moral and social wrongs, educating and guiding others. This is because they do not trust anyone else to do it correctly. They have classified almost everything as right or wrong, and expect others to do as they are told. They have the zeal of a missionary. They are articulate and love to debate points of view. They want the rational mind to rule everything. Meticulous and precise sticklers, to them life is serious business. They cannot delegate work.

The unhealthy One can be very self-righteous, intolerant, dogmatic, and inflexible. He cannot stand to be wrong. He preaches one thing and does as he pleases. Cruel, punitive, condemning others, an unhealthy One is obsessive/compulsive. The One can possibly experience sudden nervous breakdown and depression. They think, in error, they have attained the unattainable ideal for which they strove. They think they alone can do the job or have the truth. They are argumentative. They view people as malleable to their will. Nothing is ever good enough. They are dogmatic. They are so aware of their thoughts and impulses they can become obsessed because of impulsive thoughts of sex, heresy, and violence. They may even think these are demonic. This is also a way of shifting blame. They have no mercy, love, or sympathy. When others don't act according to the One's moral code, they can have others burned at the stake. In their fear of being condemned, they will quickly and mercilessly condemn others. Selfish, egocentric, aggressive, arrogant, bullish, bossy, proud, they are sometimes unable to admit mistakes.

Ones will act out by setting very high standards and obsessing about not living up to them, and by rationalizing their way out of admitting their shortcomings. They have feelings of bitterness and disappointment at having fallen short of some mark. These feelings are often blamed on others, or the world in general. They become angry, impatient, easily annoyed, and rude, judging others, and feeling "put upon." They become rebellious and tyrannical, leaving no room for any opinion but their own. They won't listen to reason. They think everything is imperfect, and it's their job to tell others the best way to set things right. All of this is the projection onto others what they are actually feeling about themselves. They feel imperfect, yet driven to be perfect. Anger and despair can be the only result. Ones need to let go of unreasonable standards, the fear of losing control, being blind to their own inconsistent thoughts and ways and disappointment with themselves and the world. They need to relax, enjoy life, and stop driving themselves and others too hard, and being easily annoyed. The One should focus on his ability to be independent, self-motivated, creative, pioneering, capable, and a leader.

Ones will work out their problems by reminding themselves it is all right not to be perfect; others count just as much as they do. Ones must learn to differentiate between the rights and lives of others and themselves; to relax and trust others to do things their own way in their own lives. It will take much pressure off. Slow down and be softer, more compassionate, more concerned for others. Enjoy life more. Understand that the feelings you have about your self-image are not facts. They are the echoes of long-past voices of those who had their own ego problems. We must all learn feelings are not facts. Feeling only become facts when they line up with reality. If the Ones stop right now and make a checklist of what most people consider normal and correct, they will find that they fall well within the limits of being an exacting person. This being fact, now they must work on adjusting their feelings accordingly. In a nutshell, they should be less critical of all, and that includes themselves.

ONES - ASCENT/DESCENT

Fault line: Self-centered and prideful approach will lead to the inability to see or admit mistakes. They are unable to learn from their own errors in life. Unable to put themselves in another's place.

Positive: Ones are self-assured natural leaders, reliable, productive, motivated, self-starters, and idealists.

Negative: Ones are judgmental, inflexible, self-righteous, critical, controlling, perfectionists. They can't stand to be wrong. The release from anger and the need to be right will lead to a freedom and spontaneity that will open up new experiences and energies. You will be lighter and more carefree.

Ascent: from One to Eleven - As the One learns how to apply his strength of will and leadership abilities, he can expand his influence to include leading others toward the direction of peace and altruism. They become a central form for change.

Descent: from One to Three - As the One begins to become more and more self-centered, he will enter a childish, unreasonable stage, turning toward narcissism and the selfishness of a spoiled child.

TYPE TWO – THE TRIBE OF SIMEON

Gift: Diplomatic, Adaptable, Patient

Motives: Helping, partnership, winning the love of others, seeking the approval of others, needing to belong to someone, diplomacy, peacemaking. Fear of being emotionally alone. Fear of not being needed.

As a Spouse/Lover: Twos are patient, understanding helpers. They prefer a peaceful, tasteful, cozy home, with close friends. They need a neat, clean, quiet, environment. Twos are able to sense the feeling and ambiance in a room or group of people. Twos need to couple and to be close, to share their feelings.

As a Parent: The Two is a parent who is sensitive, patient, kind, and tactful. They try to be like a friend to their child. Twos can complain and be nervous, making you quick to snap. As a parent, Twos can be manipulative or passive/aggressive. They may have appeared weak so as to put the child in the position of being a necessity to the parent's well-being. The child may have felt the parent was childish and the child became the parent to the family. The lack of balance here is in diplomacy, tact and helping others, being the boss.

As a Person: What a dichotomy! This type can be a diplomatic statesmen or a dependent manipulator. According to his balance and integration, the Two is a person who is diplomatic, a peacemaker, and a buffer for others.

They crave affection. Twos are gentle, patient, considerate, passive, and possibly nervous. They are sympathetic. They want someone to be the center of their world. They are tactful, having a slow temper and possessing a sense of rhythm and harmony. Some Twos have musical talent. They are tolerant, and able to see both sides themselves if dominated during their childhood, they can be overly dependent or unable to make decisions. Their world is made up of family and a small group of friends.

Twos can make good teachers. They have the ability to sense the needs and feelings of others and are drawn toward serving others. If they go too far, or if they get involved with a person who is too strong or demanding, Twos may start to lose their identity. They will repress their needs in order to continue to mold to the one they wish to serve. This can build up resentment, anger, or other unexpressed negative emotions to the point they lash out, or become passive/aggressive. Twos have a fear of rejection that keeps them trying harder. They also tend to take blame too easily, but this is because they think, if they are at fault, then they still have a chance to fix the situation and make peace.

If affected by lack of expression or understanding, Twos can become rude and insensitive, with bursts of temper and sullenness. There are times that Twos will show most of what the reverse of Two is, for example, when they are alone and do not want to be or are unhappy with themselves. This also stems from lack of self-certainty and confidence. Twos could have a sensitivity enabling them to deal with fine details in colors, textures, or sounds.

Twos need a peaceful, placid existence. Their family is a group of friends and loved ones. The Two seeks companionship, love, and marriage. Some Twos are apt to deal with logistics because they are precise. For the most part, Twos are faithful and forgiving in love. They seek harmony, balance, unity, and love. They are drawn to dominant mates. Art, music, and painting are usually loves of theirs.

Some Twos like collecting as a hobby. They may think of the past too much. They may do intricate or detailed work with their hands.

TYPE TWO - THE COMPLETE STORY

Twos are kind, tactful, patient, cooperative, diplomatic, and sensitive. They are slow to anger and able to see both sides of any given situation. They may often be placed in the middle of a fight to make peace. This may aggravate the oversensitive Twos. They may seem to have the "middle child complex," lacking proper emotional attention in their childhood, especially if they are too shy or quiet. They may feel overlooked at times, but they overcome this by being able to sense the feelings and emotions of others, then mold themselves to the needs at hand. This, however, could allow them to lose their identity in others.

Twos often get caught up in details. Not only can they lose the "big picture," but it could lead to pettiness. They may seem naive and insecure with relationships. Two is the receptive type. They are often dependent on others. A sense of harmony and rhythm is part of the Two, so talent with music or color is indicated. Their interests are in religion, art, photography, science, decorating or music. They are able to retain detail and have an above average memory. Detail retention is best with art, music, types, dance, banking, statistics, or logistics. These people often make good teachers, though they may be blunt or outspoken. A paradox exists if emotions are submerged for too long; the expression may become repressed.

The temper is often soft-spoken and passive-aggressive. They have an easy-going nature, and are patient and considerate, but if affected or under stress, could lose tact and become blunt or resentful. If stress is long-term, Twos may vacillate from being quiet and patient to being rude and short-tempered. This is due to nervousness which is a part of the Two's makeup. Twos are faithful and forgiving in love, possibly to the point of blindness. The harmony experienced or sought after by the Two may be best expressed through Eastern philosophy, metaphysics, or religion. This goes along with their search for inward peace.

They need to experience balance, harmony and unity with others. Proper expression may not be possible with a docile nature. Emotions, especially anger, must be properly vented or the anger may be later directed toward themselves. This may occur when the Two fails to speak his mind or he becomes too caught up in trying to please and mold himself to the one he has chosen to serve. Twos repress their own needs and feelings which givesway to passive/aggressive acts as they find ways to covertly express the emotions they are afraid to openly share due to a fear of rejection. Twos tend to be neat people. They are drawn to neat, clean environments. They are able to pay close attention to detail, rhythm, balance, harmony, and others' needs.

Twos want to be loved, to express their feelings for others, to be needed and appreciated. They will coerce and manipulate others, using guilt or passive-aggressive acts to get their emotions out and keep others where they want them. They also expect others to need and want their love; they need to think they are emotionally correct and will hide their true motivations from others and themselves. Healthy Twos make wonderful mates. They are capable of sensing and serving the needs of their mates, at times, even before they verbalize them. They are individuals, yet are able to be very empathetic. If the Two is not healthy, they will put on blinders. They will ignore negative aspects of a relationship and focus only on the positive. This leads to obsessions and self-deception. Twos may be blind to their own aggressive feelings, making them manipulative and selfish in the name of love.

The negative Two is the most insidious of personality types. Their love is not free, but has strings attached. This is because the parent communicated his love in a conditional way; the parent withheld approval and affection if the child disappointed, or did not approve of the child's actions or decisions. The child grew up expecting this and thinking it was correct. Yet they feel hurt and anger, and are ill-equipped to reason out why. They grow up on the emotional edge of love and anger.

They are an extroverted feeling type. As Jung stated, often only a small change in situation is needed to cause a large emotional shift. This is because of an unacknowledged anger present just below the surface. There was an ambivalence to the father or father image. This sets the stage for ambivalence toward those who can give them love. This problem of relating to the father makes their love conditional. They seem to think they have to be absolutely good to deserve love, even to love themselves. This may explain why they must ignore the bad in themselves and others. It can get bad enough that they will defend their manipulation in the name of love, even against the facts. Religion plays an important part in many Twos' lives. It gives them a value system they can relate to, and with which to express their emotions. Some will become addicted to religion in a negative sense.

Unbalanced Twos are busybodies and meddlers, not knowing the difference between what is good and what is God. They wear themselves out being good, and can be heard to say, "I believe God told me to do this." We must be very careful not to use phrases like that lightly. It leaves others in a position of not being able to help for fear of having it said they are fighting against someone who is following a higher leading. Twos must also be aware that, since the super-ego is the internalized parent, and God is the ultimate parental image, we can easily confuse the echoes of what our internal parent is saying with the leading of our higher power.

It is easier to hear the Two using catch phrases such as, "I'm just trying to make things easier for you" or "I'm doing this for you." They usually have ulterior motives. Most of the time we all have an aim for doing our good deed and we should acknowledge it, at least to ourselves. Honesty to ourselves is the most important thing. If we were totally honest about our actions and goals, we would find the early church fathers were correct when they said every action and thought of man stems from some form of selfishness. The Twos won't acknowledge this in themselves but will remind you of your problems and prick at your heart's wounds while saying they'll be there for you because you need them. They are forever trying to create a need so they can fill it.

Twos need to be needed. Twos often feel a pull between heart and head. If it gets too bad there are obsessions, psychosomatic headaches, migraines, or stomach problems. As a last word, we should "love and do what you will" and not let the word "love" be a license to do what you want.

Twos tend to be extroverts. The superior function of a Two is emotional or feeling; the inferior function is mental or thinking. Twos need to feel liked and important in the lives of others. As children they felt as though they had to earn the affection of the parent by service, compliance, and by being careful not to go contrary to the emotions of the parent. They may flatter and serve in order to "buy" a person's love. They need approval. This may be a transference from the fact they worked so hard for a parent's approval. They then tend to transfer that action over to others they love. Twos will try to become what others need.

They will say what others want to hear. This suppresses their real personality, as well as spawning an insecurity about being "found out" not to be real. This may drive them deeper to the point of losing their identity to their partner's will. They trade this for security and protection that is associated with the partner, who has usually been chosen for his strong will and personality. They believe they know the innermost feelings of others, and they strive to serve and anticipate the needs based on that feeling .

Two is the most subservient of types. Those in the subservient role have to develop a sensitive empathy or a feeling of being almost telepathic at times in order to better fulfill the role of helper. The mature Two is a model of the caring, sensitive person who is still an individual. It isn't until Twos are mature that they realize what they want out of the relationship is what they are putting into it. Obsession comes from the transference of ego to someone or something else. They will swing in their personality traits from extreme to extreme – saint to sinner, happy to angry – as they try to find a balance in themselves. It reveals situations where love was used as a tool, a reward system. Love, respect, and approval were used as a carrot in front of the child's nose to motivate him.

When unresolved anger is the driving force, there is always going to be pain inflicted. It can come with a gift, such as a comment like, "Here is a gift for you. Boy, did it cost, and I'm excited at having to go through so much to get it." This give and take, or rather give and hurt, is very common with Twos until the anger is dealt with. The catch is, since open anger is equated with doing better in school, being a good child, or performing better, they continue this in adult life by trying to anticipate their mate's wants and desires in order to be a good little boy or girl and to get the love they need. As they grow more insecure, they will stoop to flattery, manipulation, and passive/aggressive pressure to get the mate to feel as if he owes the Two something.

Rejection from the Two's point of view is very bad and is to be avoided at all times. If the feeling of this is repressed in the Two, you may hear things such as, "I'm not angry. I've forgiven the loser…" Twos can serve so intently they lose part of their identity. They put their needs on the shelf in order not to disappoint, and therefore lose connection with what they want or need. This yields the insecurity of being found out, and the stress of suppressing part of themselves. Thoughts and statements such as, "They wouldn't like me if they really knew me" can be common for the insecure Two. Even if they flirt outrageously, they usually just want attention, to feel wanted or needed. Twos watch for clues to see what people want or like, so they may be the provider of it and earn a place in the life of the lover or friend.

They are truly givers. In the romantic phase of a relationship Twos are totally committed to serving and fitting themselves to the mate, but as pressure starts to build there can be emotional, hysterical, or angry outbursts which may seem unprovoked or out of proportion to the stimuli. It has only been "crow-barred" into activity by the present problem, and like a snowball headed downhill, it has no relevance to the people who started it.

Here is a test for any type to see if you are talking about the base issue that is bothering you. Ask yourself if talking about the issue non-confrontationally is helping to dissipate the emotions.

- Do you keep going around in circles so that in the same conversation the same issues come up over and over?

- Does the argument get side-tracked? That is, does it branch into unrelated but volatile areas?

- Are you having the same arguments many times, thinking it is taken care of, only to have it come back up again?

If the emotions peak instead of recede, if you find yourself back at the start with nothing accomplished, if you find yourself arguing about many things, and if you continue to have the same fights after thinking an issue is resolved, you are probably not fighting about what is really at the base of the issue. Twos are good at hiding in the role of the victim, even though they may have created the hostile environment by reminding their mate about their mistakes and giving rise to their pain only to point out how good the Two is because they have forgiven the spouse and will help them to be a better person. Sounds good on the surface, doesn't it? When God said He would forgive us, He said He would throw our sins into the sea of forgetfulness, and He would remember them no more. We must all strive to be more God-like. This doesn't mean we should let someone hurt us over and over. God's prerequisite was that we were repentant, and a truly repentant person will strive not to make the same mistake again. That is not a guarantee that they will be successful, only that they will try.

The Two (in fact, all of us), should follow this simple rule: If you can forgive a shortcoming, then forget it. It may not be easy, but it should be put behind you. If you can't forgive it, then tell the person openly you can't, and you will probably nag him about it. You could try a time of honest "in the face" anger and vent what is really bothering you. I would be willing to bet it will clear the air and a healing will start. Just be sure you know the real issue.

Healthy Twos are unselfish, altruistic, caring, empathetic, and helpful. They are capable of unconditional love. They understand love is a gift. They find genuine joy in giving, able to love the sinner and forgive the sin. These are philanthropic, uplifting, the good parent image, looking out for others first, enjoying healthy emotional attachments, sympathetic, patient, diplomatic, receptive, considerate, maternal, sensitive to rhythm, detail-oriented, collecting and assimilating information well.

Average Twos are emotional, demonstrative, friendly, overly personal, mothering, possessive, thinking their emotional input is more important than it is. Twos are somewhat histrionic. They have the ability to declare their feelings. They can meet people. They like physical and emotional contact. They can meet people and immediately regard them as friends. The average Twos talk about love and caring more than they act on it.

Unhealthy Twos are manipulative, using guilt or casting themselves as martyrs or victims, or using hypochondria to get their way, showing feelings of anger, bitterness, resentment, especially if others don't feel the way the Two wants them to. When they do not feel loved, it hurts the Two and he calls into question his self-worth. They can jab at the soft spots of others with one hand and soothe them with the other. This passive-aggressive action confuses others. They can love and hate the Two at the same time. The Two will remind others of their shortcomings and bring them to self-doubt. All the while the Two will be telling the other person that the Two is good and forgiving enough to stay with them. The unhealthy Twos are self-deceived and do not believe they are anything but good and caring, even while they kill you with their manner of kindness. Fearful, dependent, overly sensitive, shy, petty, sullen, pouting, apathetic, Twos may try so hard to please and appease they make themselves into slaves.

Twos will act out through emotional outbursts that may be triggered by a relatively small and unrelated issue, which is used as an excuse to vent their feelings regarding the real issue. They will point to the secondary issue as the cause of their rage and emotionally destructive behavior. The real problem is they feel unappreciated, unloved, or unneeded. They are angry that they have not achieved the desired response from their efforts. They will attempt to manipulate or force the wanted feelings and reactions from the other person. Twos need to let go of feeling abused, of being taken advantage of. Feelings of resentment, and anger drive the Two toward hidden agendas, passive/aggressive behavior, and manipulate others into feeling or doing as they wish. The Two fears being alone or unloved. They may whine and complaining to get attention. Twos should focus on being a balanced, integrated part of a team effort, sensing what would help others, being a true "helpmate."

Twos will work out by understanding their true feelings and why they feel them. They must then understand no one has a right to manipulate the feelings of another. They must realize, just because others don't react in a particular way, it doesn't mean they don't love them. The Twos must see they are whole, complete, and lovable, even if no one is "coupled" with them at the time.

TWOS - ASCENT/DESCENT

Fault line: Emotional repression. Unsure of their own feelings, taking on the feelings of others, trying to control though passive/aggressive manipulation, they can become hostile if they don't think they are properly appreciated, even though they have manipulated to get things done.

Positive: Twos are loving, helping, caring, empathic, and supportive. They pay close attention to detail. They are the diplomats.

Negative: Twos are passive/aggressive, manipulative, emotionally weak, and are given to feelings of martyrdom. They have the egotism that comes from thinking they are secretly behind the scenes making things happen. They have the idea that people could not get along without them.

Ascent: from Two to Four: By attending to their own feelings and learning how to be assertive, the Two will uncover a genuine warmth and earthiness. When the repressed emotions are swept away, a discerning logic and emotional intelligence will show through.

Descent: from Two to Eight: As the Two's emotional repression and manipulation continue, he declines into an insensitivity, aggression, and crassness. If he can't get his way through compromise or manipulation, he tries a demanding, aggressive approach.

TYPE THREE – THE TRIBE OF LEVI

Gift: Aesthetic, Outgoing, Optimistic, Artistic

Motives: Needing self-expression, having an artistic view of life, Threes are artists: light, optimistic, flighty, and intuitive. The Bible states, "Without a vision my people perish." Threes have imagination and vision. Fear of being ignored, not liked, or rejected.

As a Spouse/Lover: Popularity is important. Friendly, outgoing, vibrant, fun, spontaneous, artistic, "right brained," communicative, and chatty.

As a Parent: Usually light and happy, but also can be jealous and envious. Art and self-expression, or fashion could play a role in the Three's life. The lack of balance here is in flights of fantasy. Imagination must be tempered with reality. You can live a bit too much with your head in the clouds.

As a Person: There is a part of the Three that refuses to grow up. They want to hold on to those good times and live them out in a pure, childlike state. This may make them appear to be "ditzy" at times. These are the types who are drawn to the new-age concepts and religions. They want to believe in fantasy and the fantastic. Magic and mystery feed their imaginations. Threes make good artists and writers. They are optimistic and outgoing, but may seem superficial. Threes may be influenced easily, especially by flattery.

Threes are cheerful, but sometimes flighty. They are proud and say they desire candor, but often get their feelings hurt from it because of their child-like way of taking criticism. Someplace deep inside, they are still innocent children. Threes are drawn toward other people and are very social, loving parties and chit-chat. They love sharing ideas and adding to their world of the miraculous. They meet people well, and enjoy socializing, dancing, music, parties, and other social events. They are able to mingle, fit into a number of environments, and make people feel at ease.

Threes are an interesting type because they are light and airy, which means they can be very fun-loving and able to uplift others. They tend to take life as it comes and not to take things too seriously. They may not be rich, but they may have a happier life. Threes put on a happy face and cover their true feelings with an outward show of lightness even if they are sad at times. Although they appear to be superficial and light, it must be remembered that they are caught up in a world they do not like or trust. They much prefer their fantasy world. To them the world is rough and abrasive. They do not easily accept this, so in their minds this must not be all there is. This is the path by which they buy into the invisible and mystical world.

TYPE THREE - THE COMPLETE STORY

Through self-expression, art, music, creativity, a flair for languages, painting, drawing, writing, charm, social graces, flirtation, or performance, they may bid for the spotlight. Most Threes end up at the center of attention. There is an insecurity when it comes to their mates. They wonder if their mate really loves them or needs them. Threes exude lightness and optimism. They may want their mate to be candid, but they get hurt because of it. They are stylish and place a lot of importance on style and flair. The Three wants to make people happy. They may sing well. Scattered energy and a tendency to get sidetracked are problems for Threes. These people can have a vibrant, radiant personality. They may love acting or role-playing.

They have many "faces". They seek to surround themselves with groups of people. One of their finer attributes is the chameleon-like ability to fit into most social environments. If affected, they may be superficial, lack concentration, or exhibit gaudy taste and false vanity. They may be verbose and prattle on about nothing for hours.

Threes want to be affirmed and celebrated. They thrive on attention, usually the limelight, but it all centers around a feeling of being admired and accepted. They like impressing others with talent and ideas. They may have grand ideas but little follow through. They are truly the idea people. They have imagination and vision, but they tend to lack the tenacity and planning to get things done. They can be status, style, and image driven.

Threes can make a person feel like the center of attention. When the other people see themselves reflected favorably in the Three, they feel good about themselves and they like the Three. They tend to see the good in people, but, again, because of the lack of staying power, the Three tends not to stay in relationships long. The other person will wonder what he did wrong. Threes must learn this instability hurts people deeply. In childhood Threes identified more closely with their mother image. They were given much attention when young. They were praised for performance, image, looks, or social skills. Because of this they have a high and strong self-esteem. They expect others to accept and love them the same way the parent did.

Threes tend toward pouting, or vindictiveness as children would. Threes need assurance and to feel like the spoiled child they were with their mother image. Threes are actors. They strive to be the consummate type of the image they have chosen. If they choose to be a yuppie, they will be the epitome of a yuppie. That is why there can appear to be a wide variety of Threes. They are activity and achievement driven. As children they could have been "Shirley Temple" types, and as adults they may be socialites or workaholics, but they will perform in whatever they do.

Like type Two, they can get lost in their own games. They can easily come to believe they are the characters they play. If they dig deeply enough, they will find the role they play is chosen to produce a certain kind of reaction from the "audience." They play for attention. They can play the part of the sympathetic or suffering person, and not feel nearly as deeply as they can project. Their true identity becomes eclipsed by the game. They become detached from the way they really feel. They tend to think they have to be happy to make others like them.

They tend to keep a surface optimism. Activity is an antidepressant for them. They are capable of doing and thinking of more than one thing at a time. If handled well and focused, this can be a great asset. If left unfocused, they can be scattered "air-heads." They try to fill as much time as they can with activity in order to keep inner emotions at bay. The actress or chameleon tendency is highest in the struggle to be accepted in the teens and young adulthood years. Threes can become convinced they see the world and all of its hidden power and mysteries. They may think they can channel, be a medium, or foretell the future. They can cling desperately to their world since they do not like the real one.

Threes have a lot of energy and can think or do more than one thing at a time. In this they resemble the Five type. This can keep things lively, or it can be a source of undirected energy where there is much activity and little accomplishment. Until a Three can look in the mirror and know in his heart who and what he is, he may easily and frequently fall victim to self-deception and the waste of time.

Threes tend to be extraverted. The superior function is emotional – feeling or perceiving; the inferior function is intuition.

Healthy Threes are inner directed, artistic, creative, visionary, adaptable, and energetic. They like self-improvement and knowledge. They have very quick minds that function on an intuitive level. They can motivate others to be like them since they have many qualities to emulate. They are expressive, social, conversational, inspirational, charming, gracious, artistic, creative (through words, music, dance, sculpture, painting), and romantic.

Average Threes are concerned with self-expression. They want to establish their superiority over others, usually through arcane or intuitive knowledge. Being acknowledged by others as better raises their self-esteem. They may tend to be late and distracted as if to say, "My time is more important than yours." They are marketing, public relations, and art-oriented.

Unhealthy Threes are exhibitionists, shallow, verbose, superficial, airy, unreliable, and not grounded in reality. A tip-off to this is the large number of relationships they go through, none of which are long-term. If the deterioration into unreality continues, a sociopath becomes psychopathic, and they end up believing anything. The unhealthy Three is selfish, unreliable, narcissistic, lying, careless, gossiping, flirtatious, a dilettante, shallow, and insincere.

Threes act out through flights of fantasy and unfounded imagination. This includes exaggeration, verbosity, and self-deception. Threes need to let go of fear of the "real world" and fear of failure. They need to focus on their ability to meet and interact with people; their flair for fashion, communications, or art; their persuasive personality, spontaneous creativity, and social sense.

Threes will work out by trusting the real world has more value than a world of imagination.

THREES - ASCENT/DESCENT

Fault line: Pride and flights of fantasy goes before the fall. The superficial will perish when the presentation fails.

Positive: Threes are optimistic, confident, energetic, outgoing, artistic, and creative. Negative threes are vain, deceptive, shallow, vindictive, superficial, and unreliable.

Negative: Threes have little root in reality, deceitful of self and others. An identity crisis occurs when they can no longer hide from reality. The need to fit into the world they have created means they can lose themselves in their fantasy. When the world they have imagined does not work, they deny and then come apart.

Ascent: from Three to Six. By dropping all pretense and facade, along with the need to be accepted, the Three will be loyal and caring. They will climb from the childlike approach of the Three to the parental caring and solidness of the healthy Six. Being true to their feelings brings the Three to a place of likable solidness.

Descent: from Three to Seven: As the Three identity crisis reaches its breaking point, the Three starts to shut down. They start to vacillate between depression and flights of imagination. As they lose hope in the world, they sink into an unassertive despair.

TYPE FOUR – THE TRIBE OF JUDAH

Gift: Precise, Practical, Solid

Motives: Stability and order. Emotions confuse them. Fours tend to hide from feelings. They exhibit fear of loss, fear of being abandoned. Fear of being a failure.

As a Spouse/Lover: Plain, realistic, stable, the builder, the one who implements systems, down-to-earth, Four's practical approach leads toward solutions. In emotional control, disciplined, orderly, methodical, systematic, and logical approaches are important. Working with their hands is rewarding.

As a Parent: Fours are stern, unemotional, logical, and method-driven. They are disciplinarians. They may have addictions to food, drugs, alcohol, or religion. Fours are given to depression or self-pity. In a small percentage of parents, the work habit may be off-balance, being either lazy or workaholics. The lack of balance here is in the expression of emotion, addiction, depression, and the work ethic.

As a Person: Practical, orderly, methodical, stern, and enduring, Fours are mechanically inclined, good with money, logic, and math. They are hard workers, practical, and down-to-earth. These people make good welders, engineers, carpenters, plumbers, butchers, mechanics; performing, sewing, knitting, refinishing furniture, painting, editing music, or most any job requiring good manual dexterity. Many Fours, especially women, are repressed emotionally and do not have a good outlet for venting their feelings. They may read books to relax, cook, watch TV, be involved with team sports on TV, or have some other non-physical outlet.

That is not enough to relieve the pressure, however. Because of the emotional blockage that some Fours have, women can have problems in gaining satisfaction through intercourse. They need to work on letting go emotionally and enjoying the act itself. Fours are tolerant of the faults of others; but they should avoid flighty and superficial persons. They have little interest in metaphysics or abstracts. If something cannot be touched or seen, it does not exist to the Four. Falling into ruts or routines is common among Fours. This may lead to escapism through drugs, alcohol, sex, food, or eating disorders. If this escapism is more balanced and less destructive, it will turn toward reading, movies, and working with their hands in order to escape.

At times, their emotional needs are filled by religion, sports, or partying. If they are faced with too many changes of pace, they could suffer mentally or physically. Their body clocks and sense of regularity are sensitive. They require a certain amount of routine in order to function normally. They need to learn to express themselves freely with the gifts they have and avoid becoming lazy, stubborn, or narrow-minded. They should be careful not to hold back their emotions too much; this leads to escapism and swings of emotion, such as appearing to be a cold, logical person one moment, and effusive the next.

Four is a good military type with a good memory and learning ability. It has been noted that a large number of type Four women have problems with their legs (circulation or joints). This may be due to the kinds of jobs they are drawn to.

TYPE FOUR - THE COMPLETE STORY

Argue for your limitations and sure enough, they are yours.
Richard Bach

Control, restraint, discipline, order, form, precision, and reliability are musts. Fours may not like abstracts or philosophy, yet they have a great sense of ethics and are conservative. They have fixed opinions and are stubborn. They are drawn to technical, mechanical, or construction fields. They may like to work with their hands – cars, contracting, building.

They don't trust their intuitive or emotional responses. Due to an inability to get in touch with their feelings, the Four can be an escapist, with habits of drinking, drugs, or eating to relieve tension. All of these must be kept in balance. If the escapism is turned to the positive, they will tend to escape by reading, watching movies, working with their hands, playing or watching sports, fishing, and hunting. They will swing between sternness and tolerance. They know the limits of self and others. They may become frustrated with a fickle or flighty mate. They are down-to-earth and can do plumbing, welding, farming, architecture, construction, carpentry, electronics, and refinishing furniture. When immature, they will be intolerant if they haven't learned their limits. They think people should carry their own weight and they may have a do-it-yourself attitude. They are motivated by a sense of duty and responsibility.

Fours are given to above-average memories because they have minds that can organize and categorize facts (law, drafting, medicine). If the Four is afflicted with a low self-image due to abuse or neglect in childhood, he can have a subservient, worker ant mentality. They can get stuck in the work-a-day mentality because of this subordinate frame of mind and a lack of self-worth.

Women tend to be dominant or less lady-like. If affected, they may be lazy, resisting change, lacking emotional expression, too serious, or shiftless, thinking the world owes them a living. They usually cannot stick with one thing too long (marriage, money-making, schemes to make a quick buck). They are usually quiet with people they don't know. Four females are usually breadwinners or co-workers. Stubborn and insecure, they may lack true self-appreciation.

Fours want to understand themselves and to express this in some way that has beauty. They withdraw to attend to emotional needs first before anything else. They are craftsmen.

There are two motives for the Four's creative or artistic work: to communicate or to lose themselves in their work. There are two results from their artistic or creative output: one is to transcend self, and the other is to become self-aware. If they choose to run from themselves, the result will be delayed growth, lessened self-evaluation, lack of dependability, and escapism. It is only the healthy Four who takes the high road. The average Four instead turns inward to understand himself. In doing so he becomes trapped in a subjective viewpoint. Entrapped in their emotions, or the urge to understand and control their emotions, they withdraw and have an increasingly difficult time coping with the world. They have emotional difficulties more than other types. They sense both the full human potential and the depths to which we can descend; they view themselves as having missed their chance and potential and are destined to stagnate well below their station. The despair grows.

The Four is driven by a search for identity. They want to sort out their emotions and answer the basic questions of, "Who am I?" and "Is this all there is?" There is so much repression going on, due to confusion or pain, they may not even be aware of their feelings until they are expressed through a medium. On first impression they may seem shy or vulnerable, or you may see that they try too hard to fit in. That is their insecurity, but all of that fuels the inner conflict you'll see later. They will say, "I'll live the way I want and do things when I want," but that's an excuse to procrastinate because of uncertainty, or to be lazy or irresponsible.

Most Fours lacked a role model. They didn't identify with either parent enough. There is a deep, unconscious anger because a parent didn't nurture them. They are angry with themselves for being so defective the parent left or ignored them. They could have had a feeling of aloneness in childhood, a piece missing by way of divorce, death, illness, alcoholism, or personality conflict with a parent. The child was forced to turn inward for his identity.

They feel they were defective and this caused the parent's lack of attention. They may try to be better, taking up the slack for the parent, making excuses for them, but in time they will begin to search themselves for the reason and turn within. They feel powerless and frustrated. This causes tension, self-doubt, and aggression. If the doubt or aggression is turned within, there will be compulsions, habits, "isms" such as eating, drinking, drugs, or sex. These are the primary vehicles for escapism.

The ambivalence toward the parent can cause a rebellion in the child that is most clearly seen in the teens and twenties. They will defy authority, may even break the law or drink to excess. They are acting out anger against a dysfunctional home. Some Fours come to believe they lack value. They tend to accept others for what they are without judging them. They hope others will do the same for them.

Other Fours sink to displaying a tough-guy type of exterior and even appearing to be "thugs." Mostly, Fours are needy people with a protective shell. They feel an isolation yet are trapped by a fear of intimacy brought on by a childhood feeling of not being worthy of stable, loving closeness by both parents. The central cause of pain is an insidious type of emotional abandonment. The child always assumes the parent is in the right and therefore the child must be wrong. Their self-esteem plummets. They feel worthless and alone. The despair that comes is partly because they search for reasons why the parent doesn't love them when the problem is with the parent. They end up lost within themselves in despair trying to find a way to be good enough to make Daddy or Mommy love them. This leads to anger, and fatalism. They may dwell on the past, wondering where they went wrong, and lamenting what might have been. It is melancholia, and is fought by outdoor activity and escapism.

Now and then there is a loop formed in which the despair, which is really unresolved anger, leads to escapism in the form of drugs or alcohol. The escapism reinforces their own poor self-image of being worthless, which drives them deeper into despair. Even if drugs or drink are not involved, they need to watch for such cycles of thought and habit. As blocked as the emotional expression usually is, Fours can make the best artists, sculptors, chefs, or musicians. They seem to do it from the very core of their heart.

I want to encourage all of the Fours in the world to let go of their parentally caused pain and to view themselves as people of potential, realizing no child is bad enough to warrant cruelty, neglect or abandonment. The Four needs to lay the blame where it belongs. Be angry, then get it out and go on with your life. Be expressive and open with your newly found freedom. You have much to offer, not the least is an ability to put ideas into form.

Fours want to have close, intense relationships but are self-conscious. They may not be able to convey or demonstrate their love. Even to say "I love you" may be very uncomfortable for them. Their emotions are literally hog-tied, and remain that way until the despair overtakes them or they learn how to express feelings through a medium such as music or art.

Many Fours have a rough exterior. They may work in a tough, blue-collar job, such as construction, trucking, farming, factory work or the like. This may be easier for them since no one expects a steel worker to open his heart and express his feelings although no doubt there are exceptions. Fours tend to be introverts.

The superior function is judging. The inferior function is sensing or perceiving.

Healthy Fours are inspired and creative. They are emotionally honest. Funny and serious, emotionally strong, in touch with their inner impulses, and able to vent them creatively and without anger, they view both good and bad experiences as a growth process. They see all people as individuals and let them seek their own path without judgment. Disciplined, practical, orderly, methodical, industrious, conventional, honest, and reliable, they fit in well with social norms.

Average Fours can be into art or music and try to express their feelings through a medium. Sculpting, woodworking, gardening, or just manual labor to relax are included. They can get self-absorbed, moody, depressed, self-pitying, or indulgent. This gives way to decadence, impractical actions, escapism, or irresponsibility. Because this cycle is difficult to break, many Fours gravitate to blue-collar, mill work, construction, truck driving, labor-intensive jobs to keep down emotional or mental pressures.

Unhealthy Fours are emotionally blocked by self-hatred, depression, or hopelessness. In being unable to get in touch with their emotions, they don't love or accept themselves, abusing drugs, drink, eating, sex, or even religion to escape, showing no social values and no responsibility to society or others. They are undisciplined, procrastinating, stubborn, have limited viewpoints, over-indulgent, crude, violent, vulgar, withdrawn, or unable to express their feelings. It is a dichotomy that on one side Fours are so attracted to beauty, art, self-expression, and feeling, and on the other hand, they are introverted worriers whose emotions are blocked and repressed to the point of self-destructive behavior in the name of controlling themselves, their emotions, others, and the environment .

Fours will act out through anger turned against themselves. This leads to hopelessness, despair, and self-destructiveness. They may show withdrawal from others through a tortured silence, drinking, drug abuse, overeating, and overindulgence in the worst cases.

Fours need to let go of hurt feelings turned inward, escapism, self-destructiveness, hopelessness, despair, feeling inadequate, being shame-driven, fatigue brought on by depression, dwelling on past mistakes or what could have been laziness. They need to focus on their ability in logic, order, method, good memory, hard work, putting ideas into form and action, working with their hands, their ability to accept others for who they are, and down-to-earth common sense.

Fours will work things out by getting an aim or path in life and starting to walk it. Without getting a direction and starting to make a difference in their lives, they are lost in their feelings and aimlessness. They must be gentler on themselves, not thinking they have missed life or it is too late to change. Decide what you want to do, then go for it without self-condemnation.

Don't judge yourself by your past; just do your best each day, and before you know it you will have accomplished your goals.

FOURS - ASCENT/DESCENT

Fault line: A feeling of being wronged or held down, self-pity, a dramatic or uncentered way of expressing feelings such as addictions.

Positive Fours are warm, physical, creative, logical, and down-to-earth, with a realistic approach to life.

Negative: Living in a rut. Afraid or confused if anything out of the ordinary happens. Feelings of persecution. Cold, depressed, guilt-driven, stubborn, moody, self-absorbed, and obsessed with what they think they could have been.

Ascent: from Four to One - By taking responsibility for their own actions and consequences, Fours take control over their own lives. They become leaders and reliable, self-disciplined people.

Descent: from Four to Two - From depressed to repressed, the Four devolves from being self-absorbed to emotionally weak, from having feelings of being wronged and held down to martyrdom.

TYPE FIVE – THE TRIBE OF DAN

ECC 7:29 Lo, this only have I found, that God hath made man upright; but they have sought out many inventions.

Gift: Free-thinking, Progressive, Exciting

Motives: To reclaim and hold on to a less stressful and happier time, to see the absurdity of life, and to enjoy life. Personal freedom at all cost, or until they find something worth trading it for. Always keeping their options open. Fear of being confined or trapped by a situation. Fear of being held back from life.

As a Spouse/Lover: Lively, magnetic, able to cope with change, mystical, free, finding life is a sensual adventure, casual, teaching, and communication of ideas, Fives love new experiences. They get bored quickly. They like travel. They are able to think quickly, even if on the move. New ideas excite them as inventors or investigators.

As a Parent: Fives could be quixotic, changeable, sexual, sensual, or overly prudish. They might be critical or sarcastic. The lack of balance here is in self-gratification, appetites, and responsibility. As a parent you could be quick-witted and even impatient.

As a Person: From Dante: "Man is driven to discover, explore, and know by a *divine discontent*." This drive to know was one of the reasons for eating the forbidden fruit in Eden. To decide to take one path does not mean you will not mourn the passing of the millions of paths left untrod.

Quick in thought and deed, the free spirit; impulsive, moody and high-strung if tied down. Fives are curious and like travel and variety. They learn best from experiences of life. They are outgoing, somewhat sporadic. Fives are able to cope and adjust to new situations. They have high personal magnetism, sensual and sexual appeal. They are charismatic. They may confuse sex and love. Five is a physical type, so will work in two different directions. Some will work with their hands in repair, installation, building, or traveling; others will go toward selling, teaching, investing, speaking, preaching, politics, or writing. Fives are in constant need of activity and new experiences.

They like to keep moving and doing. If the Five is in a situation that does not allow him to express his free spirit, or if he is emotionally or physically squelched, he can become snappy, harsh, critical, or judgmental. Fives can be critical or temperamental in love. This usually indicates repressed emotions or needs. They may feel something is missing in their life, but not know what it is. This is cause for frustration and anger, causing them to lash out at times. The Five absorbs the environment and flows with it.

Fives are jacks of all trades. They are quick learners. Fives are good with public relations, writing, and investigating. They convey ideas well. They can practice until they've mastered a skill. These people will be faced with choices between the world and the spiritual realm, that is, lust and habits versus love and spirit. Some Fives will become mystics or spiritual people, usually after they've run the gamut of the world and are dissatisfied. Some will have to fight addiction and lust for many years. The energy of the Five may be intense but short-lived because it burns itself out quickly. These people may renounce the world for the spiritual, or the spiritual for the world. One must remember, if morality is disallowed or spiritual law is disobeyed, it will be paid for in some other form.

TYPE FIVE - THE COMPLETE STORY

Fives are on the outlook for new opportunities. They have developed a sense of things new and possible. They are involved in a series of projects, each having great potential. They are so caught up with the development and "birth" of the project they never think about how to present it to the world. Thus, great impulsive energy gives way to ideas whose fruit can die on the vine because the public will never know about it. They sow but have trouble stopping long enough to reap.

Fives have the ability to cope, change and be fluid. They like to travel, and enjoy the experiences of life. Personal freedom is a top priority. Five is the type possessing a strong sensual and sexual appetite. They are impulsive, critical, sometimes irresponsible, and given to excess. They tend toward immediate gratification. They adjust well. They are fickle, free-spirited, and curious, and they like to investigate. They wring their hands if there is nothing to do. They would rather learn from life than from theory or books.

They are jacks of all trades and will have numerous jobs and experiences. They have a critical and/or temperamental disposition with their mates. Fives feel deeply but may confuse sex and love until spiritual growth or maturity moderates them. This may indicate a number of brief romances and/or affairs. If the Five finds himself confined or in a stifling situation, he will become harsh, critical, judgmental, or moody. They can be quick to judge, but an underlying softness is evident with regrets if their actions are too rash.

The critical and moody attitude may extend into the work place. Because of the ability to adapt, Fives may appear not to stand up for their rights at times, letting others seemingly take advantage of them. This is because they know they will adapt and they ask themselves, "Does it really matter or affect me?" If it doesn't, they do not bother to correct it. If affected and not spiritually sound, the Five tends to repeat mistakes and disregard values or morals. The unbalanced Five is uncertain in change, and has a fear of the unknown. They become nervous, overindulgent, and irresponsible. Five represents a drive to express the self physically and through action. Fives may be teachers, especially in a technical field, speakers, preachers, and politicians.

Five sits at a pivotal point of growth and direction. He may be drawn toward religion and religious teaching. It is the type of renunciation or debauchery. Some Fives will swing to the mystical and religious side, others will seek self-gratification. They have charisma and an ability to make people feel better, happier, and interested, but this may lead to the possibility of promiscuity and difficulty with faithfulness and lessen the chances for a happy marriage because they may flit from one person to another. They may seem emotionally fickle. Part of Five's purpose is to understand and master his emotions.

Type Five wants to be happy and to escape anxiety. They will do this by experiencing and getting "acquainted" with as many things as possible. Because of this they are considered the "generalist." They have a wide range of knowledge and experience. Fives tend to act in the immediate. This usually leads to more doing, since one action or search will lead to another. This type does not think about conscience very much. In extreme cases they could be somewhat sociopathic since they are involved with immediate gratification. Being the extroverted sensation type, their frame of reference is the "real" world of sensory data. Input is directed from the environment to a person, more so than other types. This sets them up for becoming addictive personalities. They will consume more than they need, and need more than they can possibly appreciate, feeling the world exists to fulfill their appetites.

If they are balanced, they will get great joy out of life and its experiences. Their thrust is toward productivity; however, if their focus shifts, it will go from producing to possessing. This is where experience becomes consumption. They will then stay busy trying to keep their sensations high. But there is a type of narcotic effect which demands more, better, faster, longer since the lower level has been reached already. This will bring the Five to overextend himself. Not finding happiness through these experiences, he becomes insecure, unhappy, and anxious. At this point he will become enraged and desperate, claiming he had been in some way deprived of happiness, unfairly so. He will lash out at those who deny him.

In public, Fives tend to be charming and disarming. As children they escaped into a world of imagination. Fives don't broadcast anxiety; they look lighthearted and happy. They love playing and planning. Fives are likely not to worry much. They are perpetual Peter Pans, giving way to a bit of narcissism. They love new adventures. They view the world with infinite possibilities, and become nervous at the idea of losing an option, or narrowing their possibilities. This is why they tend to make commitments with "back doors." They always want an alternate plan. They are masters at going with the flow, as long as the flow doesn't limit their personal freedom. This, to a Five, is the greatest sin.

Fives have the ability to see connections between seemingly unrelated ideas, methods, and disciplines. They have the unique ability of problem solving. Inventive and imaginative, they possess the ability to synthesize unusual veins of knowledge. They must watch for rationalizing the escapism and boredom. Some Fives like escapism and having fun so much that, instead of acquiring things, they will use their money to get away or just have fun. They approach relationships by sharing life's experiences, especially the good ones. This seems to confirm their own experiences, memories, and feelings, and in some way validates them just that much more.

The Five seems to feed off experience, and another's reaction simply expands the feast. It also reflects to the Five the way he already feels. There is a problem, however. With all of this living behind them, they are likely to become jaded and unflappable. At this point the Five can get in trouble. They are apt to become apathetic or depressed, or, in seeking a better high, they can turn to things illicit to break the monotony of the same old excitement.

If a Five is in a restrictive situation, for instance a bad marriage, he will become moody, cranky, angry, even suicidal, as he blames others for holding back his freedom. If you can hold a Five by keeping his interest, marriage to a Five can be interesting. It should consist of a lot of activity, food, fun, travel, and sex.

Fives seem to be given to situational ethics as they go through life, seeking what feels good. This is doubly true when it comes to love, which can easily be confused with sex. They will rationalize their actions by saying, "But I love him or her, so what else counts?" It is difficult for Fives to be tied to needy or emotionally dependent people unless they are along for the ride and don't tie the Five down. The Five, like the One, finds it hard to take blame. Confrontation and accusations bring a loud inner voice of failure. Since they use others' opinions, or desire of them as a meter of their self-worth, this affects the basis of their worth in their own eyes. It is good that they can divert their attention easily; something bad can be covered up by something good fairly quickly, so the pain doesn't last long.

Fives have good memories of childhood, but this is because they tend to focus on the happy side of things. They don't usually cleave to hate or resentment very long. There is a slight tendency to be closer to the mother in childhood. As children the Five was spoiled. This is why some exhibit rebellion against authority that could make them feel tied down by work or commitment. Fives hate boredom. They usually have several projects going on at the same time. They go from one to the other, seeing parallels and similarities between all of them. Casual commitments are made easily, but permanent commitments are hard, even frightening.

Fives want a little taste of everything that is best. They are gluttons for experience. They tend to think of more than one thing at a time by putting an unsolved problem on the back burner while working out a second problem. At some time the foreground problem will, in some way, spark a connection with the background issue, and the answer will bubble up to the conscious mind. This is how one problem or project is, in some way, bound up or connected to another.

They love talking, intellectualizing, and brainstorming. If given a new fact, Fives will try to fit it into many different scenarios. This leads to a viewpoint that sees the interdependence and interrelationships of things. They are editors, writers, communicators, linguists, philosophers, and idea people. Eternally young and sometimes immature, they love doing and experiencing, but fear having their projects judged. Because of their charm and ability to communicate, they can lead others to believe their knowledge has more depth than it truly has. In fact, they have a wide base of knowledge, but usually not a lot of depth.

At their worst they can be charlatans. They are afraid of being revealed as less than what they appear to be. They are happy with situations in which no one is above or below them, and all are on the same level. They are good at promoting ideas, and networking with others.

There are two possibilities for the formation of the Five. The first possibility is the Five had a very pleasant time during early childhood, maybe spoiled or pampered during the early years. They were encouraged to question and explore the new world. They found most new experiences to be pleasant and desirable. Then there was a drastic change in their world – a move or estrangement setting them on a path where the majority of the earlier experiences became just memories. The Five continues to try to recapture those good, carefree times of the past by searching out experiences as an adult that will make him feel like a child again.

The other possibility is Fives were formed, in part, by a negative orientation to the mother image. Due to a number of reasons – from poverty, war, illness, divorce, neglect, smothering, or being aggressively controlling – she frustrated the child. The child found himself not being nurtured and secure. The child then had to find his needs and nurturing by himself. His world and its experiences had to substitute for his mother's love. The id got stuck in instant gratification, with no restraints on himself.

Fives are extroverts. The superior function is physical – sensing; the inferior function is intuitive.

Healthy Fives concern themselves with satisfying their true needs. They add to the world, not consume it. They are productive and have great minds, as well as large areas of knowledge. Healthy Fives assimilate reality and experiences into themselves. They affirm life and are joyous, full of wonder and reverence. The spiritual life becomes a reality to them. They acquire faith and look for the good in situations and people. They are swept into an awareness of the metaphysical. The inner world of the Five is made up of impressions, a catalogue of experiences. They are multifaceted. They usually have refined tastes and a sophisticated air to them. Language and writing skills aren't uncommon. They are very observant and have quick, dry senses of humor.

Adaptable, active, resourceful, versatile, curious, investigative, sensual, sexual, and able to take a chance, average Fives have a vibrant love of life. They want to try it all. To perceive it is to know and enjoy it. They pay attention to the finer things of life, such as food, clothes, music, and sex. They can be elegant people. Most of their activities deal with appetites. There is something of the comedian or performer in the Five, usually driven by insecurity. They are sassy and irreverent. Their brashness may offend some, but others find it refreshing and humorous. They are not subtle people and can be tactless, simply speaking their minds. They tend to push activities and experiences past the bounds of good taste. They may be manic, high on their illusion of life, or full of grandiose plans, which are difficult to carry out.

Unhealthy Fives are jealous of what others have. They are wasteful with excesses in their lives (can never be too rich or too thin). They started out getting high on life, but now life can't offer enough, not even in excess. Not even entertainment or food is safe from this. They become jaded and insatiable. Unhealthy Fives stay in motion. Since all of their "reason" is extroverted, they can't figure out why they are unhappy. They become indiscriminate in their desires and consumptions; depravity is the order. They act out, doing and saying things to hurt others without concern or restraint. Having wasted their energy, they slow down and become very depressed, even suicidal, given to excesses, over-indulgence, impulsiveness, and restlessness. They become fickle, critical, discontented, and noncommittal.

Five will act out by impulsive, consumptive behavior. He will accuse, blame and strike out at others to hide his own frustrations and unhappiness of not being satisfied by anything very long. Fear of losing personal freedom can lead to lying, adultery, and lack of commitment.

The Five needs to let go of recklessness, impulsiveness, addictions, a Peter Pan outlook, not taking responsibility, venting frustration on others, burnout, a need for instant gratification, impatience, escapism, lack of self-discipline or restraint, and overextending self. They need to focus on their quick minds, ability to communicate ideas, charisma, spontaneity that energizes others, ability to motivate, ability to investigate, curiosity, sense of humor, and resilience.

Fives will work out by realizing, once and for all, any happiness that comes through the senses is transitory at best. All ups will have an equal down, so it is best to seek the center path. Commitment to someone you love will keep you from losing him and having to look for a "second best" for the rest of your life. To be willingly committed is not to be bound; it is only to love. You don't need a back door if you really mean the commitment.

FIVES - ASCENT/DESCENT

Fault line: A pervading feeling of emptiness is the force which drives the Five to try to find an experience, or something in the physical world to fill the void. Greed and gluttony is the fault line.

Positive: Fives are fun-loving, spontaneous, imaginative, productive, quick, confident, curious, and charming.

Negative: Fives are narcissistic, impulsive, undisciplined, restless, rebellious, unfocused, critical, and curt. They are masters at rationalizations.

Ascent: from Five to Seven. By realizing the void within can't be filled from the outside, the Five becomes stable. He turns experience into wisdom and impulsiveness into objectivity.

Descent: from Five to One: As more and more experiences are taken in, the Five begins to fear nothing can fill the emptiness, so there begins an anger. This is acted out in the form of a critical, anxious, inflexible attitude.

TYPE SIX – THE TRIBE OF NAPHTALI

Gift: Responsible, Devoted, Protective

Motives: Dedication to home, family, and friends; loyalty, serving society, doing what is ethically right. The Six is driven by fear of not measuring up to society's standards. They fear of moral, or ethical failure.

As a Spouse/Lover: Family and justice are important. They are good teachers, guides, counselors, doctors, nurses, social workers, authority figures, police, and ministers. Sympathetic, jolly, and devoted, this is the parental type. A solid individual, this type is an emotional yet reliable person, dominating with a need to have at least the look of a stable family.

As a Parent: As a parent, this type could be very concerned with "doing the right and honorable thing," always wondering what people will think, a nurturing and strong influence that tends toward meddling, gossiping, or nosiness. The lack of balance here is in the area of being judgmental and begrudging service to others. There could be a need to place blame and punish those who are perceived as guilty.

As a Person: A helper, homebody, and minister to the needy, the Six likes quiet pleasures. They are idealistic about relationships. They are always ready to help a friend. There is a love for music and art. They also have a concern for fairness and justice. If this goes too far, it will yield a judgmental, self-righteous, tyrannical person. Six needs to be coaxed in love to full sexual expression. They have a quick and/or emotional temper. The Six has a peaceful nature unless home or principles are at stake. If they are insecure, this type can be very jealous and possessive.

This is the type of ministry, law, teaching, medicine, nursing, counseling, and protecting others. If they are healthy, these people are the healers of society's afflictions. They are the parent image, loving the home life. Sixes are down-to-earth and make good community leaders. If adversely affected, they can become short-tempered and meddlesome. They may try to dictate or be overly conventional. Although this type is called upon to be a shoulder to cry on, they may resent aiding and listening to others, if they are overtaxed. Most, if given a chance, can make good homebodies, parents, or spouses.

TYPE SIX - THE COMPLETE STORY

To ask is to know, and to know is to accept responsibility. Romance and family are top priorities. The Six has a parental attitude toward others. They are concerned with values and rules of conduct. The Six identifies emotionally with things, so he is opinionated. Sixes are reliable, drawn to healing and teaching, listening well but could be meddlesome. They are crusaders and can be obstinate. They may offer advice when it isn't wanted. They like taking responsibility for others in the role of a father or mother image. They want to be leaned on. They are idealists, especially in home and love affairs. Like the type Three, the Six is very concerned with their image. The community and church image is to be protected at all times.

Sixes are good at doing and fixing up around the home. They like to "nest." They are usually conformists, good money-makers, and homebodies. They have emotional tempers, mostly when the welfare or tranquility of the household, family, or mate is in question.

Most Sixes don't get depressed often. They tend to maintain at least an outward appearance of mental stability. Because of their reliability, they usually manage money and people well. Friends and family may lean on them. They tend to be happiest at home with the family. If they are affected or unbalanced, there will be over-involvement with others' problems and a self-righteous attitude. They can also be dictators or resent service to others. They will feel held down at home. The balanced Six is concerned with doing what he perceives to be morally right. Their purpose is to learn to love people as a whole, to find a place in the service and giving of mankind.

Type Six respects loyalty. They will watch and test others and their attitudes before trusting them. They have to watch their feelings of anxiety and insecurity. This is a type full of contradictions. They want trust, but they test others first before trusting. They honor authority, yet fear it. They do not like aggression, yet they are at times aggressive. They search for security, yet feel insecure. They fear being rejected, yet will reject others who do not measure up to their moral and social value structure. Anxiety causes this vacillation. They feel more secure with "big brother" to watch out for them, be it the corporation, political party, or church. They need to trust and believe in something.

Sixes want approval from others, so they resist being in positions of inferiority. They fluctuate from obedience to rebellion; likable to cranky. They are actually in conflict with both internal authority (superego) and outward authority. They tend to look outside of themselves for direction, yet don't like being in a subservient position. They can be openly hostile to an authority figure if the distrust or anger at the father image has built up. They will appear rebellious and defiant at the authority figure, as there is transference of feelings acquired in childhood. We should again point out there are two sides to the Six.

We see conformity and rebellion, honor and anger occurring in the same person. Sometimes they happen at the same time causing fear and loyalty, love and hate to come into a dynamic balance, and it is all based around the father image. Almost always the child tried to love the father even though he may have been demanding or unfair. This did not leave a way to deal sufficiently with the negative feelings. As the child tried harder to reach a level of approval in the parent's eyes, anger built because of the harsh, disciplinarian, or unapproachable posture from which the father image operated. It may have been a morally high or correct issue, but the way it was enforced did not convey love. This sent a double message to the child.

It is very important to do the right and just thing, to be loyal and good. But the intense striving formed an image of fear and suspicion in regard to authority figures. This creates a push-pull relationship. This tension forms the basis of their anxiety. When it builds, they want the security they missed, but since they have come to trust in only themselves on the deeper level, they did not trust the authority on an inner level and either can become aggressive and belligerent, or try to serve and placate to assure the authority's continued goodwill and protection.

Sixes are an introverted, feeling or perceiving type. They, like the Eight type, want to be the protector. Sixes are more parental in this quest than the bossy Eight, though. Also, like the Eight, they are looking for someone to be their protector. The Six is looking for a guardian, a father image to trust and rely on. Isn't it fitting and reasonable that the things we seek to become are the very things we seek in others?

So many times we could learn from ourselves if we would recognize the simply stated truth of a song by the Beatles which holds the key: "...and, in the end, the love you take is equal to the love you make." We should carry it further and say what we need, are missing, and hope to find, is what we try to become for ourselves and for others. It is just another way of trying to fulfill our own needs. When all is said and done, all we can rely on is God. We may think we can rely on ourselves, but, in time we will fail us, too.

Sixes tend to swing emotionally and are hard to anticipate. They may get close to someone, then become concerned about being taken advantage of by them. This brings anxiety and the need for reassurance; so back to the person they may go for assurance. The Six child identified positively with the father image. They gained identity and security by being approved by him. Anxiety arises if approval isn't forthcoming. They learned that by following rules and being responsible and obedient, they gained positive strokes from the father image, and this strengthened their feelings of worth and security. If they did not please this authority, Sixes learned retribution would come. This means they have a very strong super-ego (inner parental voice). In time, this father image is transferred to other authorities such as law, business, government, husband.

Sixes fear being left, so they place great value on long-term relationships. Family, church, and community are the symbols of the emotional stability and commitment the Six stands for. If they veer into disobedience, they will worry about what others think. There is a fear others will turn on them.

Sixes can be either introverts or extroverts but tend to be introverted. The superior function is emotional-feeling or perceiving; the inferior function is intuitive. The need to be the authority, so there is less authority over them, coupled with a need to serve and be protected by an authority image leads some Sixes into becoming police officers, nurses, doctors, preachers, priests, or managers.

There are two distinct directions a Six might choose, based on which most affected them – the morality and loyalty issues, or the harshness and authoritarianism. They can seek to serve and protect the moral standards, or they can rebel against authority and become lawless, tyrants, or bullies, serving another kind of group or family such as gangs or mobs. It isn't surprising Sixes are likely to be involved in long-term relationships. Their loyalty and tenacity can allow them to survive a long time even in a dysfunctional relationship.

Healthy Sixes are reliable, trustworthy, loyal, trusting, and independent, yet cooperative. They take commitment seriously. They elicit strong emotional responses from others. They will fight for others as they would for themselves. Good-natured, good-humored, friendly. The image they try to emulate is their father image within. Capable of 50-50 relationships, they are good leaders since they know what others are looking for in authority. They can reassure others and be emotionally open, loving, and caring.

Some Sixes lost faith in authority as a child. Something resulting from the parents' actions spawned fear, feelings of being powerless or overpowered. The parent, usually the father, may have had an explosive temper or have been very controlling. This is carried over by the child into adulthood in the form of a hesitancy to act and a suspicion of authority. Sixes tend to doubt their own ability. The anti-authoritarian stance forms a split path. On one hand, it makes them gravitate to the underdog. They will go to extremes to beat the odds. This can even drive them into feelings of heroism, or even martyrdom, in the search to beat the system, pull together, and set things right that the authorities have fouled up. This is the rebellious stance. It is fueled by feelings of oppression and anger of past misuse by authorities. This can be summed up by a "you and me against the world" attitude.

The other path is one of being devoted to an authority figure or group, as long as the Six feels the group or authority is going in the correct direction. They become loyal servants, able to follow a chain of command well. They are dutiful public servants and parental types. This is a strange type of self-protection. They like serving and thereby affecting others. That is because they think if they are on your side, they won't be harmed. Sixes are afraid of being ganged up on or harmed by an unexpected attack by those outside the control of the Six. So they serve the more powerful group or person in exchange for their protection. This type of Six tries to do what is right in society's eyes.

Sixes do not give in order to get something back. They give in order to feel safe or for others to owe them allegiance. They fear betrayal. These are also persons who fear intimacy. They can easily project their fears and suspicions onto the partner, accusing him of not wanting to be close or doubting of their true feelings and intentions. Sixes need to know the partner has respect and faith in them. They need to know the partner feels safe with them. Sixes will bask in the reflection of the feelings of the partner spawned by them. These are feelings of "nesting" in a safe place. This is what the Six wants to feel first-hand.

This should be a lesson to all of us, that we all tend to live assuming others feel, need, and want the same things we do. This narrow view can lead to misunderstandings and wasted time. We must all learn to see things from others' points of view. Real communication is to speak to people on their own level and from their own point of view. Sixes should be careful not to project their feelings or fears on to others to make them see ulterior motives that are harmful to the Six. This even goes for their mates. Because of the background of the cause of this type, it is difficult for Sixes to trust and be intimate without fear. Yet they need and want closeness, and have the capacity to feel deeply.

Healthy Sixes are devoted and protective without being meddlesome. They are interested in being patient and fair. "Truth, justice, and the American way," is the battle cry for the healthy Six. They are domestic, reliable, tenacious, and conservative. They are good listeners and, therefore, good teachers, counselors, and ministers. Education is important to them.

Average Sixes identify with authority figures and follow their lead. They are traditionalists, family and company people, both dutiful and responsible. Sixes on this level begin to show contradictions in personality. They are ambivalent and passive/aggressive. They want authority over them in order to feel more secure, yet they fight against authority and rebel at times. They may become defensive, authoritarian, partisan, blaming others if things go wrong. This is an over-compensation for their fear and insecurity. This fear may be seen in the Six's becoming dependent, even comfortable being ordered around. This vacillation between dependence and independent leadership urges makes them very unstable. When they make decisions, they are likely to look for precedents such as rules, regulations, scriptures, by the book. This adds to their security.

Unhealthy Sixes are insecure and dependent. Anxiety and feelings of inferiority are high. They can become sadistic as they over-react due to insecurities. Archie Bunker types, fraught with prejudices, bigotry, and blustering, they try to recreate the security they had in the past but to no avail. They overcompensate for their fear and insecurity and become tyrants. They deal harshly with the mistakes of others while letting themselves off the hook. Everything becomes a crisis because of insecurity. Things are blown out of proportion. It ends in a masochism in which the Six seeks union with others in a twisted way by saying, "I've been bad. I didn't follow all of the rules. Punish me so you can love me again." If there isn't punishment from another source, they will punish themselves in order to substitute their punishment for a punishment they fear would be more severe from the authority. If this isn't enough, they will provoke the authority by turning to violence, becoming meddlesome, irresponsible, unyielding, self-righteous, and tyrannical.

Sixes will act out through a rebellion and hardness that hides a fear of authority. They will have a quick, judgmental temper. A tyrant-like need to bully or control hides a fear of being abandoned, misused, or persecuted.

The Six must let go of fear of abandonment, feeling trapped by obligations, anxieties and worry about themselves and others, judging others, a tough facade to hide feelings, being negative about situations or people, the need to boss or mother others, and stubbornness. They need to focus on their abilities to guide and care about others, to serve the family or community, showing their true concern for others, a nurturing heart, a parental sense of fairness.

The Six will work out by realizing no one can take control or exert authority over them. That is something that has to be given. They are safe to be their own authority. They must be encouraged to be secure with themselves and find security in others.

SIXES - ASCENT/DESCENT

Fault line: The fear of not being approved of, along with the fear of authority figures, can get strong enough to taint the entire outlook. This is paranoia.

Positive: Sixes are loyal, caring, practical, parental, responsible care-givers.

Negative: Sixes are judgmental, rigid, defensive, unpredictable, and paranoid. They distrust authority but need approval. This sets up a love/hate relationship.

Ascent: from Six to Nine: Freeing themselves from the need of approval and the fears associated with this, Sixes become less limited and more universal in their outlook. The result is more open-mindedness, generosity, and inner peace.

Descent: from Six to Three: As the fear of being approved of by their authority figures increases, the paranoia starts to show itself. The Six becomes more jealous and competitive, not wanting others to have more friends or approval than they. Judgmental attitudes become vindictive as they slip into a shallow, vain posture.

TYPE SEVEN – THE TRIBE OF GAD

Gift: Analytical, Spiritual, Rational

Motives: To observe and gather information, to know how and why, to manipulate reality or knowledge to one's own benefit. Fear of failing due to lack of knowledge. Fear of opening up to others.

As a Spouse/Lover: Reserved, cerebral, and elegant, a refined thinker and philosopher. The use of the mind, knowledge, and quiet environment is important. These people value truth and straightforward, objective ways. At the same time, they can be elusive or two-faced. The lack of balance here is in the area of emotional aloofness or expression, suspicion, lack of trust, and stress relating to education or resistance to it. They are intelligent, observant, and deductive thinkers at best or cynical, sneaky, and devious at worst.

As a Parent: As a parent, Seven tends to be aloof. The ideas regarding sexuality could have been out of balance in either direction. Learning and school were areas of concern. This parent could encourage the child to hide or not discuss feelings.

As a Person: The mind is calculating and probing. This "calculating" can be applied in deviousness, or insightfulness. Seekers of truth, or dealers of deceit, Sevens can twist the truth to fit their needs or examine the facts and seek the truth. The pivotal point of the Seven is knowledge; therefore, there is usually an interest in science, medicine, nursing, lab work, psychology, technology, math, or other similar fields. If using truth with malice, the Seven will speak the truth at the chosen time which can destroy another person and leave the Seven without blame because, "after all, it was the truth." They will gossip and call it "getting the facts". Information used wrongly is manipulation.

"Did you find everything?" the clerk asked with a smile in her voice. "How is one to know if something was missed?" was the contemplative reply. Appalling power, terrible control, this emotional detachment. Uninvolved emotionally, watching the scene play out, and feeling nothing. They know the relationship is controlled by the one who cares the least.

TYPE SEVEN - THE COMPLETE STORY

Sevens are trapped in their own minds. Since thinking about feelings is easier than and less threatening than actually exhibiting the feeling through action, the Seven simply stops at the "thinking" phase. Sevens are constantly on guard against the world and people around them for fear of being taken by surprise and overwhelmed.

This type is the balance of what is precious and terrible about truth, analysis, aloofness, and secretiveness. Sevens respect knowledge for its own sake. They may study, research, observe, or analyze in their daily way of life. A quiet storm is formed from the vortex created by introversion and introspection, along with a loneliness that is brought about by their own subjectivity. They need love and closeness, yet their introverted nature does not allow them to adequately express themselves. They must stretch in order to communicate their deep feelings to others. Seven needs solitude and a quiet home. Sevens are observant and have quick minds. They seek to perfect their beliefs and understanding. They tend to withdraw when in crowds and they hate noise and confusion.

The Seven may harbor hidden sexual or emotional needs. Sevens often hide their feelings, finding it hard to express themselves. They will probe to find out what their mate feels, yet they cloister their own thoughts, feelings, and actions. Through the aloof nature of the Seven, there is a loneliness within and a need to be with people. Sevens vacillate between needing time to themselves and needing to hide from their loneliness in the midst of people.

They can become stubborn if pushed. Some Sevens mature slowly. They should not marry until they are older. This allows for maximum stability. Their quiet sensitivity can get them hurt by infatuations. Seven tells things on a need-to-know basis. Their thoughts are abstract, but the Seven can use them, as well as their silence as weapons against those with whom they are unhappy. They withdraw their attention and emotions and become a cold wall, saying nothing is wrong, but hurting others in a sneaky, passive/aggressive way with silent aloofness and coldness. Faith in themselves is the challenge. There is an undertone of feeling less than adequate, emotionally or physically, that haunts them. This adds to the fact that it is hard for them to express themselves. They would rather have an intellectual world than an emotional one. They don't trust their feelings. The depth and aloofness of a Seven makes them an enigma to others.

This mysterious air is a lure to many and they will be attracted to the "sexiness" of it. Because of their detached nature, Seven is life's strategist. They sit, emotionally removed from the battles of life, and plan the next step. Due to this view of life, they can use people and situations to their own ends. This is a rather devious trait the Seven must guard against. He should remember not to use people or the secrets friends have told in any selfish way. If you hurt, you will be hurt. Things always come back around. Be honest and up front. Sevens may find it hard to open up; some may seem melancholy.

At times, they feel the questions of others are distracting and irritating or a nuisance. This results in short, clipped answers. The Seven child may be hard to control because of a silent stubbornness. Some will take their punishment and not cry in order to do what they want. Sevens are skeptical and find it hard to accept anything unless proven. They tend to live within themselves. Indecision is possible at times because of the analytical need for more data. Watch for a devious or violent tendency if outlets of self-expression and emotions are blocked. A type of intellectual snobbery is seen in an off-balanced Seven.

Their purpose involves searching and understanding to gain maximum expression through learning and teaching and balancing a reserved nature and a lonely nature. Seven can be outwardly open but inwardly closed. On the outside they may appear as outgoing, funny, and able to communicate, yet they still won't show their true feelings.

Maybe the Christian faith does better among its enemies
than having to endure the indifference of its friends.
Garrison Keillor

Sevens are observers and can be very private people. Their world is a mental world. Even if they are not "mental giants," they tend to think and not to speak. Financial interaction is uncomfortable, obligations feel coercive, and relationships threaten their stance of emotional aloofness. Emotions are to be controlled. Intense one-on-one competition is to be avoided. They remain aloof in a self-protective posture. They are independent people who can be comfortable being alone for days at a time. Being observers, they have a rather objective view of things.

They may seem emotionally cold or distant as they watch and observe people or watch situations develop with an air of cool superiority, thinking they would never get involved in such foolishness. But the skeptical or cynical attitude that may develop is just a way of remaining emotionally removed – for that matter, so is the intellectual snobbishness that some Sevens exhibit. The truth is, they are uninvolved, not because they are wiser, but because their fear of opening up and trusting is so low it keeps them at a safe distance.

There is a saying in the sport of Judo: "To throw an opponent, you must put yourself in a position to be thrown." It is the same with affairs of the heart. You can only be in a position to be loved if you are in a position to be hurt. Sevens have trouble taking that gamble. This same thought process and fear of being taken advantage of can extend into any situation in which there are heavy demands or expectations. Fears can be reduced somewhat if the limits, rules, and expectations of a situation or relationship are laid out at the start.

To prevent a chain of perceived intrusions and betrayals from growing into fear or paranoia, the Seven views life as a string of snapshots, all related yet isolated. What happens tomorrow may not be what happened today under similar environs. This type of outlook, where nothing is taken for granted, lends itself to the skeptical posture of the Seven. The Seven wants to know. He wants to understand everything. He wishes to be able to interpret everything. This is a way of defending himself from his environment.

Genius is to fuse knowledge, insight, and reality. Madness is when these oppose one another and a split occurs. The Seven can go to either extreme. Sevens can see patterns, gain insights and relate things in one context to another context. Genius sees and recognizes patterns in things; madness imposes patterns on things, which leads to distorted reality. In this they are like the Five, but unlike the Five, Sevens may emphasize thinking over doing. Saying or doing reveals their position, and there may be a weakness there. It may be used against them. This is something the Seven doesn't like to risk. Many times this is because their words have been used against them by trusted friends or family. This balance has to be watched so their mental world doesn't become all consuming.

In the pursuit of pure ideas, Sevens do not want others to influence their thinking because this seems to diminish their self-worth. However, they tend not to totally trust their own ideas. If the Seven thinks he is the only one with the answers, he can drift into error by relying only on unchecked ideas, and can go further and further away from reality. They can project their anxieties and impulses onto their reality, making them paranoid, timid, aloof, or off-balance.

They are the Jungian introverted thinking or intuitive type. This makes for too much subjectivity. The thoughts start with the subject and flow back to the subject, meaning facts are collected in order to form a theory and not for the facts themselves. A better explanation of the Seven is a subjective thinking type. Sevens were ambivalent toward their parents, who may have nurtured them erratically.

They may have received conflicting signals in childhood, such as parents who drank, partied, were in and out of church, or off and on as far as dependability. The stress of an unhappy family would lead to this feeling of ambivalence toward the parents and the world. The result is the Seven lives in a constant state of alertness. They fear being controlled by others. They watch their environment and all in it in order to foresee trouble and protect themselves. Love/hate of parent and the world makes them detached; they retreat to their thoughts. There is a duality then between objective and subjective reality that can lead to schizophrenia.

If the Seven is uptight, he will have danger on his mind, but because he is looking for it, he feels safer. Sevens believe if something can be seen (perceived), it can be understood and mastered. They enjoy using knowledge, being naturally ingenious, inventive, and technical. Since there is always more to know, the Seven has trouble putting thoughts to action.

They never feel comfortable with their level of knowledge since they realize there is always more to know and learn. They fear the world yet are fascinated by it. The Seven, like the Two, has a passive/aggressive streak. They will use silence and the withholding of their attention to control others. This is a good way of getting a point across and yet not disturbing their precious peace and quiet; they don't even have to display their suppressed emotions to do it.

As children they felt intruded upon. This could have been because they were very sensitive to noise and activity in their home or because they could not get privacy because of a large, intrusive family or small living space. They learned to "tune out," or hide out in order to find peace. The other family pattern is one in which there was abandonment, so the child detached from his emotions and kept occupied mentally in his own world in order to survive. Their idea of controlling a situation is to be aloof or emotionally removed from it. Interactions drain them. They take offense at having their time or energy put at others' disposal. Sevens are often scholars in obscure fields. The expert in a field, having spent years compiling data, the Seven's reclusiveness turns to feelings of isolation and loneliness if depression or enforced separation goes on too long.

Sevens have a feeling of superiority over those who like competition (as in sports), believing it to be a waste of time. Since they are introverts they need quiet time at the end of the day to sort out their feelings and wind down. They may calm down by thinking, reading, or working on projects. Since they are mind-centered, they connect with others through special interests or knowledge. They tend to interface with the world the same way. They are attracted to systems such as psychology, math, occult science, or natural science in order to explain and understand the world. At times they will realize how destructive the misuse of psychology or other knowledge can be, especially to the insecure, but it is worth it to them to be able to secretly hurt someone without becoming actively emotionally involved.

Sevens tend to be introverts. The superior function is mental – thinking or intuitive. The inferior functions are feeling – physical (doing).

Healthy Sevens are visionaries, profound and comprehending thinkers. They love discovery. They are able to concentrate and become involved with a project. Innovative, genius, secure enough not to detach from their environment or cling to their own ideas. They have open minds with intuitive foresight. They are closer to being contemplative than thinkers. They can convey ideas and information in simple, clear form. Wise, knowledgeable, and dignified, they have a sense of the self and the universe in an interactive role through interest and research in philosophy, psychology, science, and mysticism. Able to observe, analyze, draw conclusions and applications, specialized fields, scientific and research writings are their strengths. Seven needs time to be alone and to sort out the acquired data and associated thoughts of the day.

The average Seven is intellectual, analytical, and specialized, making a science of things, research, philosophy, and scholarship. He can be detached or eccentric. He enjoys speculating on ideas and theories. Sevens tend to interpret everything around a set of pet theories which may lead to error. They tend to apply their theories to everything. They may break things down to study so much the big picture is lost. They are bookish. Intellect is their forté. There may have been a lonely period in their childhood which urged them to turn inward. They tend to be high-strung, their thoughts flowing in a stream from one thing to another in a chain of seemingly (to the observer) unrelated thoughts. This takes their conversation over a scattered, branching, detailed path at times. Their thoughts may be hard to follow.

The unhealthy Seven can be reclusive and isolated from reality, cynical, aggressive, obsessed by strange ideas, and affected by phobias, paranoia, schizophrenia, or genius gone to insanity. Nothing is certain because every angle is examined, and all things are possible. They may think that one grand idea holds the key to all answers. Or they may reduce things to such a point the "awe" is gone, and the truth is lost. They love to take ideas to the limits, sometimes for the shock value.

They can become antagonistic with anyone who disagrees with them since this actually threatens their reality. They are rejected because of their ideas and self-righteous attitudes, and so feel contempt for people. They may display skepticism, fear, dishonesty, melancholia, pessimism, false pride, sarcasm, mental disorders, or uncontrolled anger.

A Seven will act out by retreating into a shell, a nervous recluse hiding from the world. They escape into imaginations and fantasy worlds which have their foundations in the mind. Feelings of betrayal can drive them further inward. A person who is hypersensitive to activity, noise, or environmental disruptions produces a snappy, grumpy, like a silent hermit. The basis is a fear of not being able to take it all in and protect themselves from a hostile environment.

Sevens need to let go of isolating themselves, rejecting others, snobbishness, thinking others cannot be depended on, cynicism, feeling powerless, being violated or taken advantage of, suspicion, aloofness, deviousness, and lying. The Seven must focus on his ability to find the truth, and using his fine mind to reason. He should lean of his ability to reason. He has a sense of class or elegance, ability to research, form strategies, and glean spiritual insights. Science, medicine, math, and teaching others are all in the Sevens abilities and reach.

Sevens will work out by balancing physical and mental activity, developing a sense of humor, and accepting the fact they can't know everything or see everything coming so they might as well relax and laugh at it.

Sevens will act out by withdrawing into their minds and living in fear of emotions and human interactions.

SEVENS - ASCENT/DESCENT

Fault line: An attempt to fill the emptiness within is done with knowledge. As long as they are involved with the mind, it takes their attention off what they are feeling (and what they are not feeling). They believe completely in the old adage that knowledge is power, especially when it is a secret to control another. Skepticism and paranoia develop when there is too much confusion.

Positive: Sevens are objective, wise, self-contained observers.

Negative: Sevens are snobbish, arrogant, stingy, critical, aloof, and emotionally removed.

Ascent: from Seven to Eight: As the Seven gets more evolved in the world, he starts to put to use all of his knowledge. He stops living in theory and starts applying himself. The result is a person to be looked up to and reckoned with – capable, confident, direct, and in charge.

Descent: from Seven to Five: As the Seven is wearied of more and more information and its lack of application to improve the human heart, he becomes restless. Nothing seems to satisfy. They descend into a critical curtness. They become unfocused, sensing the primary reason for gaining their knowledge is abandoned.

TYPE EIGHT – THE TRIBE OF ASHER

Gift: Authoritative, Enterprising, Efficient

Motives: To take control, to be boss, to gather money, power, status, or control, to fight for what can be obtained. Fear of being out of control. Fear of poverty.

As a Spouse/Lover: Success is important to the showman, boss, or organizer. Loyalty is looked for, and ability is admired. This type is power driven and needs to be in a position of authority. He is an executive who thrives on pressure, possessing staying power, perseverance, drive, tenacity, status, money, intelligence, efficiency, and control. The household is run like a small business.

As a Parent: This parent must be in control of others, and leans toward materialism or emotional abuse. This parent fears being controlled or influenced and sees emotional displays as weaknesses so they tend to be cold and harsh. Some parents wouldn't change their minds or admit their mistakes if it killed them. As the child matures, the parent struggles to retain control.

As a Person: The organizer and disciplinarian, Eights likes a challenge to show he is capable and efficient. He strives toward high ideals and has ambitious drives. People are drawn to this. They want 100% efficiency. Eights are businesslike, aggressive, and confident. They often take responsibility for the work of others through the position of a boss, owner, C.E.O., or supervisor. Eights usually don't pamper or cater to weak mates. They must strive for a 50-50 relationship since they have a natural drive to be in control. Many Eights will set a stage and demand others accept them in the part they will play or get out. They can be ruthless. They may like psychology, law enforcement, human resource management, business, money management, bookkeeping, quality assurance, inspection, or banking. They can be lawyers, judges, or executives, since these people have power over others. They usually have sound judgment in affairs dealing with business. They may be drawn toward status symbols or expensive tastes.

If the Eight is not healthy, everything is for them and there is no giving. The off-balance Eight is like her "mental sister," the type One. They are egocentric to the point of having a subjective viewpoint in life that doesn't allow them to see what effect their decisions have on those around them. This can lead to them hurting or angering those closest to them and not accepting any responsibility for it. What is worse, they are very proud and usually would not apologize even if they do come to realize they were wrong. Obviously, to overcome this problem, the Eight must be objective enough to put himself into the other person's position and concede that he can be wrong about many things.

The balanced Eight can make an excellent supervisor, entrepreneur, or business owner and has good potential in business as a real estate broker or stock market investor. Eight also relates to sports, athletics, or martial arts. This is because he strives to compete and be the best. Winning and achieving are important to Eights. They may think they know all the answers. They may consider a mate on the basis of income if they are too materialistic. Eights are devoted people and are capable of much love and caring, yet they are also a people of appetite. Since they value efficiency, strength of will, and control, they tend to suppress their emotions and put on a hard exterior. They may be more interested in the quality of life rather than the love in it. Although they seldom show it, there is an underlying softness and need for love.

TYPE EIGHT - THE COMPLETE STORY

Eights have a high sensitivity to "justice" in regard to the actions of others. They are preoccupied with the potential others have to exert power and control. They have a willingness to issue orders and administrate. They can be ruthless.

Eights focus on money, finance, and controlling others. Although Eight is the balance of physical (or material) and spiritual, Eights are usually inclined toward the material. They are confident, businesslike, authoritarian, and are drawn to efficiency and quality control. They can be in law enforcement and other positions of authority. They can be drawn to the legal system as a point of control. They look at people asking, "What can this person produce or do for me?" The executive type, given to management, bookkeeping, and ownership position, he takes responsibility for the actions of others as the manager or boss. He can be intimidating and may come across as a know-it-all. Eight can be aggressive or outspoken. Because they tend to dominate, they need to strive for a 50/50 relationship; otherwise they may take over the household.

The Eight doesn't like to pamper or cater to a weak mate. They can be materialistic, but very giving to loved ones. Eights are usually strong-willed. They like the finer things of life. Quality is very important. Things must be systematic and logical. Eights like big houses and nice cars. Finding the best system and putting it to use with money and/or people is a forté. Eights are ambitious.

Eight women need to marry strong-willed mates since they will be inclined to try to dominate their partners, yet they will not respect them if they can dominate them. Men will need to marry a strong, stable woman so she would not be outmatched and dominated to an oppressive degree. If affected, disrespect for authority, dishonesty, callousness, and materialism will set in.

They are status symbol and wealth-driven. Many times, Eights relate to sports and/or simply being the best and most efficient in what they do. The material outlook leads many Eights to put a price on security. They need money in the bank and the bills caught up to be secure. They may even take the income of someone into account before allowing themselves to care for him or her. They may be overly concerned about the quality of life instead of the love therein. The Eight female tends to break the mold of most women. She is more "male" in her thoughts and ways than most. She is strong enough to "get ahead in a man's world."

Some Eights may have drinking or motivation problems because of the intensity of the personality being like an overload at times. Eights like to have power over people. The more rigid Eights view children as an inconvenience and would rather not bother. These people have a lot of money pass through their hands, but the philanthropic Eights will give much to others.

Eights vacillate between philanthropy and greed. The Eight who is out of balance will be self-absorbed to the point of ignoring or not considering the feelings or views of others. They will be blind to what their expectations, demands, or decisions are of anyone else. If it is brought to their attention, they will usually have too much ego and false pride at stake to admit mistakes or faults, even if it means the loss of a friend. To guard against this, the Eight needs to practice looking at things from the perspective of others and always remember, like all of us, they are working from a subjective point of view, so they can be wrong as easily as anyone else.

Eight types want to be self-reliant, to act in their own self-interest, to have impact on people and their environment. Love of power is the love of self. They attempt to conform the environment and those in it, to their aims. They relate to the environment in order to prevail over it. They take charge, imposing their will. Getting their way is very important to them. The Eight's sense of self is stronger than his sense of others. He is steely and single-minded, the extroverted, mental or thinking type.

Eights have a keen sense of things in the making. They are always seeking new possibilities. Stable conditions suffocate them. They cannot be frightened away from a new possibility, even if it goes against previous convictions. They are the champion of the underdog, confident that by their will they can reach their goals. Although this presentation may sound harsh, if motivated correctly it will yield experts, athletes, and gold-medal contenders. However, if they go astray, they usually get caught up by their own egotism. They can't see or believe there is anything wrong with them, even though they may not take the needs or wants of others into consideration.

One possibility of the formation of the Eight type is as follows: The Eight may have learned one parent in his life did not respond to him unless he asserted himself. This assertiveness may have had to increase to aggression from time to time until the child got the parent's attention and also got his way. He learned a strong-willed child could dominate even an adult.

Soon this same process was used in other areas of life by being aggressive and strong even if one was wrong, in order not to face the fact or punishment for being wrong. They then began to walk on other's feelings. If the ego is unchecked, they will view life only through power and its use, so they will take advantage of any weakness they see. The preferred position is to charge in, take control, and maintain a situation. Eights believe the truth comes out in a fight. A clean fight is exhilarating to them. They feel anger, fighting, intimacy, and truth are all related.

The Eight's tough exterior covers a heart of a child who had to fight for his space. He would like to stop fighting, but doesn't trust others to take control and be just or fair. This is because his parents were not consistent or fair. Blame and punishing the wrong-doers are preoccupations with Eights. They have an all-or-nothing way of approaching things. Security to an Eight means knowing all of a situation and having power over things. The Eight is intent on power or control. Power can be in the form of money, possessions, people, or simply control and authority to act.

A possible formation of the Eight is a result of dealing with hard knocks and simple survival. A parent who was a disciplinarian, harsh, or emotionally distant, meant the Eight had difficulty in expressing the vulnerable side of themselves. This is a childhood reaction to being pushed around, treated unjustly, or ignored by a parent, sibling, or friends.

A bad school, a tough part of town, or a poor childhood could exacerbate a survival instinct. The feeling is the person in control did not act with the child's best interests in mind. There could have been a divorce or other situation involving a parent's harshness or anger the child took personally. It damaged the child's faith in authority and security figures. They learned the world was not safe. The Eight child had to be old enough to stand on his own or think for himself in order to become self-reliant. This means at least part of the mistreatment would have occurred between the ages of six and sixteen.

Another possibility for the formation of the Eight type which can, at times, exist side by side with the other patterns is as follows: This type can be caused by one parent turning the child against the other parent by having no faith or anything good to say about them. This suspiciousness can also be caused by a parent or adult abusing, neglecting, or molesting the child. This disregard for the child's welfare makes the child suspicious of them. Then Eights feel they should be in control because they have been taught not to trust the authority figure. They think they can do it better than others, and they will protect instead of exploiting others. Yet, due to their strong personality and will, at times they can do just that by running roughshod over those of less strength.

No matter how Eights are formed, they can become so focused on a goal they can deny pain, fatigue, opposition, even the odds against them. It does not let them determine reasonable measures of success or accomplishments. They can't see what is enough so they keep pushing forward. At times it can go so far as to create a type of tunnel vision. The Eight will not see the full picture. They can repress feelings and even incoming data until the truth overtakes them. When they are knocked down by truth, they realize the signs were there all of the time. They may even find that others' ideas, opinions, or views simply annoy them, not because, like the Seven, they know all the answers, but because they are in control and calling the shots.

The Eight is the type of the judge since they demand justice. They always want the wrongdoers to be punished and vengeance to be done. But, it is their justice they try to impose on others so they appear to be judgmental. They can be irritable and dogmatic. If the Eight is not balanced, the right and wrong of a situation will get totally lost in the effort to win the argument. Eights are very competitive, even in discussions. It is difficult for them to restrain their expression, whether it is through anger, sex, or competitiveness. They are a consumptive type and are often classified as loners. Although it might not be their preference, it is what is easiest for them. They become attached in slow painful steps of testing and trials for the mate.

They value open honest arguments. If you can't take anger expressed in your face, don't pick an Eight. Much like type One, they will test the mate to see if they can dominate him. If they can, they won't respect him as much. Once trust is established, there is a bonding that is very deep. We can see why Eights would not be so good at diplomacy or "sweet-talk." They aren't emotionally attuned, and if they think you aren't being up front about everything, they will attack. The attack comes from an insecurity that they are being blind-sided or manipulated, and a feeling of frustration of having to waste energy on things as frivolous as emotions, especially when it can all be avoided if all of the cards were really put on the table.

The Eight, like the One, hates being wrong. One of the favorite tricks of the Eight who has been caught in a situation where he is proven wrong or has made bad choices, is to attack first. Accusations will be directed to the innocent party. Eights will often pick an area of the other party's behavior that can be brought into question so the discussion will be redirected away from their weakness. The sad thing is the Eight's pride may be such that he refuses to inspect his own behavior. Eights will let you know exactly where you stand, and they expect the same. They are possession, power and territory-driven, and that goes for work as well as romance.

The mature Eight will have learned to give a little and meet in the middle. They have an overriding fear of having to submit and depend on others, probably because they did not think they could depend on one of the parents. Eights grew up in a situation of having to fight for their rights. It could have been a physical fight such as with siblings or other kids, or it could have been a battle of wills with a parent. The child may have had to simply set his mind that the situation would not break his spirit.

Eights don't like compromise. They tend to view things as black and white. The middle ground leaves them feeling vulnerable.

Eights tend to be extroverts. The superior function is mental thinking; the inferior function is feeling.

Healthy Eights are magnanimous, leaders, self-restrained, courageous, self-assertive, confident, and inspiring. Self-restraint means not kicking people when they are down; knowing when things are appropriate, and restraining self until then. They can better the lives of others. As benefactors and visionaries, they can thrive on and learn from adversity, turning setbacks into opportunities. They can create and maintain social order, material success and personal achievements. They are fair, ethical, and responsible for their actions, especially as others are concerned.

Average Eights are enterprising, rugged, forceful, aggressive, domineering, willful, and combative. They are builders and power brokers, they think there can only be one person on top, and they are it. They are not team players. They are the entrepreneurs, business and political movers and shakers. They are self-made persons. Money, for them, is the means to the end of being self-sufficient so as to not depend on others. They are negotiators (buying, selling, trading). They love risk, danger, and excitement, especially in the financial world. To make money is to make more of themselves. Female Eights tend to dominate their mates since they have the same ego structure as the male Eight. Cultural restraints stand in their way, however.

Eight men are ambivalent toward women, seeing them as they have seen their mothers. They tend to dominate them, even becoming aggressive. They can easily become womanizers. Eights describe a combative childhood, a situation where the strong survived. They learned to protect themselves by becoming sensitive to the intentions of others. They grow to ignore the odds, and even become blind to the issues at times, as they pursue a goal single-mindedly. They come to think of themselves as the righters of wrongs, the enforcers of justice. Fairness, justice, and control are the central issues.

Unhealthy Eights are relentless, ruthless, vengeful, belligerent, violent, megalomaniac, and intimidating. Only money seems to be reliable to them; even the love of friends and family is secondary to power, control or money. Their view is so narrow that they are blind to what they and their demands inflict on others. Their pride will not allow them to even examine the possibility of being wrong, much less to admit it. This same pride and need to be in control makes them refuse to ask for help from anyone. They have very poor judgment when it comes to others and their emotional needs. They use and hurt people and are blind to everything except the thing they want.

Unhealthy Eights are viewed as unstable. They begin to believe their own bloated image of themselves. They swagger, bluster and are self-important. They hate softness in themselves and even more so in others. It is viewed as weakness. Might makes right. Treacherous, immoral, they will do whatever they have to do to reach their goal, including violence. The more power a person has the less need a person has to justify himself; therefore, the acquisition of power is a means of combating guilt. The more the Eight sinks into megalomania, the more he is likely to think he is above the law and even the instrument of God, or God himself.

Eights will act out through aggression and a bid to control the environment and all that are in it. They will be bossy to the point of rage. They will attempt to physically compel others to obey. If a person resists, they will escalate their effort until someone gets hurt, all in the name of control. Eights need to let go of abusiveness, anger toward others, trying to control or bully others, bossiness, thinking theirs is the only way. The need to see perfection in performance leads to hard-heartedness and thinking everyone is incompetent. The fear of being controlled by others leads to greed, intimidation, and territorialism. Letting pride, ego, coldness, or hardness come between them and the ones they really care for. The Eights need to focus on their ability to know the potential of people and help them achieve it. They have the ability to organize to make people's lives easier, to make money in order to give and share, and to exercise philanthropy. They should use their strong minds to allow others to understand. They possess the ability to inspire confidence, leadership ability, management ability, and ability to direct.

Eights will work out by allowing themselves to feel and putting themselves in the shoes of others. How would they like to be hurt, yelled at, hit, or abused? Then why do it to others? You don't have to be right and in control all of the time. The gift is always for the giver. Do unto others as you would have them do unto you! Remember?

EIGHTS - ASCENT/DESCENT

Fault line: a lust for power and control of their environment spreads out to include the people in it. There is an anger at not having everything in control and operating correctly, or according to their wishes.

Positive: Eights are direct, authoritative, driven, self-confident, capable, and assertive people with a strong sense of self.

Negative: Eights are controlling, insensitive, self-centered, domineering, aggressive, intimidating, and bullies.

Ascent: from Eight to Two: When Eights become truly secure with themselves, they drop the bravado and bossiness. They can then let others make their own choices. They will become supportive. They will use their abilities to help and support others.

Descent: From Eight to Seven. There are two problems with needing an ever increasing power base. First, there is no end to the desire. Secondly, as the area of control increases, so does the energy requirement it takes to keep and run the territory. This will spread the Eight so thin he will eventually collapse or stop and be dissatisfied. When this happens, the Eight becomes even more critical, negative, and arrogant. In an attempt to keep what they have, they become stingy and emotionally removed.

TYPE NINE – THE TRIBE OF ISSACHAR

Gift: Altruistic, Selfless, Generous

Motives: To try to see all sides, to preserve the status quo, to keep harmony at all costs, to maintain peace even if it is an illusion. To serve the greater good is always a choice between self-sacrifice and self-pity. Nines fear breaking the status quo. They fear of taking a chance. They fear of the unknown.

As a Spouse/Lover: Giving, compassionate, understanding, artistic, warm, generous, altruistic, philanthropic, emotional, a social worker type, Nines love to help others and need to be needed. Self-expression is important for a tender heart with a passion for life.

As a Parent: Softhearted and emotional. Be careful, a child could view the Nine as unstable or overly changeable. Nines can be creative or artistic. Because they tend toward being emotional, they could have a bad temper. Nines can be fickle or turned by emotional winds. They should not deny their temper and aggression, and they should not blame others. The lack of balance here is in the area of emotionally hiding from reality, being childish, refusing to act until things get bad, or being spread too thin.

As a Person: Nines hate being cooped up. Some have an explosive temper, yet they have compassion and understanding, too. They are givers, often giving too much of themselves. This can lead them to lose a part of themselves, much like the type Two can. They may have too many irons in the fire. The Nine may judge on first impressions too often. If they have a point to make, they won't stop until it's made. They are warm people and may be too generous. Nines can be emotionally needy. Reassurance in love is important to them. The Nine likes pampering and being pampered. They must guard against self-pity. They tend to be governed by the heart rather than the head. Some of them are given to theatrics and to dramatic scenes. They can be histrionic.

They are a type that may, at times, appear in plays and movies because, like the type Three, they like acting and role playing. Because of their wide and altruistic viewpoints, they want to be impersonal in the way they love, but they become distressed if they are not loved. They have the ability to inspire trust. Nines are able to put themselves in the place of others. They are helpers, artists, ministers, nurses, doctors, psychologists, or social workers. They can be generous, passionate, and compassionate. They may overreach themselves at times and spread themselves too thin. They can also hold a grudge for longer than most people live. Nines are idealists. They are driven to help humanity.

The other side of an unhealthy Nine not often mentioned is the need to keep the peace and to preserve the status quo, even at the expense of happiness. Nines will tolerate many things in order not to move out of a given situation and into the unknown. It looks, at times, like slothfulness, but it is not. It is based in the fear that what they have is the best they can obtain. They may not feel they deserve any better than what they have.

The Nine will go through a list of "good points" about a situation, and then still state how unhappy they are. This is akin to making a comparison between apples and oranges because the first list was facts and the second list feelings. The ability to weigh their feelings against a list of tangibles seems to confuse Nines. They may feel like there is a bad situation, but there is always another reason to stay. So the struggle remains to preserve even a living hell. They may manipulate through dramatics or they could be quiet and insecure.

Nines need to maintain an aim in order not to become scattered. Their concentration tends to wander if they don't keep focused on a given objective. At the same time, it is their nature to keep a wide vision of humanity. Even though they feel guilty when they put themselves first, they must learn at times that will be the proper thing to do. There will probably be hard luck in love. Although it is hard to say which causes the problems of the Nine first, his choice of mate or his actions toward the mate, it is likely Nine will have major disappointment in love. No, this is not a cliché that can be applied to most people on the planet; this is a type of trouble you get yourself into by your choices and interactions regarding relationships. The Nine must learn that not to make a decision is in fact a decision.

The Nine is subconsciously drawn to people who mimic dysfunctional problems in their childhoods. This is true for all of us but is much stronger in Four and Nine types. Most type Nines come from broken homes and are missing a stable father image.

TYPE NINE - THE COMPLETE STORY

Many of this type may have been subjected to trials of a painful childhood: very strict or alcoholic parents, a broken home from death or divorced parents. Emotional, generous, idealistic, compassionate, and understanding, Nine is a giver and intuitive (trusting first impressions), but is also bull-headed, sometimes sneaky, and maybe given to self-pity. They have had hard knocks. They worry about failing in love. They are insecure and need continual reassurance. Nines do well in the medical field, such as physical therapists, lab technicians, social workers, or nurses due to the humanitarian aspect of the work. They tend to have too many irons in the fire. This type has warmth, depth and emotion. Giving, humanitarian, idealistic, motivated in too many directions with few results, partly due to their idealism and partly due to the choices of their emotional involvements,

Nines may seem to get hurt or used in love more often than most. It may seem to them they come out on the short end of things, as if the other person always gets more out of the relationship than the Nine does.

I would like to remind the Nine he cannot "fix" anyone. It is up to the other to fix himself. This goes for the Nine looking for someone to make him feel "complete and happy" or for his efforts to try to help the dysfunctional person his heart may have gone out to. One who came from a dysfunctional home may be drawn back to a dysfunctional home. The mind may know it is wrong, but the little child inside the Nine who was hurt or stunted in that environment is stuck there trying to figure it out. So the situation feels familiar. Be careful not to be drawn to cold, abusive, or emotionally unstable mates as your parents may have been. Parents may have been very strict, religious types. The father may have abused alcohol or drugs, or appeared to be emotionally distant. One parent may have been missing in the formative years of the child.

Nines have a gift for painting, art or music, refinishing furniture and antiques, or other expressive abilities. They may favor psychology and writing. A few can be emotionally and mentally scattered. There is a very high percentage of personal divorce or divorced parents associated with this type. Nines may be impractical and fickle amblers. Dramatic, especially in fights; indecisive about future plans due to fear of the unknown.

Nines want union, harmony, and peace. They want to preserve the status quo. Tension and conflict are to be avoided. They tend to ignore things that upset them. Their sense of self comes from being in union with and helping others. Their view of life is open and optimistic. This causes an easy-going attitude that doesn't see the need to change things. They may even ignore the wrong staring them in the face. They are a relating type but they have a hard time relating to reality. Nines tend to blur their own identity because they want union with others. They may not reach their full potential because of this. To better conform to others, the Nine represses part of self. They equate self-assertiveness with aggression, so they have difficulty in expressing self as they should. They are the introverted sensation type. They are conspicuously calm and passive because there is a kind of detachment with reality.

The formation of the Nine type seems to have two patterns that run sequentially. The identification with the parental image is comfortable for them. Early childhood was a comparatively idyllic time which the person would like to recapture. In the second part of the sequence, or the second scenario, the later period of childhood could have been shattered by illness, death, or divorce. This propels the id to try to hold on to its better days where union and reliance on another met all of their needs.

Many Nines may have been close to their grandparents and felt a parental bond with them, especially in their early childhood. This love could have filled the void of a missing parent and provided for the emotional needs of the child. I have noticed a very high percentage of Nines who come from broken homes. In many of these instances the grandfather took the place of the father. If there was not a divorce, there may have been abuse (either emotional or physical). This, to the child, is tantamount to an emotional divorce. Normally these emotional changes would have occurred between ages four and nine. In another scenario the Nine child was overlooked. His needs, opinions, and point of view were not taken into account.

At times, when they expressed a view, they were told to shut up or their opinion was stupid. Their ideas were ignored. After too much of this, the Nines began to repress their feelings and preferences. They let others make the choices for them. They developed a keen sense of what others want. A type of emotional diplomacy keeps them from going against the flow and being reminded their opinion doesn't count. That is always very hurtful. They take comfort in small physical "pampering." They begin to emotionally withdraw as they learn nothing helps their cause, not even anger. They try to set up ways of not having to choose by setting up routines and operating on a kind of ritual.

Nines try to operate through this numbness to the extent that they have trouble keeping their minds on things or sticking to things. Nines "feel" their memories, they are so strong. Therefore they are not likely to fade, and neither are any grudges they may have. They are not fully in touch with any feelings they have. It is almost as if a partial filter is set up. Anger is one way for the wants and wishes to become revealed. They may say, "I didn't realize I felt so strongly about that." Without this direction it leads to scattered energy, teetering, not being able to direct and motivate themselves over a long period.

Nines are very susceptible to inertia. They have trouble with commitment and follow-through. They feel a need to keep the status quo. They will go to extremes to not act on or change things. This goes for relationships, situations, and even weaknesses in themselves. This can cause serious problems in relationships as the Nine "flakes out." They can't come to a firm decision because they were emotionally punished for it as a child. In one scenario of a Nine's childhood, the parents viewed the child's wants as an intrusion or an interference with their desires. The parent then ignored or chastised the child for having desires that might conflict with the parent's wishes. The parent could have been selfish, or given to "martyrdom." Yet, on the positive side, this has forced them to develop the ability to see all sides of a situation.

We must realize repressed feelings and preferences are like water - they will always seek a way out. This lends itself to a number of passive/aggressive strategies. One is to take control by being late. This puts others on your time schedule. Another is to refuse to make up your mind or make a commitment. This puts others temporarily under your control since they are waiting on you to decide. That is, until they get mad and give up in anger. Nines can use their diplomatic sense (which allows them to know what others expect) against others, by simply not performing.

Healthy Nines are self-possessed and fulfilled. They are content, optimistic, emotionally stable, supportive, good natured, and unpretentious, having overcome their fears of becoming an independent person, at one with themselves, even with their aggressions. Able to bring more of themselves to others, they do not idolize others but are able to love realistically. Love of self and others can bring a mystical overtone. They have no guile and do not understand lying or cheating in others. They are positive and generous. They actively play a part in the cycle of life, growth, and death. It is embraced, and they age with dignity. They are idealistic, tolerant, giving, forgiving, compassionate, generous, and universal in their frame of thought. They are artists, thinkers, and romantics.

Average Nines are self-effacing, accommodating, passive, minimizing problems to appease others, perhaps fatalistic and resigned to the fact when nothing can be done. They love to commune with others and nature. They love the outdoors: hiking, sailing, camping. They have a mystical side, a magical, mythical sense of the world. Elves, fairies, and such are shown to others through them in paintings and stories. The average Nine sees himself through the eyes of others. This may cause them to subordinate themselves. They fear asserting themselves. They do not want to disrupt the perceived communion. They can begin to live for the other person.

They take the middle-of-the-road stance, morally and socially, in order to be accepted. Respectability is very important to them because of this. They love the past and the old-fashioned ways. They are nostalgic, sentimental, and take things at face value. They never want to upset the status quo. This is taken to such a degree they tend to ignore negative things and say "Oh, we don't have to worry about that." They develop a happy-go-lucky outlook.

The further step is to detach themselves from reality and form a take-it-or-leave-it attitude. It is an easygoing style gone one step too far. They diminish their feelings and keep things on an even keel. Things don't sink in. This makes them part of the problem and not the solution. In relationships they idolize the other, then begin to substitute the idolized person for the real person. This makes them put less and less energy into the real relationship. They will do or promise whatever it takes to resolve a problem with others to appease them, but since they really do not want to deal with the problem, it isn't resolved and will show up again. The discussion simply bounces off their heads. They have sacrificed their loved ones and friends to the need for peace, the status quo, and not dealing with reality.

Nines can be either introverts or extroverts but tend to be introverts. The superior function is intuitive or feeling; the inferior function is mental - thinking.

Unhealthy Nines are repressed, neglectful, obstinate, and disassociated from reality. Severe cases can be catatonic and have multiple personalities. There can be a strange type of obstinate pessimism in that they go too far to avoid conflict. They repress their aggression and become adamant in not facing problems. They flake out and sacrifice relationships, making others angry when they try to force the Nine to do anything about fixing a problem. They may strike out at the person, but more than likely, since they wish to maintain the status quo, they will be passive/aggressive. They will accuse the other person of causing trouble and making waves. They will use lines such as, "Everything will work out," or "We've made it fine up to now," or "You're making too much out of it," and "You're causing trouble and putting too much pressure on me." For people who do so little, unhealthy Nines have less energy, probably because it is spent in internally walling off reality. When reality does show its head because of their neglect or having hurt someone through it, they will be plunged into despair, denial, even suicide. They can become bitter, fickle, selfish, irresponsible, and given to emotional extremes.

Nines will act out by realizing their passive/aggressive behavior. Like the Two, they must dig to find their real motives. They will have fiery tempers if they are not in touch with their feelings since the feelings will connect and explode. They need to see themselves as peacemakers and altruists so badly they will deny anger or its results. They will control by passive means, even to the extent they will get satisfaction in seeing someone struggle all the while knowing they have the solution. While they could help, they will stand by and do nothing but gloat over the other person's stress. Nines carry grudges. They can be flaky and forgetful when they don't want to face reality, even if it causes others to carry more than their share of a load.

The Nine should let go believing bad situations will just go away, ignoring unpleasant situations, being afraid of changing things, being emotionally detached, denying their own aggression and temper, not being in active control of their life, dependency, getting lost in doing the same routines and habits. This prolongs and promotes the numbness of life. Living vicariously or pouring themselves into others so as not to face themselves or a situation, and having too many irons in the fire takes away the time needed to focus on themselves or their problems.

Nines will grow by focusing on his talent to give, his altruism, intuition, far-reaching views, humanitarianism, art, acting, passion, the ability to get in touch with feelings and truly live life, psychic ability, emotional content, and the heart light.

Nines will work out by getting a grip on how they really feel, and not playing silly games with others, by fighting cleanly, taking an interest in the reality of things, approaching the world head on, and being dependable and straightforward when dealing with others. Above all, they mustn't scatter their energy. They need to pick one thing and do it, then go to the next item.

NINES - ASCENT/DESCENT

Fault line: Nine has the tendency to "zone-out or space-out." They think if they do nothing, then what is bothering them may go away. They can become passive/aggressive as they try to put away or ignore their anger and disappointment. They fear change and want to keep things as they are. A known condition is preferable to them, even if it is bad.

Positive: Nine is pleasant, peaceful, generous, receptive, and open minded. Servant of the needy.

Negative: Nine is apathetic and forgetful. They vacillate between being unassertive and stubborn to becoming obsessive, apathetic, and slothful.

Ascent: from Nine to Three: When the Nine takes things in hand, he frees up all the energy it took to keep his feelings suppressed. This energy shows itself as an outgoing, social confidence.

Descent: from Nine to Six: No feelings can be kept hidden without causing damage. In this case the strain takes its toll, starting with unpredictability and emotional swings. The control of emotions turns to rigidity. The weakness cause by repressed emotions deepens the need for security and love that would bolster and soothe the Nine. If they do not get the security, the Nine crystallizes into judgmental defensiveness.

TYPE TEN – THE TRIBE OF ZEBULUN

On the surface, the Ten has much in common with the Three, so look closely.

Gift: Outgoing, Influential, Compelling

Motive: To influence people toward their objectives, to lead by persuasion as a means of control. To sell oneself and what one has to offer.

As a Spouse/Lover: Vibrant, able to meet people and sell them on oneself, prideful, appearances are important. Can be self-centered.

As a Parent: Tens may be concerned with looks, appearances, and fitting in. They are usually light and happy, but also tend to be jealous and envious. Sales and meeting people could have played a role in this life. The lack of balance here is in jealousy, pride, and concern with fitting in and being accepted or admired. This may be a perfectionist. Because they are concerned with appearances they may say or do one thing in public and another when away from people they know.

As a Person: Tens can be perfectionists. They can be very picky and uptight at times. They can drive themselves much too hard and the people around them a little crazy. This is usually from the child within them trying to win the parents' approval. This type can be repressed at times. There is a need to loosen up and care less about what others think. Maybe seeming superficial,

Ten wants to be the center of attention. Tens tend to seek the "perfect" lover or relationship. They want candidness but often get their feelings hurt from it. Tens are drawn toward people and are very social.

They are very concerned with the way they appear. Because of the concern with outward show, they may be somewhat stingy since money buys status. They meet people well and enjoy socializing and parties. They are able to mingle, fit in to a number of environments, and make people feel at ease. They sell themselves by acting in the way the social strata and circle they want to move in would approve. They may tend to alter their personality to suit the group.

Tens' problem is in taking themselves too seriously. They can become vain and narcissistic to the point they are so self-absorbed there is no room left in them for having fun. As a general rule, Tens who don't get too caught up in how they look to others and having everything just right, socially, will have a happier life. If not, they will probably look back at all of the time they wasted.

Tens put on a happy face and cover their true feelings with an outward show of lightness. They use chit-chat to keep people from getting too close. Although they appear to be superficial and light, it must be remembered they are caught up in being accepted, and what you see is a cover-up. If they are in touch with their true feelings, they will be hidden for fear of rejection.

TYPE TEN - THE COMPLETE STORY

Charm, social graces, pride, jealousy, learning quickly, and flirtatious. Popularity is important. Tens are the consummate salesmen. They belong in the public eye and they love it. They may bid for the spotlight like the hams they are. Most Tens end up as the center of attention. Tens tend to be picky at times. They seek to be perfect in whatever area they are pursuing. They can change their stripes to fit into any group. They are social chameleons. They can drive themselves too hard because of this. Tens can be the smooth and polished salesman or the lounge lizard with open shirt and gold chains. They can wear thousand dollar silk suits or gaudy fashions and loud colors. They can be persuasive or pushy. These are opposite points of the same type.

Insecurity may arise leading to a need for the attention and/or affection of others to strengthen their own image. They wonder if their mate really loves them or needs them. Tens exude lightness and optimism in public. Tens are stylish and place a lot of importance on associating with the "right" people. Status symbols are important in the way of clothes, cars, and jewelry. Some tend to be verbose and don't know when to shut up. They may have many "faces," seeking the approval of the group. Tens may be superficial or exhibit false vanity. Tens are very socially competitive.

Tens want to be affirmed. They thrive on attention. They like impressing others with looks and possessions. They can be status, style, and image-oriented. They tend toward being narcissistic. They interact with others well, but it is to defend against rejection which they fear. The interaction is only on a superficial basis. This is important to understand since it is the key to many Tens. They do not easily open up to others since all of their interactions are based on prima facie issues and appearances. The fear of rejection drives them. If rejection occurs, to remain only superficial will keep the pain superficial also. They are able to sense and respond to the emotions of others the way plants respond to the sun. This is a way of always keeping the approval of the other person.

Tens must learn to go beyond this and respond out of love, not out of fear of not being liked. Like chameleons, they respond to the attention of others by imitating the values, ambiance, and psyche of those they are with. In childhood Tens identified closely with their mother image.

Some Tens were given much attention when young. They were praised for performance, image, looks, or social skills. Because of this they have a high and strong self-esteem. They expect others to accept and love them the same way the parent did. If acceptance is not forthcoming feelings of rejection develop. This adds to an arrogant air. Some Tens can manipulate and use others without remorse. They get in the mode of making the "sell" at all costs. If others don't admire them they will strike out in anger, pouting, or vindictiveness as a child would. Tens need assurance to continue the special feeling they remember from childhood. When the Ten matures enough to turn inward and examine themselves they will develop a balanced view of their self-worth and their abilities, acknowledging their faults and the equal worth of all. They will be modest, real, genuine, adaptable, and social people.

It matters to them that a good image is presented – a perfect home, a perfect family, the storybook lover. They learned to suspend their feelings in order to focus on getting attention and status. Tens work toward material and financial acquisition in order to feel more secure about self.

In relationships, the Ten is competitive, with a type of competitiveness which lends itself to gossip, back-stabbing, and being seen with only the right people. Tens are narcissistic. They are convinced their way is right because they are superior and competent. This, however, is pride based on the false persona, not the real one. Emotional intimacy is held at a distance due to the fact they are afraid the real self won't be loved. They, like the Twos, might say, "If they really knew me, they wouldn't like me." This is due to a false or "salesman's" face too often presented by the Ten. But Tens have too much pride and an image to maintain, so they will continue until their ship sinks. The saddest thing about this type is the way they manipulate people, and they know it. They are angered because people are fooled by their false face, yet they are afraid to show the real one, even though that is the only way they may be truly loved for who they are. In a crisis, such as a mid-life crisis, a Ten may wake up to the fact they were just playing a game, or not expressing the real self who has been bottled up for so long. At this point one should prepare for a change because the Ten isn't the type to take it in stride. Tens will act.

Tens should ask themselves, beyond the games and below the masks, what is my true face? Until a Ten can look in the mirror and know in his heart who and what he is, he may easily and frequently fall victim to self-deception and the waste of time and pain it can bring for all involved. We all play games at one time or another. We all want to be something or someone else now and then, but we must keep in mind it is only a game. Trying to make it permanent is a lie and is dangerous. Ten, show your true face!!! It will help the Ten immensely to know most of us see through the exaggerations and games, and we have already accepted them in spite of the "garbage" (and we all carry around garbage).

Tens tend to be extroverts. The superior function is emotional feeling or perceiving. The inferior function is intuitive.

Healthy Tens are inner directed, authentic, self-assured, energetic, adaptable, and ambitious. They like self-improvement. They can motivate others to be like them as they have many good qualities to emulate. They are people in their potential state, in the process of making something out of themselves. They spend time on making themselves better, more desirable, more attractive, smarter, socially better. They are the All-American boys or girls – expressive, social, ambitious, conversational, inspirational, charming, gracious, and romantic.

Average Tens are concerned with prestige and status. Career and success are important. Image is top on their minds. They can be calculating manipulators, arrogant, pretentious, and narcissistic. They want to establish their superiority over others, usually through competition or tangibles such as house, car, clothing, jewelry, income, or even spouse. Being acknowledged by others as better, raises their self-esteem. They compare ability, and looks, as if to say, "Mine is better than yours." They have an egotistical air. They feel comfortable only around those with whom they feel superior. They are usually very successful since they pursue being the best with all their strength. They plot advancement relentlessly. Some have a "whatever it takes" approach. They are marketing-oriented persons, selling themselves. They seek to perfect their image instead of themselves. When an image is practiced, it takes on a false and empty life of its own.

Unhealthy Tens use sex, appearance, or attraction to influence others and get admiration and their way. They may hold themselves away from others in a "look but don't touch" frame of mind. They like frustrating others. They will do anything to "make it." Their battle cry is, "It isn't enough that I win, but others must fail." They enjoy lying, even if about nothing important. It gives them a rush. If the deterioration continues, the sociopath becomes a psychopath and they could do anything. Since the problem stems from their mother, most acts will be against women. The unhealthy Ten is a bragging, lying, superficial, jealous, careless, gossiping, flirtatious, shallow, and insincere person. They will marry for status or drive their mates into the ground to get it. Their image is tied up in what they wear, who they are partnered with, and what they drive.

Tens act out through jealousy and revenge. They care so much about their image in the eyes of others, they will do or say anything to get it. This includes exaggeration, verbosity, conspicuousness, and driving themselves too hard toward being the ideal of what they have chosen as an image. The image is not truly them; it is what they think others want to see.

Thus, the unhealthy Ten is histrionic and demanding. Tens need to let go of jealousy, envy, fear of rejection, fear of being humiliated or being inadequate, denying their feelings in order to fit in, thirst for admiration, need for constant attention, arrogance, driving too hard to be perfect, and not being their real selves. They need to focus on their ability to meet and interact with people. Their flair for fashion, communications, or art; their persuasive personality, spontaneous creativity, and social sense are their gifts. They must be real and authentic people before the gifts can be used.

Tens will work out by trusting the real self has more value than a fake self. If people like you when you are real, they will like you for life. If they like the false you, they only like you as long as you are "playing." Realize, if you are secure in your own worth, you will not be threatened by the success of others.

TENS - ASCENT/DESCENT

Fault line: Deceit of self and others. Histrionic, hypochondriac, acting out emotions without feeling in order to convince others and get their way. An identity crisis occurs when their likes, dislikes, and feelings are suspended in order to portray what they decide is appropriate. The need to fit into the character they have chosen means at times they lose themselves in their part.

Positive Tens are optimistic, confident, energetic, outgoing, and social, being both good networkers and communicators. Negative Tens are vain, deceptive, shallow, vindictive, jealous, and competitive perfectionists. They play the part they have chosen to the hilt.

Ascent from Ten to Six: By dropping all pretense and facades, along with the need to be accepted, the Ten will be loyal and caring. They will climb from the childlike approach of the Ten to the parental caring and solidness of the healthy Six. Being true to feelings brings the Ten to a place of likable reliability.

Descent from Ten to Two: As the identity crisis reaches its breaking point, the Ten starts to shut down. They start to vacillate between apathy and obsession. As they lose themselves, they sink into an unassertive despair.

TYPE ELEVEN – THE TRIBE OF JOSEPH

Gift: Persuasive, Intelligent, Insightful

Motives: To act as the diplomat, peacemaker, statesman, politician, leader, idealist, or inventor. Driven by ideals and vision. Determined to make a difference.

As a Spouse/Lover: Elevens may appear to be patient, but they are working toward their goals. Their mates may think they have reached a compromise, but make no mistake, the Eleven got his way. Elevens prefer a peaceful, tasteful, expansive home, with friends who are intelligent. They need an orderly, quiet environment. Elevens tend to be workaholics. Even though energy seems limitless, they tend to work to the exclusion of the family.

As a Parent: Elevens are parents who are sensitive but demanding. They provide a structured environment for the child. Education is very important to them. Chaos makes the Eleven nervous, so the child is kept away or on a short leash. Elevens may be quick to snap at those making noise. As a parent, they can be manipulative. The lack of balance here is in being so demanding that the child is not allowed his childhood. There is also a tendency to be the boss since the Eleven does not trust others to "get it right."

As a Person: What a dichotomy. This type can be a diplomat-statesman, or a demanding manipulator. Eleven is a Benjamin Franklin type; renaissance men and women of wisdom. They have wide areas of knowledge and are usually very intelligent. This can lead to an elitist attitude. They must remember there is no need for the intelligentsia if there is no one to teach, train, and lead.

Sensitive, diplomatic, peacemakers, buffer between warring factions, Elevens are tactful, possessing a sense of rhythm and harmony. Some Elevens have musical talent. Elevens are diplomatic and able to see both sides. Their personal world is rather small compared to their public life. They prefer a small group of friends.

Elevens can make good teachers, lawyers, politicians, doctors, inventors, and engineers. They are drawn toward serving others on a large scale as public servants. Many will fall into the trap of forgetting who is the servant and who is in charge. Position and authority tend to eventually go to their heads. If affected by lack of expression or understanding, Elevens can become rude and insensitive with bursts of temper or by becoming demanding, and prone toward violence or drinking.

Elevens need a peaceful, quiet port in the storm where they live. Most Elevens, like Sevens, are logical and precise. Many have a gift for languages. Other gifts could be communication and writing. They are charismatic to an unusual degree.

TYPE ELEVEN - THE COMPLETE STORY

Elevens are some of the finest movers and shakers. They are driven and tireless, diplomatic and able to see both sides of any given situation, but – don't be confused – they have their own ideas and agendas. They are often placed in the middle of conflict to make peace between conflicted people, corporations, or nations. They are able to sense the feelings and aims of others. They understand the intricate games people play and the posturing they do. The Eleven can see through these things and get to the heart of the issues. Elevens have a macrocosmic view of life. They can get caught up in details because they would rather deal with the big picture. They sense the issues they deal with on a large scale. Talent with music or language is indicated. Their interests are in politics, economics, religion, or science. They are able to retain detail and have an admirable memory. Their detail retention is one of the best.

They may be blunt or outspoken. A paradox exists if emotions are submerged for too long repression occurs. The temper is often soft-spoken but deeply felt. They may appear to have an easy-going, friendly nature, but they are tigers and have a plan of attack. If affected or under stress, they could lose tact and become blunt or resentful, rude, and short-tempered. They need to experience balance, harmony, and unity in their environment. Emotions, especially anger, must be properly vented. They are very impatient with slow minds and those of little vision or intellect.

Elevens tend to be very neat people and are aware of how important first impressions are. They are drawn to neat, clean, quiet, peaceful environments. They pay close attention to people, word choices, body language, and hidden meanings. If lacking in morals, they will coerce and manipulate others, or use strong-arm tactics or brow-beating to get their way. They may try to overpower others by sheer intellect. They must keep in mind this will only lead to ill feelings.

Healthy Elevens are world class people, but may not make the best mates. They will be shared by the community, city, state, and world. The family must take its turn. They exude a sense of self-assured confidence. They are very empathetic. They are able to intuitively sense the underlying motives and goals of people. This is what allows them to be master diplomats and statesmen.

If the Eleven is not healthy, he will have strong feelings that tend to be over-expressed. They will become fixated on the problem. This leads to obsession and depression. They may be blind to their own aggressive feelings, making them manipulative and too forceful in the pursuit of solving the problem.

The negative Eleven is the most dangerous of all personality types. They usually have enough influence to make them a powerful foe, and they are not afraid to use the power. Their friendship and favors are not free but are doled out for paybacks. Their parents had high expectations and may have used bribery and influenced the child with favors to get what the parent wanted out of the child. The child grew up expecting this and thinking it was proper behavior. They grew up expecting others to give in. Political subterfuge and exploitation is the standard.

They are an extroverted intuitive type. There was ambivalence toward the father image. This set the stage for ambivalence toward those who can give them love. This problem of relating to the father makes their love conditional. They seem to think they have to be absolutely brilliant to deserve love or respect. Power and influence play an important part in many Elevens' lives. It gives them a value system they can relate to, with which to verbalize their ideals. Most of the time we all have a selfish aim for serving and we should acknowledge it, at least to ourselves. Honesty about our own plans and schemes keeps us from believing we are as great as what is printed about us. Elevens need to feel as if they alone can solve the problem. Elevens are given to headaches and heart or stomach problems.

Elevens tend to be extroverted. The superior function of an Eleven is intuitive or thinking. The inferior function is physical.

Elevens need to feel important in the lives of others. As children they felt as though they had to earn the affection of the parent by performing at a high level. They worked very hard for a parent's approval. They then transfer that action to others they love. Respect and approval were used as a carrot in front of the child's nose to motivate him.

Healthy Elevens are unselfish, altruistic, caring, capable, influential, and astute. They are capable of universal love. They are able to serve mankind and to be philanthropic humanitarians. They look out for the good of the whole. They are wise, diplomatic, receptive, progressive, and leading reformers. They are idealists, inspiring the people around them to higher levels.

Average Elevens are competent, quick-witted, friendly, and progressive. They have the ability to lead others. They can meet people and immediately size them up.

Unhealthy Elevens are manipulative, demanding, arrogant, power-hungry tyrants. Feelings of anger, bitterness, and resentment arise, especially if others don't go along with their plans. They will use their insights into human nature to hurt and manipulate others.

Elevens will act out by angry outbursts and tirades when others stand up to them. They are angry if they have not achieved the desired position of power over people. They will attempt to manipulate or force their way into the position they want. Elevens need to let go of feelings of resentment, anger, and hidden agendas, as well as trying to manipulate others into doing as they wish. Elevens should focus on being a balanced, integrated, helpful part of society.

Elevens will work out by understanding their true drives and ambitions. They must then understand no one has a right to manipulate or brow-beat others.

They must realize intellect is only a small part of us and, just because others don't think as clearly or in a particular way, it doesn't mean they are any less important.

ELEVENS - ASCENT/DESCENT

Fault line: Intellectual snobbery. Over-emphasis on intellect and position at the expense of emotional clarity. Trying to control through aggressive means, they can become hostile if they don't think they are properly rewarded, even though they have manipulated to get things done.

Positive: Elevens are serving, thinking, helping, and supportive. They pay close attention to detail. They are the diplomats.

Negative: Elevens are tyrannical, aggressive, manipulative, emotionally weak, and given to feelings of megalomania. They have the egotism which comes from thinking they are secretly behind the scenes, making things happen.

Ascent: from Eleven to Twelve: By attending to their own feelings and learning how to balance assertiveness with the good of the whole, Elevens will uncover their greatest potential.

Descent: from Eleven to Two to Eight: As the Eleven becomes frustrated at being held back, he will become negative and aggressive, like the negative Two, except he will be driven toward anger and revenge. As the Two's emotional repression and manipulation continues, it declines into an insensitivity and aggression and crassness. If they can't get their way through compromise or manipulation, they try a demanding, aggressive approach.

TYPE TWELVE – THE TRIBE OF BENJAMIN

Gift: **Inventive, Enlightened, Visionary**

Motives: To overcome and find the answers to life's questions in science, intellect, and reason. To struggle with expressing emotions. To add something that will endure and help mankind.

As a Spouse/Lover: Distracted, Twelve is always working, even when he's not at work. Twelves keep their minds on the problem even when at home or asleep. Disciplined but distracted, methodical and systematic, the logical approach is important as Twelves work with their minds. Absent minded, distracted by the problems they are thinking about.

As a Parent: Twelves are loving but emotionally distant at times. They may have an obsession with finding the answers to the issues in the discipline they are in. Given to depression, overworking, and lack of social contact, a small percentage of parents have a work habit that may be off balance, being workaholics. The lack of balance here is in the expression of emotion due to a heavy emphasis on logic and reason.

As a Person: They are scientifically and/or artistically inclined. Builders, scientists, systematic, dreamers, their practical approach leads toward solutions. The passion may be for physics, math, cosmology, or engineering.

The artistic realm may be sculpting, music, or painting. Although the description of this type may seem broad, it is in fact very narrow. This is the smallest percentage of all types. These people are geniuses in their fields. They will be conductors, master musicians, theoretical physicists, cosmologists, master chefs, inventors, engineers, and scientists. The interesting thing that sets them apart is the way their minds function. There is a high function of memory and recall. These people are bright enough that social skills may be lacking. They also seem to think several steps ahead and see issues and problems before they arise. There is also an ability to see the interconnectivity in various areas of science and art.

Twelves live within their minds. They can think in several dimensions. Their focus can block out the world around them until all that is left is the task at hand. The only major problem is they live an intellectual and introverted life. Many Twelves, especially women, are repressed emotionally and do not have a good outlet for venting their emotions. Because of the emotional blockage some Twelves have, they exhibit problems relating to one-on-one relationships. They are quiet, introverted, eccentric, or even emotionally androgynous. If they are faced with too many changes, noise, or chaos, they become nervous and emotional.

Their challenge is to learn to express themselves emotionally, to be careful not to hold back emotions too much; this leads to depression and fatigue through overwork. Good memory and learning ability give this type of person a foot up in our mentally driven society.

TYPE TWELVE - THE COMPLETE STORY

Control, restraint, discipline, order, form, precision and reliability dominate, just like the Four type, but add to it a large dose of insight, intellect, and tenacity. Twelve is like the best of the type Four and type Seven combined. They deal well with abstract ideas such as cosmology, theoretical math, physics, and philosophy. The Twelve has a great sense of how the greater systems work. They dig for insights and knowledge. They have keen intellect and intuition, two things normally not seen together. They are stubborn and tenacious when it comes to projects. They are drawn to math, medicine, physics, mechanical and electrical engineering, and there are even some found in the higher area of architectural design. Although they would never rely on their intuition, there is an inner sense of the balance and working of things which leads them into advances in their fields. They pound at the door of human knowledge and can become frustrated when they suspect the answer is just beyond the next discovery.

Twelves are the Einsteins, Newtons, and DaVincis of the world. They are bright and they are needed, but they may be difficult to live with. They can be so directed and focused that time and schedules slip away. Their minds are always working even while they are going about their daily lives. They have a problem working it out in the back of their minds, even as they sleep. As focused as they seem, they are distracted and absent-minded, unaware of how they look or if they have eaten lately. They seem to snatch ideas and inspirations out of the air like someone grasping lightning. Likeable, disconnected with reality at times, unaware of the environment, focused on the interior world of the mind and the landscape of the problem; they can spend days without missing the outside world. When immature, the Twelve will be intolerant if he hasn't learned his limits. Twelves think people should carry their own weight and think for themselves but the Twelve will have a measure for this most will not live up to. Oddly, their loved ones can be somewhat exempt from the measuring rod since the Twelve wants to love and protect them from the world they see as useless and harsh. Many have a do-it-yourself attitude. They are motivated by a sense of discovery.

Twelves have immense memories and can visualize in three dimensions and solve complex problems in their heads. They have minds that can organize and categorize facts. If the Twelve is afflicted with a low self-image due to abuse or neglect in childhood, he can have an escapist and unrealistic view of the world. They can retreat so far into their interior world they become insane.

Women tend to be dominant, throwing off the common perceptions of female stereotypes and taking on a more androgynous role. They are usually quiet and intense people. Twelve females are usually breadwinners or co-workers. They can be stubborn and sexually insecure. They may lack true self-appreciation. Twelves find it difficult to relate emotionally although they feel deeply. They appreciate beauty, balance, and harmony. They want to understand themselves and to express this in some way that has beauty. Some end up putting their full talents into music. They become conductors and great musicians. They play to put voice to emotional needs and feelings, as stated in the profile for the type Four: There are two motives for creative or artistic work–to communicate self or to lose oneself in work. There are two results from artistic or creative output–one being to transcend self, the other to become self-aware.

The Twelve has problems with connecting thoughts and feelings to the outside world. They can have a difficult time coping with their own emotions. It is the intellect and logic that tends to be their world. It may be because of this struggle to emote that some Twelves spend their entire lives either inside their own minds or trying to perfect the expression of emotions through a medium such as sculpture, painting, or music. Like the Four, they sense both the full human potential and the depths to which it can descend.

Many Twelves had rough childhoods. They did not fit in. The way they thought and acted seemed foreign to the other kids, so they were looked upon as different. They may have been rejected and, thus, became loners. They didn't identify with either parent. They spent many hours in their own room alone. They read, thought, wondered, and began a journey of the mind. There is a deep feeling of emptiness at times and loneliness their strong minds focus away from. It is in the hours of deep concentration on a problem or on their art, that they find relief from the feelings of loneliness. The child was forced to turn inward for his identity. He may have reasoned that he was defective and this caused the parent's and peer's lack of attention. He feels isolated, yet he has much that people envy. He has a clear, sharp mind, a determined approach, and a sense of what is possible in mankind.

Twelves tend to be introverted. The superior function is intuitive but can be mental–thinking. The inferior function is sensing.

Healthy Twelves are inspired, brilliant, and creative. They are emotionally honest. Both funny and serious, they know and understand their feelings and are able to vent them creatively. Disciplined, methodical, industrious, tireless thinkers, imaginative, visionary, and bright; they fit in well with social norms. They have broken free of the trap of depression, introversion, and anger. The Twelve is an enlightened, goal-oriented, ingenious, masterful individual.

Average Twelves can be involved in science, art, or music. They express their feelings through a medium such as sculpting, woodworking, or painting. They can get absorbed in their work and the passion of solving the problem they are working on. They must watch for irresponsibility, absent mindedness, and impatience.

Unhealthy Twelves feel emotionally blocked, depressed, and hopeless. In being unable to get in touch with their emotions, they have cut themselves off from their emotions and live completely in a mental, interior world. They can become loners, undisciplined, given to procrastination, unkempt, and unaware. It is a dichotomy that, on one side Twelves need art, self-expression, and emotional feeling, and on the other hand they are introverted thinkers who must strive to get out of their minds and into their hearts. They can become intellectual snobs who have given up on humanity.

Twelves will act out because of depression and by a feeling of being alone and detached from everyone else. There is despair, self-destructiveness, and insanity. Twelves need to let go of the fear of emotions that cannot be understood. Not all things can be quantified. They need to understand it is OK not to understand everything.

Twelves will work things out by getting in touch with their lost feelings and learning to balance the mental and emotional sides of themselves.

TWELVES - ASCENT/DESCENT

Fault line: A disconnected emotional flow and lack of ability to express feelings.

Positive: Twelves are warm, creative, logical, bright, and engaging.

Negative: Twelves are depressed, driven, sullen, moody, absorbed in their work, and obsessed with their thoughts.

Ascent: from Twelve to Four to One: By taking responsibility for their own feelings and examining them, they become leaders in music and science, capable of interaction, teaching, and relating their findings and feelings to others.

Descent: from Twelve to the negative Four to Two: By the exclusion of emotions from their lives, there can be such a pressure built up that depression and insanity set in. The Twelve becomes self-absorbed and neurotic.

TRIBAL DEDUCTIONS

All people have a choice to accept defeat or welcome greatness. We all have extraordinary gifts to exploit and deep flaws to identify and overcome. It is my deepest hope in these pages, you have found some signs of yourself. I hope you have seen your dragons and your demons and resolved to defeat them. Most of all, I hope you have seen your potential and how to reach it.

One of the most frequent causes of friction in relationships is the misinterpretation of another person's intentions, based on their words or actions. More often than not, we attribute *our* motives to *their* actions. We fail to realize each type functions from a different base of motives. The worst thing we can do is to apply our basic motives and drives to their responses.

As an example, let us assume a situation of conflict or disagreement between an Eight type and a Two type. As the issue heats up, the Two, operating from a base that seeks to help and empathize and is afraid of rejection, is likely to take a more passive, even manipulative stance. Women are more likely to be passive/aggressive than men, probably because in the societies of the world women used to be, on the whole, less educated and usually physically weaker. Those who are weaker, or see themselves as being weaker physically and/or educationally, find other ways to persuade and to preserve their individuality. This is done with emotional manipulation.

Twos hate confrontation; it frightens them on a deeper level, so they turn more toward manipulative means in order to get their way. After all, people want to have their wishes granted. Everyone has an agenda. The Eight, on the other hand, is likely to become aggressive and will seek to control the situation from a base which is more power and control-oriented and operates from a fear of being taken advantage of. The Eight will view the Two as being unsure, weak, and even cowardly, though he is not. The Two is probably quite sure of how he feels and knows what he wants. He is simply going to try to keep harmony and try to help the Eight. This does not mean he won't try to manipulate the Eight, but it will be a passive/aggressive stance the Eight is not likely to see.

The Eight may interpret the actions of the Two as a retreat. Eights will attempt to advance to fill the space in the argument they think has been vacated by the Two. The result can only be the Two is going to view the Eight as a bully who cannot be reasoned with. Actually the Eight loves to reach a compromise by "banging heads" at times, believing in a peace through testing and trying one another. This is a type of territorial behavior.

The Eight will be confused by the Two's lack of steadfastness. He will assume the Two doesn't care about the issue as much as the Eight, or the Two isn't willing to fight for what he believes in. The Eight may lose respect for the Two, simply because he interprets the actions of the other in the light of his own motives. The de-evolution of the relationship into the bully verses the victim is one possible outcome of this scenario. Yet, if at any time either of them had stopped and truly understood the basic motives of the other, they could have saved themselves from this. By understanding other persons we can try to speak and understand their language. We can know their fears and work around them. We can gently try to reassure them we are not trying to do to them what they fear most. By knowing where the other person is coming from, we can help and not hinder the aim of harmony and peace in our families, workplaces, and lives.

Here is a quick reference list of the types, and their likely base of operations and how it will manifest in a fight:

- **One**: Intolerant of others' ideas, fears being wrong and the condemnation it may bring. Egocentric, arrogant, judgmental, critical, and cold. The base is one of being unsure and the fear of coming up short of their ideals and being judged harshly. They fight against the parents' critical attitude of them which they hear in the voices of others.

- **Two**: Histrionic, prying, emotionally intrusive. Insincere, uses false flattery, and manipulative. They beat around the bush, and express aggression in an indirect way. They try to put themselves on the moral high ground and act like the hurt puppy. From here they will fight the side issues they can win without directly attacking the main argument which they may lose. The base of the Two is a fear of abandonment and rejection. They want to keep the peace and be a helper. They need to know they have a place in the hearts of others, but this is only to insure they will not be disregarded.

- **Three**: Haughty, holier-than-thou, arrogant, sarcastic, these assume they should be admired all of the time, even when they are wrong. The basic drive is fear of losing face. They refuse to be just one of the crowd. Their egos are very strong, and they demand attention.
- **Four**: Escapes through drugs, alcohol, sex, or religion. Stubborn. Hides feelings. Trouble in expressing emotions.

- **Five**: Quick-witted, sarcastic, tries to jump quickly between subjects to confuse the opponent. The motive seems to be a fear of losing their freedom.

- **Six**: Tries to take control as a parent or authority figure. Self-righteous, possessive, and passive/aggressive.

- **Seven**: Can be devious and sneaky. They tend to hide and/or distort the truth. Their favorite game is to tell part of the truth in order to back up their claims. They are brooding and withdrawn when angry. The drive is a type of paranoia.

- **Eight**: Will not admit they are wrong. No compromise. Tyrant. The boss.

- **Nine**: Scattered energy. Wants things to remain the same. Fearful of change. Temper and theatrics when threatened.

- **Ten**: Some will immediately remind you of how much pressure and how many demands they are under. They will blame you for making things worse in their lives. They hope this will redirect the problem by placing blame on others.

- **Eleven**: At first they will be in disbelief you dared to disagree with them, and then try to convince you of the errors of your ways. The final stage will be an emotional outburst in an attempt to regain power and control.

- **Twelve**: Confused, retreating, sullen, avoiding, they will go away and think about the issue. They will then come back to it and try to reason out the answer.

THE PARENT TRAP

As with any idea or system which attempts to pigeonhole or categorize, there are obvious drawbacks. People are not simple enough to fit neatly into any one category. If the system being used is functional and the categories are defined properly, you will be able to see yourself or those to whom you are applying the system, in one main category. There will be secondary applications in other categories, but they will be weaker and their effects will not be as strong. This rule applies to this list as well as any other system of pigeonholing.

One night while a friend and I sat and talked over our latest revelation, she mentioned that after forty years of feeling put down by her mother she realized her mother was jealous of her. This started my mind wandering. In the following days, I thought of all the parents I had known and how they related to their children. Some were very good and supportive. Others pushed their children relentlessly. The next night, I fell asleep trying to find some similarities between this plethora of parents. The next morning I had the answer. It seemed to have bubbled up from my subconscious in a way Carl Jung could appreciate. All parents interact with their children in the following ways: Supportive, Manipulative, Vicarious, Jealous, Dismissive/Permissive, Abusive. Each of these postures will produce several responses in the child.

The *supportive* parent is one with no agenda or personal expectations laid on the child. The parent allows the child to set his own goals and then supports the child in his endeavors. It takes a healthy, balanced parent to love and support a child with no strings attached. This is the kind of parent who is most likely to produce an emotionally healthy child. Before you go grabbing this label for yourself, let me point out only ten to twenty out of a hundred parents can even come close to this type, so dig deeper.

The *manipulative* parent is one of the most common. These slowly eat away at the child's self-esteem and confidence by trying to tell the child what to do, sending a clear message to the child that he doesn't know enough, isn't capable enough, or isn't adult enough to run his own life. This is very damaging to the ego and can only end in resentment for both. The parent will raise the kind of child he is fighting so hard against, and the child will be resentful for not being able to simply be a person without having to wage a war to get that right. The manipulative parent is the one who tries to interfere, run, orchestrate, detour, plan, or otherwise meddle in the child's life. It can be as apparently kind as showing up uninvited to clean the house, which says to the child he can't even clean correctly; or as intrusive as always offering an opinion when not asked. The manipulative parent wants to navigate the child through life in various degrees. The strange thing is the parent is usually unhappy with his or her own life.

The parent could want another chance to get it right through the child's life. This is a form of the *vicarious* type. The vicarious parents have many hidden agendas they heap on the child. All of their wishes and dreams, even those things they always wished they could have done, are written into the child's life plan. Fathers drive their sons in sports. Others coax them to follow in their footsteps. Mothers drive their daughters to be beauty pageant contestants, cheerleaders, or other favorite dreams. Parents demand the children exceed all normal expectations in academics. The parent has many reasons for doing these things. Among them is ego. The parents demand the privilege of being proud, even to brag about their child. It is as if the child were their property to be displayed. The child feels driven. If the children can live up to the parents' demands, they will be constantly displayed and touted as something special. This can quickly build an over-inflated ego and an expectation, expecting to be admired by all.

The *jealous* parent could simply be a dominating, controlling type who is forever seeking to increase his base of control and power. Whatever the reason, he is attempting to take the child's life and run it to one degree or another. We all have a right to our own opinions, to learn, to live our own lives, and to be wrong while doing it. If the ploy of manipulation, which is normally covert, becomes stronger or more overt, the manipulation becomes control. This parent controls through threats, blustering, force of will, or force of intellect. He simply shouts the child down or reasons the child out of her feelings.

Like the manipulative parent, jealous parents will also steal your joy. They are convinced you should live, believe, and act as they do. It hasn't dawned on them that they are not happy in life, and anyone who follows their path may not be happy either. This parent tends to raise children who are somewhat rebellious. They had to get strong to save their individualism. Sadly, if the parent's personality overtakes the child's and the child's will is broken, the child can turn inward and become incapable of making clear or strong choices or commitments.

The jealous parents are the most dangerous of all. They are difficult to spot and covert in their attacks. These parents are usually unhappy with their lives. They are reminded of this fact whenever someone, even their child, seems to do well or be happy. They will demean, cut, and sabotage the child or his feelings. The parent may not attend significant events in the child's life, and in the more unguarded moments the parents will let their resentment slip. There is a saying that, within flashes of anger, true feelings are revealed. The child will feel as if he does not deserve to succeed, much less exceed. He may feel it is wrong because it makes Mom or Dad feel bad when he does well.

The *dismissive* parent is one who is detached from the ups and downs of a child. He is usually too caught up in his own life to give much thought or care about the problems that may be faced by a child. The parents that fit this category are either very self-absorbed or are very stressed out due to the demands of life. This doesn't matter to the child, however. All he knows is he is not important. No matter how good the child is, the parent doesn't seem to notice. He sends the message to the child that he is not important, not loved enough. This causes some children to seek more negative or destructive means of gaining attention. As a general rule, a child will try first to gain approval, and when he cannot obtain the parents' approval he will then try simply to get attention. This is a situation that can escalate quickly into acts that are designed for their shock value in order to simply get a reaction from the parent.

A subcategory of the dismissive parent is the *permissive* parent. A child that runs rough-shod over Mom or Dad is a child who does not feel cared for. The message is the child can do whatever he wants because the parent doesn't care. A wholesome discipline is a way to show love. It says you care enough to watch out for the child. It forms a feeling of love and security. It also serves as a blueprint for life choices in later years. It is sad to think there are children whose very existence is acknowledged so seldom they aren't comfortable with their own worth or personhood.

The last and easiest to identify is the *abusive* parent. He can either be emotionally abusive, physically abusive, or sexually abusive. Emotional abuse most often takes the form of verbal abuse, but not always. Sometimes it can be a mean-spirited emotional tyranny. The abuse type has anger, rage, or a need to ultimately control others. There isn't enough time to tell all this can do to the child. The abused can grow up to abuse. Abused wives can choose abusive husbands to continue the pattern. The abused child grows up to have a distorted self-image, and most of all there is pain and anger. These two feelings will be the stumbling blocks until they are dealt with.

Look at your parents from an objective point of view, and categorize them by placing them into one of the basic categories. All parents will fit into one primary place and possibly a secondary place. For example, abusive parents are often dismissive also. A jealous parent will probably be dismissive in order to vent jealousy in a passive/aggressive way.

You must turn this mirror on yourself in order to learn and grow. Keep in mind less than 20 percent of children actually receive healthy parenting, so don't be too easy on yourself. Are you supportive, manipulative, vicarious, jealous, dismissive, or abusive? Any type can be any kind of parent, but there are noticeably higher percentages of correlations between certain personality types and parent types. This makes sense when we consider there are types of people more prone to nurture, and others more prone to abuse. The nurturing types are usually manipulators, by the way, so they don't get off that easily either. Any healthy type can be a supportive parent, but the other types, which represent specific anomalies, are more prone to be parents of certain types.

The manipulative type is prone to be a Two, Three, Eight, or Ten. The Eight and the One will step over the line into the area of becoming controlling; however, I have placed these two types together since I view them as greater and lesser degrees of one another.

The dismissive parent is usually the One, Four, Five, or Twelve type. They are too involved with their own life to be bothered by others.

The jealous parent can be a Three, Six, Eight, or Ten. Any unhappy person tends to be jealous or envious, but these types show a greater bent in that direction.

The One, Three and Nine can get more from vicarious living than others. They do it for their own pride in the child as if it makes them look better as parents.

Four, Six, Eight, and Ten are the tyrannical and abusive types. They are so because of anger, rage, or a need to control. Within the context of relationships, there are many ways of classifying reaction.

More Ones, Sixes, Eights, and Tens tend to express anger, aggression, tyranny, and confrontation in their relationships.

Fives, Sevens, and Nines tend to express appetite, sensuality, and a peculiar drive to consume things, including the relationship.

Twos, Threes, Fours, and Tens are prone toward control, ownership, and control of the relationship. This can be overt or by passive/aggressive means.

Since any person can express any type, these are only a higher percentage of occurrences. Don't assume that just because you are not a number mentioned for that type of parent, you can not still be classified in that category. You can be anything you choose to be, good or bad.

WHAT TO DO NEXT?

So you have read the personality profiles and the psychological overview, and you are thinking you may have a problem. Don't we all!

The first thing to do is to allow the shock of having identified and admitted it sink in. This is the first in a three-step procedure. Most people will not admit to having a problem; therefore, most people never start getting better. You must hold on to the realization. Write it down in detail. Keep it, and read it over again later when your zeal for improving yourself starts to wane. Be specific in your insights, and don't let yourself off the hook. If your problem relates to choosing a particular mate, don't excuse yourself by saying you didn't know how he was when you married him. I want you to understand you did indeed know. There is no way a person can hide all he is from anyone who is around him for more than a few days. Our subconscious is more observant than that. It picks up on every nuance, slip of the tongue, and faux pas.

The axiom that should always be remembered is, you are as damaged as the people you choose. It is difficult to take responsibility for the actions that get us into bad situations, and even more difficult to take responsibility for actions that keep us in abusive situations. Weak and trite excuses are those such as, "I stay with this person for the children." This is a "hot button" of mine since what you are saying is you are staying in an abusive relationship so the kids can experience a bad childhood, and by being exposed to abuse within the home, grow up to be abused, or to abuse. To use this excuse means a long and insightful evaluation has been done to decide if leaving or staying is best for the children. I usually find this is not

J. Lumpkin – Healing the Tribes of Man

the case. The decision is normally made based on what is easiest for the parent. The choice is usually based in fear or slothfulness.

The next most stated excuse for staying is there is no place to go. There are many homes for battered women and children. The services are free and confidential. Your whereabouts are kept secret. Many locations will even train you for a job and allow you to start life anew. There are not as many places for the abused man to go, which is a shame as the dysfunctional woman is capable of inflicting as much harm as a man. Many people use passive/aggressive and covert means so as not to openly attack and suffer open physical conflict. It is nonetheless just as damaging and causes long term scars.

The last of the three big excuses is, "I just love him too much to leave him." If he is abusive, then you are saying literally you love him more than life itself or the lives of your children, since you are willing to allow your or their possible death. These are worst-case problems, but they are numerous and growing. I am not saying everyone in a dysfunctional relationship should leave. I speak only to those whose very minds and bodies are under attack. I do think the fastest way to start healing is to stop the injury first, and then begin the treatment. The highest percentage of success comes from couples who begin the sojourn together. Just as the abused is suffering from lack of wholeness in order to allow the actions, so is the abuser suffering from a lack of wholeness in having the rage and anger built up in him to do these things. There will be times one partner must leave the other behind and journey alone toward healing.

If you are the abuser and you are reading this right now, you may even be feeling resentment and anger at having to examine this issue. If you throw this book down, you may keep repeating the actions you yourself find embarrassing and not acceptable. You must get in touch with the fact that you are willfully hurting another human being. By your actions you are saying her battered psyche and broken heart is not as important as the

310

release you get by beating, yelling, or hurting her emotionally. The same rules apply for emotional and physical abuse.

If you are one of these people, admit it. We must recognize our problems, take responsibility for them, and then put forth the effort to fix our problem. Strangely enough, this is where the majority of people stop. Almost everyone runs into the truth about himself at one time or another, but most shrug it off and go on as if nothing has happened. They are the ones who say, "It is my life and I can live it the way I want." Some will say, "Well, at least I'm not as bad as some." Well, you're bad enough, and you might as well admit it now before things get any worse.

Of those people who enter into therapy or a self-help program, most get stuck in a stage of recognition. That is to say, they recognize and understand the problem, but they do not put forth the effort to change. The last and most painful step is the effort to fix the problem. Thus far we have looked with objectivity at our types. We have discerned from the types, along with our ability to look at ourselves, we have an area of imbalance. We have noted parallels between our childhood problems and the problems described in this manual. We can then assume the effects of these problems are also, at least in part, ours.

Some of the common causes and effects are discussed in these pages. If you do not believe there is any problem or area of dysfunction in your life, then there is no point in reading further except for the gaining of general knowledge. We can't fix other people, and it usually causes confusion and resentment when we try, so I urge you once again to attend to the log in your own eye before attempting a speck-ecthyma on anyone else.

Now we must talk about what to do. First, ask yourself how much pain, insecurity, or misunderstanding your blind spot has caused you and those you love. Next, ask yourself if you truly wish to change. Would you go through the pain of brutal self-examination? Do you want it enough to be totally honest about your motives, actions, and intentions? Do you want to change enough to police yourself and be consistent about your insights? If so, then we will begin.

Let us take an action, almost any action. Examine that action and its purpose. The purpose that is on the surface which you relate to at first, is not the true purpose. The true purpose can only be seen when you have answered the question "Why" for the final time. Let us suppose a person had an affair. If I asked him why he did it he would probably say his mate didn't love him or make him happy. This would beg the question of whose voice he was hearing and whether this feeling was due to a blind spot in him/her, his mate, or both of them. No one can force you to do anything. Anyone can do, or not do, whatever he wants, if he is willing to pay the price. The price may be high. It may mean your life. But if an action is worth the giving of your life, then there is nothing to stop you from trying.

So let us quickly bypass the trap of "They made me do it." Now, why did you have the affair? To be happy? Why did you think the affair would make you happy? Because it makes me feel like somebody loves and wants me, might be the reply. Why does the fact you are wanted make you feel happy? Because it makes me feel as if I am worth something. Why do you feel the worth others ascribe to you makes you more worthy? Because I am unsure of my own worth.

Here is a scenario: A story emerges of a child who had been alone and lonely for years. From the time he was in the first grade, he had few friends. His parents drank socially, and his father began to have a drinking problem. They were always surrounded by their friends, but the child had few friends of his own. Since the lifestyle of the parents was so different from the child's in this area, it sent a message to the child that his way was wrong. At that time he had no way of correcting it, but slowly he sharpened his social skills and developed a somewhat magnetic personality. As time went on, he amassed a group of friends. He became promiscuous. As the image matched more and more closely to that of the parent's, the person felt like he was on target. The only problem was the adoration of others was necessary in order to fulfill the image and to quiet the voice of the parent.

Inconsistency of attention and lack of insight to the child's needs produced this blind spot. It could have gone in many different ways, but with this individual this was the result. By asking why, why, and why, we get to a point where it is no longer an easy answer. At this point the digging begins, and the needed insights come. It may be painful to admit to your own selfishness. This person had to admit it was more important for him to feel good than for him to be faithful to his spouse. That is selfish, but we all have areas like that.

Why do you do those things that hurt you and your loved ones? Chances are you are being driven by voices you don't understand. The types will give you some insight into whose voices you are listening to and what they are saying. After this head start, you must clarify and focus on the area. No two people are alike, so the information contained in the types is designed to be a general starting place. As anti-climactic as it seems, the only cure for a blind spot is awareness and the discipline to look more closely at that area. Once you are aware of the existence of an inner voice that makes you feel a certain way, you must come to understand feelings are not facts.

Feelings do not have to be acted upon. They do not impel you; they compel you. In the final analysis, the difference is, you are in control. It may help to repeat that to yourself when certain feelings come up. Feelings are not facts. I do not have to act on feelings. If there isn't anything that caused the feeling, it is only an inner voice. You cannot trust your inner voices of the parent or child. Would you let a five-year-old plan and control your life? Would you let someone who didn't care for you try to make you happy? The voices of the child and parent are like that. This is not to say your real parents didn't love you, that is a separate issue, but because the voices usually come out of times of pain or trauma, where a piece of you has been left behind, they are not balanced voices.

After you have found the problem, you must start to recognize and identify whose voice you are hearing. It is only the adult who can be allowed to plan your actions, not the voice that says, "Nobody loves me" or "You are never good enough" or "You will feel like you're worth more if someone wants you." Only the adult is to be listened to and acted on. That voice is the one asking, "What will be the final outcome?" or "Is this the best course of action for the most lasting good?"

The adult can suggest we go through suffering in order to improve ourselves, but the child cannot. The parent can suggest we serve and suffer in a situation indefinitely, but the adult would not. In order not to repress feelings, the child and parent voices should be allowed to "feel and say" whatever they wish. It is normal to feel afraid at times – you know it is the child. It is normal to feel guilty for not going to work, even though you are on your death bed – you know it is the parent. The voices do not have to be acted upon.

When you understand which voice is which, you can allow expression, but not action. In this way you will learn to live your life as an adult. It takes recognition, understanding, and the commitment to examine your thoughts and feelings before they become actions. As time goes by, this will become second nature. This is what balanced adults do. They are people who may have some unpleasant feelings at times, but they are not driven by them. They are in control of their lives. Their voices are not.

FINAL CONCLUSIONS

THE BEST OF TIMES

To some, God gave a word of wisdom; to some He gave a word of knowledge. Let us pray His words come to us. When there is insight, when we see the situation clearly and God gives us the words to speak, we speak healing into the person and the relationship. It is a wonderful and blessed feeling.

The molding of a soul takes a very long time. Through constant gentle pressure one can begin to straighten the crookedness and untie the knots. We can witness the blooming and fullness of what God made before sin destroyed it. We can be the ministers we are supposed to be, which are the hands and feet of God to love His people. We should ask no more from life than this.

THE WORST OF TIMES

People can be cruel. They can be manipulative, deceitful, devious, controlling, and arrogant. Everyday, games are played in order to get what is wanted and to shift blame. Affection and approval are withheld to control or punish. Life is made a living hell as one waits out the other. The loser is the one who breaks and asks for a divorce first. Counselors are caught in the midst of the firestorm. By the time we see the patients, the battle has begun and it is too late to ensure peace. We can only hope to regain it in time.

When a couple sits down in front of us, the problem may seem obvious. Judgments made prima facie are usually wrong. We must be sure to ask ourselves why he or she is acting out. What is driving the action? Often we will find layers of problems interacting. He may be angry because she withholds affection. She may withhold affection because she is angry at his lack of attention. He may not give her attention because he is angry at insults thrown in public. She may be insulting in public because he doesn't listen to her any other time...and on and on it goes. Layers upon layers of issues pile up as the counselor digs toward the bottom. What is generally found at the bottom is a cry to love and be loved. Insecurity, a need for love, and the need of a closer walk with one another and God is the basic human need.

Make no mistake. There is evil in the world and every day men and women decide to walk in its path. You will meet evil. You may look into its cold eyes. Pernicious selfishness is without conscience, without remorse, and more than willing to pose as an innocent victim. Its face is that of someone victimized, but its actions are thoughtless and hurtful without regard. Evil lies by word, action, and deed. It distorts reality. Perception, twisted often enough, becomes insanity. Evil is contagious and the first symptom of someone living under the influence of an evil person is a loss of self and of mind.

All personality types can fall into evil. Each has its own path and expression of deep selfishness. Each lashes out with its weapon of choice. Be prepared to take a stand for the sake of their partner. There will be times when our best advice is to get out before it is too late.

MOST OF THE TIME

In this work, we merely scratched the surface of the major issues confronting counselors on a daily basis. As a panoramic work, we have endeavored to understand the personality with its manifold faces as well as the common problems that befall all of us. We have looked at basic human needs as well as what those needs are likely to drive us to do. We have removed the masks that cover our true face and viewed the ugliness that is man and the glory that is God's creation.

Most cancerous are those afflicted with self-righteousness or religiosity. Addiction to religion is a disease left over from the days of the Pharisee, but it is difficult to cure.

But the contrite and humble spirit is a blessing and hope of mankind. As counselors, we will see all types and all maladies. However, in the pages of this book, personality types are cataloged and explained. Paths are charted from sin to salvation; from disorder to health.

The most meaningful path we must walk is not charted in any book. It is the one that leads us out of the religious and into the spiritual. Religion smothers with its rules and regulations. Spirituality sets us free with a pure communion with God. In this state there is nothing to hide. All is revealed and God is right there with you. Forgiveness and resurrection power is found in God and in Him alone.

More about the journey from bondage to freedom can be found in the book, *Dark Night of the Soul, a Journey into the Heart of God*, by Joseph Lumpkin.

ABOUT THE AUTHOR

Joseph Lumpkin has written for various newspapers and is author of the books *The Lost Book Of Enoch; The Gospel of Thomas – A Contemporary Translation; The Tao Te Ching – A Contemporary Translation; Encounter the Warrior's Heart; The Warrior's Heart Revealed;* and *Dark Night of the Soul – A Journey to the Heart of God.* Joseph earned his Doctorate of Ministry from Battlefield Baptist Institute.

Bibliography

Healing The Child Within: Discovery and Recovery for Adult Children of
Dysfunctional Families (Paperback)
by Charles L. Whitfield
Publisher: HCI; Reprint edition (April 1, 1987)
ISBN: 0932194400

If This Is Love Why Do I Feel So Insecure? (Paperback)
by Carl G. Hindy, J. Conrad Schwarz, Archie Brodsky
Publisher: Fawcett; Reissue edition (July 1, 1990)
ISBN: 0449218597

Angry All The Time: An Emergency Guide To Anger Control (Paperback)
by Ronald T. Potter-Efron
Publisher: New Harbinger Publications; 2nd edition (January 2, 2005)
ISBN: 1572243929

Breaking the Patterns of Depression (Paperback)
by Michael D. Yapko
Publisher: Main Street Books (September 15, 1998)
ISBN: 0385483708

Diagnostic and Statistical Manual of Mental Disorders DSM-IV-TR (Text
Revision) (Diagnostic and Statistical Manual of Mental Disorders)
(Paperback)
Publisher: American Psychiatric Association; 4th edition (June, 2000)
ISBN: 0890420254

Discovering Your Personality Type : The Essential Introduction to the
Enneagram, Revised and Expanded (Paperback)
by Don Richard Riso, Russ Hudson
Publisher: Houghton Mifflin; Rev&Updtd edition (May 20, 2003)
ISBN: 061821903X

The Enneagram in Love and Work : Understanding Your Intimate and
Business Relationships (Paperback)
by Helen Palmer
Publisher: HarperSanFrancisco; 1st edition (January 19, 1996)

ISBN: 0062507214

The Ego and the Id (The Standard Edition of the Complete Psychological
Works of Sigmund Freud) (Paperback)
Publisher: W. W. Norton & Company (April, 1962)
ISBN: 0393001423

Archetypes and the Collective Unconscious (The Collected Works of C. G.
Jung, Vol. 9, Pt. 1) (Hardcover)
by Carl Gustav Jung, William McGuire
Publisher: Bollingen; Second edition (January 1, 1969)
ISBN: 0691097615

Psychology and Religion (The Terry Lectures Series) (Paperback)
by Carl Gustav Jung
Publisher: Yale University Press; Rep edition (September 10, 1960)
ISBN: 0300001371

National Institute of Mental Health Website   2005

The National Mental Health Association Website 2005

National Library of medicine / National Institute of Health Website 2005

I'm Ok, You're Ok (Hardcover)
by M.D., Thomas A Harris
Publisher: Galahad (November 27, 2004)
ISBN: 1578660750

Mental Health Foundation (U.K.) Website 2005

National Electronic Library for Health (U.K.) Website 2005

Apocalypse of the Psyche (Paperback)
By Joseph Lumpkin
Publisher: Picasso Pubns Inc; 1 edition (December, 1998)
ISBN: 1551974959

Twelve Tribes Of Mankind (Paperback)
By Joseph Lumpkin
Publisher: Fifth Estate (March 31, 2004)
ISBN: 097463364X

National Institute on Drug Abuse Website 2005

On Death and Dying (Paperback)
by Elisabeth Kubler-Ross

Publisher: Scribner; Reprint edition (June 9, 1997)

ISBN: 0684839385

On Grief and Grieving : Finding the Meaning of Grief Through the Five
Stages of Loss (Hardcover)
by Elisabeth Kubler-Ross, David Kessler

Publisher: Scribner (July 5, 2005

ISBN: 0743266285

Holy Bible, King James Version

Publisher: American Bible Society (June, 1980)

ISBN: 1585161519

Gifts Differing: Understanding Personality Types

By Isabel Briggs Myers

Publisher: Davies-Black Publishing; Reprint edition (May 25, 1995)

ISBN:089106074X

God's Gifted People: Discovering Your Personality As a Gift

By Gary L. Harbaugh

Publisher: Augsburg Fortress Publishers; Expanded edition (September,
1990)

ISBN: 0806624868

Growing up Straight: What Families Should Know About Homosexuality

By George Alan Rekers

Publisher: Moody Press (1982)

ISNB: 0802401562

Handbook of Child and Adolescent Sexual Problems

By George rekers

Publisher: Lexington Books (1995)

ISBN: 0029263174

Can Some Gay Men and Lesbians Change Their Sexual Orientation? 200 Participants Reporting a Change from Homosexual to Heterosexual Orientation
Robert L. Spitzer
Presentation at the American Psychiatric Association Annual Convention. New Orleans, May 9, 2001. Note.

Subsequently published in Archives of Sexual Behavior, 32(5), 403-417, October 2003.

Hero with a Thousand Faces

By Joseph Campbell

Publisher: Bollingen (March, 1972)

ISBN: 0691017840

The Power of Myth

By Joseph Campbell

Publisher: Anchor (June, 1991)

ISBN:0385418868

NOTES:

NOTES:

NOTES:

NOTES:

CPSIA information can be obtained
at www.ICGtesting.com
Printed in the USA
LVHW081342050520
655046LV00008B/967

9 781933 580074